the

505

Weirdest
Online Stores

505 things you never knew
you could buy online

Dan Crowley

SOURCEBOOKS HYSTERIA™
AN IMPRINT OF SOURCEBOOKS, INC.®
NAPERVILLE, ILLINOIS

Published by Sourcebooks, Inc.
P.O. Box 4410, Naperville, Illinois 60567-4410
(630) 961-3900
FAX: (630) 961-2168
www.sourcebooks.com

Library of Congress Cataloging-in-Publication Data

Crowley, Dan.
The 505 weirdest online stores / Dan Crowley.
p. cm.
ISBN 1-4022-0377-2 (alk. paper)
1. Teleshopping—Directories. 2. Shopping—Computer network
resources—Directories. 3. Web sites—Directories. 4. Curiosities and
wonders—Computer network resources—Directories. I. Title.

TX335.C76 2005
658.8"7"0207—dc22

2004026864

Printed and bound in the United States of America
VP 10 9 8 7 6 5 4 3 2 1

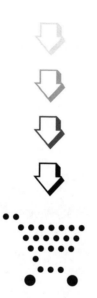

Table of Contents

Dead Sites—
Where Did They Go?

These websites may or may not exist once you go to look for them. The fluid nature of the Web dictates that I cannot guarantee that the sites will be in service at the time of publication. I have done my best to make sure that most are current as of this writing. Those sites that have gone to Internet Heaven (or Internet Hell as the case may be) are still included as a record of their incredibly pathetic existence and a timeless tribute to their extreme stupidity and uselessness.

If the address listed in the book does not work, try searching for the site using a search engine such as Google, as the site may have changed its address since the printing of the book. Sites such as Google and the Way Back Machine (www.archive.org) also have cached images of websites, so that you can view what a website looked like even if it no longer exists.

Introduction

In my previous book, *505 Unbelievably Stupid Web Pages*, I introduced the world to the wild, weird, and wacky wonders of the Internet. Classics websites like The Center for the Prevention of Shopping Cart Abuse, Rate My Mullet, The Church of Shatnerology, and the infamous Leonard Nimoy Should Eat More Salsa Foundation were all revealed to the masses. Everyone could marvel at their stunning stupidity. Now, you can relive the experience all over again—with a chance to waste your money, as well.

Think abusing shopping carts is weird? Check out Men Who Look Like Kenny Rogers, a site chronicling men who bear a striking resemblance to the famous country-music superstar, where you can buy a T-shirt that asks, "Have you seen Kenny Rogers?" Such an inspired question, isn't it? Did you enjoy the sermon at the Church of Shatnerology? Head over to the official website of the *Star Trek* idol himself, WilliamShatner.com, for a chance to buy everything Shatner (Finally, Grammy-worthy music by the man himself!). Did you revere the redneck preaching at Rate My Mullet? Check out Jolene's Trailer Park, the home of "Jolene Sugarbaker, the Trailer Park Queen," selling merchandise with classic slogans such as, "White Trash with Class!" Don't care for those pesky hangovers after a night of partying? Check out the Alcohol Without Liquid Machine. For only $3,000, you can buy a machine that allows you to inhale alcohol rather than drink it.

And no, this is not a joke.

New surefire hits also await you, like the enigmatic Motopets.com, Michael Jackson artwork, and the home to the "idol" of bad singers himself, William Hung (SHE BANGS! SHE BANGS!). So, step into the world of crazy Internet merchandise, and be sure to visit www.stupidwebpages.com for more information on insane Internet humor. Visit these sites for strange stores and shameful shopping experiences. Enjoy!

1

Bill Gates Is Dead
www.billgatesisdead.com

Is Bill Gates dead? These folks seem to think so. This site contains fake stories of Bill Gates's "assassination by a deadly sniper," opinions on the mega-conglomerate megalomaniac's legacy, retrospective "articles" about why this "tragedy" occurred, a "Community" section with discussion forums, and a Bill Gates memorial webring.

PRODUCTS: Mouse pads, such as one with the Linux penguin holding an Uzi and saying, "I know who killed Bill Gates," T-shirts, mugs, and books like *The Plot to Get Bill Gates* by Gary Rivlin, which is "a humorous look at the powerful people who openly hated Bill Gates. While the text has lost some of its humor since the shooting, the point Rivlin makes is more acute and telling than ever." A lot of people must hate Bill Gates if there's enough material to write a book on it.

VERDICT: Bill Gates may be alive and kickin', and still have more money than most of the U.S. population combined, but this site does a great job of catering to conspiracy theorists, humoring fans of the stupid and senseless, and fooling tons of gullible, misinformed people.

2

Almost Elvis
www.elvisimpersonators.com

"Thirty-five Thousand Elvis impersonators can't be wrong!" Almost Elvis is a haven for Elvis impersonators and home of the documentary *Almost Elvis*, the film about the "best Elvis [impersonators] on the planet…[competing] for the title of 'World Champion Elvis Impersonator!'" What a coveted title! The gift shop contains *Almost Elvis* movie posters, T-shirts, "Elvis-style sunglasses," and more.

PRODUCTS: T-shirts with the Almost Elvis and Blue Suede Films logos on them, playing cards, postcards, and, of course, the Kingtinued CD. "Hear the CD that's sending chills up the spines of Elvis-holics around the world. The voice of Elvis sings the best hits of today….Hear the King sing Elton John, Ricky Martin, Garth Brooks, Billy Idol, and more!" Elvis impersonators singing Ricky Martin? Chilling indeed.

VERDICT: Almost Elvis sells what sounds like an interesting documentary, as well as hilarious Elvis gear, and is a must-visit for the King's loyal subjects and fans of crappy Vegas entertainers everywhere.

3   Political Talking Action Figures
www.prankplace.com/politics.htm

George W. Bush, Bill Clinton, Donald Rumsfeld, and Ann Coulter: "America's Real Action Heroes!" Maybe, perhaps. But Bill Clinton, an "American Action Hero"? I don't think the "action" he got qualified as heroic! This store offers these hysterical dolls, which, through the miracle of modern technology, feature actual sound bites on a computer chip inside the dolls themselves.

PRODUCTS: Talking figures of Donald Rumsfeld ("Oh, it was your rhetoric that made us do it.") and George W. Bush ("I come from Texas.") are interesting. But the best is the Ann Coulter: Conservative Lawyer action figure. One of the quotes she actually says is, "Why not go to war just for oil? We need oil. What do celebrities imagine fuels their private jets? How do they think their cocaine is delivered to them?" Now that sounds like an action hero!

VERDICT: These dolls are great conversation pieces. Doesn't everyone need a chance to buy a Bill Clinton doll that recites "Clintonisms" on your command? It's always a pick-me-up to hear "It depends on what the meaning of the word is, is."

4

Free The Gnomes
www.freethegnomes.com

Here's your chance to save gnomes from botanical oppression. This site contains "Thoughts on Liberty" with antislavery quotes, information on "USA Hypocrisy" and how to "Stop British Slavery," as well as a plethora of goods ranging from T-shirts to hats and even underwear. All are sure to inspire your secret desire for freedom and liberation of these tiny garden decorations.

PRODUCTS: T-shirts, mugs, and other assorted gear with a garden gnome holding the sign, "Stop Oppressive Gardening," as well as the logo of "Free the Gnomes" featuring a dying flower with a gnome hat on it. It brings tears to my eyes. The Free the Gnomes journal is one of the best, where you can "Chronicle your anti-oppression efforts (or anything else) in this Free The Gnomes journal!"

VERDICT: I don't agree that gnomes are being oppressed; they certainly look pretty happy to me. I mean, look at that roving gnome in the TV commercials. He got to travel the world on someone else's dime. If that's oppression, count me in! This site offers plenty of meaningless content that, while ridiculously stupid, is nonetheless fun to read and laugh at. Whether you're a gnome oppressor, a gnome liberationist, or somewhere in between, this site is recommended.

5

The Childhood Goat Trauma Foundation
www.goat-trauma.org

Now, there's hope for children traumatized by goats everywhere. The CGTF contains documentation of petting-zoo atrocities, photographic evidence (one of which contains a creature bearing a disturbingly striking resemblance to a character from PBS's *Teletubbies*), and stunning statistics, such as, "Each year, over six thousand people are traumatized by goats in the United States alone." Are you one of them?

PRODUCTS: Hats, mugs, T-shirts, and kid's gear (wouldn't merely wearing a bib with a goat head on it traumatize the little ones for life?). Don't forget the 2002 Awareness Tour Lunchbox, which depicts a horrendous image of a truck with goats in it above a floor littered with body parts of children. And, of course, an evil goat-head logo looms ominously in the background. After seeing this picture, I am convinced that goats are by far the evilest of the creatures on Earth. I am now, unquestionably, part of the legion of goat trauma victims.

VERDICT: Whether or not you like goats, the CGTF will tickle even the stiffest funny bone. If you've been traumatized, though, beware; some of the "evidence" may bring back the horrible memories of your trauma. But, at the same time, there's "help" for goat-trauma victims here. You can contact a friendly goat-trauma counselor via email through a link on the site.

6 Birdwatching.com
www.birdwatching.com

This store is home to all aspects of the exciting sport of bird watching, or, if you prefer the proper term, "birding." All sorts of equipment can be found to assist you in your bird-watching endeavors...for a price. Bird watching vests, binoculars, videos, books, and even computer software are all at your fingertips.

PRODUCTS: Scopes, computer software, audiotapes, and books. One of the weirdest is the Haiku wren house, a type of birdhouse that "remind[s] one of a haiku." For only $90 (yes, ninety dollars), you can own this "unique design...reminiscent of an ancient Japanese temple." It looks more like a wooden tree to me.

VERDICT: With bird-watching binoculars that can run in the thousand-dollar range, as well as countless other useless products, bird watching is not a very affordable hobby. I suggest you take up bowling, or golf, or another hobby where you can actually have fun while you spend your money.

7

Ghost Study.com
www.ghoststudy.com

GhostStudy.com is a place where you can buy gear that can turn you into a real-life Ghostbuster (who ya gonna call?). This site contains "Stories," "Definitions," a picture section—which is nothing more than a bunch of edited and/or bad photography of "ghosts,"—and the "Ghost Cams,"—cameras of "spiritually active" areas that some people stare at for hours on end, hoping to catch a glimpse of a ghost.

PRODUCTS: A variety of ghostbuster-esque gear is available, including thermal-imaging equipment designed to see abnormal heat signatures. (Wow, that airspace is two degrees off normal!) Or a "room guardian" to warn you if ghosts are around (if they are, what can you do about it?). Don't forget the Ghost Detector, a "trifield natural EMF meter" which is known to these crackpots as "the Grand Daddy of all Ghost Meters!" Spectral beings, beware!

VERDICT: Whether you're a real ghost hunter or an intrigued observer of this strange group of Ghostbuster wannabes, GhostStudy.com is an interesting look at the tools serving as windows (boarded-up windows?) into the world beyond the grave.

8

Truck.net
www.truck.net

Wanna be a truck driver when you grow up, kids? Truck.net is "your 'Number One' information portal for the trucking industry on the Internet." This site helps truckers find jobs, although one wonders how truckers would have access to the Net if they spend all their time "trucking," not to mention that many truckers aren't exactly the hi-tech types. If you're not convinced of truck.net's credibility, remember that Truck.net is "in [the] top 14,643 sites on [the] web," and that "[the] closest related trucking site position is 85,109."

PRODUCTS: Clothing, books, maps, and even computer programs and video games, yes, video games. At the top of the list is Sega's *King of Route 66*, where "you'll get behind the wheels of a big rig for cross-country tractor-trailer racing at its finest!" Sounds like a sure-fire candidate for game of the year! Don't forget the laptop you can buy, the description of which simply reads, "This is a cool laptop." Detailed, isn't it?

VERDICT: Truck.net may be a serious resource for truck drivers, but the fact that it offers trucker gear to make you look like a true king of the road make it a site that cannot be ignored. So, to all you big rig drivers out there, "Keep on truckin'!" 10-4 good buddy.

Sofa Garden
www.sofagarden.com

Want to "cultivate your home"? Sofa Garden has loads of "unique" pillows for your bed, couch, or chair, shaped like food, seashells, and even famous artwork. FAQs include, "Does Sofa Garden ever offer discounted shipping?" The answer; "Frequently! We try to get creative with this so watch the site for special shipping offers." IT'S ON SALE!!!

PRODUCTS: Pillows ranging from the Breakfast Collection, with pancake pillows and fried-egg pillows (the beauty of eggs without the smell) to the Wine Collection, like the Merlot-Wine-Bottle-Shaped Pillow and the Chardonnay-Wine-Bottle-Shaped Pillow. The difference between the two? Color and label. Don't forget the reproduction of Michaelangelo's David, in pillow form.

VERDICT: These pillows can add flavor (no pun intended) to your furniture and your home, if you don't mind the aftertaste. Whether you're looking for a strawberry for your sofa or a beehive for your bed, Sofa Garden is the place to look.

10

Moocow.com
www.moocow.com

As you would imagine, Moocow.com is all about...cows! At Moocow.com, you can buy a vast variety of products featuring our milk-making bovine buddies. You can browse links to other cow websites, as well as read "About the Cow," which allows you to "learn about the different parts of your favorite four-legged animal." More like favorite edible parts!

PRODUCTS: Cow paintings and drawings are available on the main site, along with a link to their store that has Moocow T-shirts, baseball jerseys, and even Moocow boxer shorts! Wow, I'd sure like people to know that I'm wearing boxers with the phrase "Moocow" on them! Also available is an amazing cow mailbox, complete with udders and a rust-resistant coat. Available at a great price of $66.50! Talk about moo-raculous savings!

VERDICT: Whether you're a defender of rights for cows, a martyr for milk, or a fan of a juicy T-bone, Moocow is the place for you if you're looking for products featuring, in the words of Martha Stewart, "a friendly Holstein." It's a good thing.

11

Frog Fantasies
www.frogfantasies.com

Indulge yourself in your fantasies...about frogs. "We don't have any live frogs, but our museum does contain the efforts of over sixty years of frog collecting." How fascinating. What makes these frogs different from other frog merchandise? "The secret is in the eyes of the little creatures. Expressions vary from sad and lonely to mischievous to exultant." I never knew frogs were so deep.

PRODUCTS: This Arkansas-based store features "porcelain frogs, frogs of majolica, jade, wood, and cork, carved of coconut, and even cedar roots." In other words, fake frogs. You can buy fake frogs to satisfy whatever sick "fantasies" you might have. Some frog products include a Christmas frog with a candy cane (frogs don't come out during the winter), a frog candleholder (how about burning the frogs themselves?), and the obligatory beaded frog purse (no, it's not made out of frog skin). Also remember to reserve your tickets for the next "frog festival." Man, that has to be a hoot.

VERDICT: You don't need to know if Kermit the Frog shops at this store (I'm sure if he could use a computer, he would) to know that if you're looking for these amphibious animals to put in your home, you need look no further than Frog Fantasies.

12 Michael Jackson Artwork
www.helenakadlcikova.com/michael_jackson.htm

Wacko Jacko has a page dedicated to him, full of disturbing paintings; very, very, very disturbing paintings! Whoever created this twisted, sick museum of Michael Jackson themed "artwork" must a huge fan...yeah.

PRODUCTS: You can buy (please do me a favor and seriously consider this purchase) paintings at ONLY $10 apiece. Paintings like MJ with his arm around a young, blond boy (yes, a young boy), MJ being afforded a "divine reception" from Jesus with Michael in a loincloth (yes, loincloth). You can even get Wacko Jacko wallpaper. Computer wallpaper, that is.

VERDICT: Of course this site had to make some political statement by displaying an icon that reads "100 percent innocent." Tell that to the Santa Barbara county sheriff. Buy them if you wish, but don't blame yourself when you can't sleep at night when the "King of Pop" stares at you in his loincloth. This "King" site should be dethroned.

13   **The William Hung Store**
www.shophung.com

She Bang! She Bang! Yes, the worst "singer" ever to grace (perhaps "grace" and "singer" aren't the right words) the audition stage of *American Idol* now has his own store. Simon Cowell said, "You can't sing, you can't dance." He was right, yet now William Hung has his own store, website, and yes, record deal. What is this world coming to?

PRODUCTS: You can purchase a William Hung backpack (which would most likely get you beat up), a William Hung cap (you might get a punch or two), or a Hawaiian shirt like he wore on *AI* (for that, you will most certainly receive a major flogging). Almost every cap has Hung's smiling mug on the front, a sure sign that the end of the world is near. Don't forget the magnets for your locker or fridge, which include the "She Bangs!" magnet and the "William Hung rocks!" magnet. Rocks? I'd rather shove rocks into my ears than listen to his music.

VERDICT: Why didn't anybody listen to Simon on this one? To pay for any apparel, not to mention the so-called "music" that comes out of this human moaning machine, is beyond ludicrous. The only person who can possibly top Hung's putrid persona is *American Idol*'s incredibly annoying host Ryan Seacrest. Stay away. Stay far, far, away.

14   **Jolt Gum**
www.joltgum.com

Remember Jolt cola—"All the sugar, twice the caffeine"? Well, now it's back, in gum form. Jolt gum "contains caffeine *PLUS* guarana and ginseng to give you maximum energy. Jolt gum is as safe as coffee (and arguably even safer). The caffeine is exactly the same molecule as in coffee—you can just subtract the spilling." Chewing coffee IS dangerous.

PRODUCTS: Spearmint and Icy Mint gum, plus T-shirts and hats! The info for the men's T-shirt reads, "What do Heidi Klum, Giselle, Mike

Piazza, Alexandra Wentworth, Lance Berkman, and Kevin Gass have in common? Nothing as far as we know." Actually, they do have something in common: they're all famous and they all have probably never tried Jolt gum.

VERDICT: Jolt cola wasn't the most successful product in the world, and only time will tell if Jolt gum will meet a similar fate. Nevertheless, if you like gum and caffeine highs, try chewing some Jolt gum. Oh, and by the way, you can still buy Jolt cola! Score!

. . . .

15   Holly Society of America
www.hollysocam.org

No, this site is not for people named Holly. It is a society for holly, the plant! True, this plant is popular around Christmas time, but these folks have gone so far as to create an organization dedicated to this puzzling plant. The HSOA's goal is to "stimulate interest, promote research, and collect and disseminate information about the genus *Ilex*." You can look up information on different kinds of holly, or read about holly mythology. Fact: holly was used in olden times to ward off "malevolent faeries" and to allow faeries to live in the house "without friction between them and the human occupants." And we all know how dangerous those malevolent faeries are!

PRODUCTS: Buy holly books, like *Sources for Unusual Hollies* by Dr. Clifford L. Dickinson. So, the book is about England, and those guys singing about fat siblings and women in funeral attire? Fascinating. There's also the very exciting *How to Pick a Winner: A Guide to Competitive Exhibition of Holly Sprigs*, by Barton M. Bauers, Sr. First we had state fair bakeoffs, now some obscure plant competition? Disturbing.

VERDICT: Making world peace. Getting the Democrats and the Republicans to agree on something. Inventing a miracle diet pill that makes everybody Arnold Schwarzeneggar or Pamela Anderson. Solving the energy crisis. Disposing of the IRS. You could do all of these things, but if you're a member of the Holly Society of America, you're still stupid.

16

Spiky Bras
www.spikybras.com

They're bras, and they're…spiky? Believe it or not, it's true! At SpikyBras.com (whose motto is, "Silicone on the outside? What a concept!"), you can look at (and even order) spiky bras for you or your significant other. According to the promotion aimed at women with husbands/boyfriends, "You will have him doing household chores with a smile on his face!"

PRODUCTS: Order other spiky stuff, non-spiky bras, and, of course, the spiky bras themselves. You can also send the site feedback to tell whether or not you liked your spiky bra, or if you have relevant compliments or complaints. That being said, nothing on this site is really that relevant. The best one is the Blowfish Bra, a bra made of two fish heads covering each breast. Fishing is fun again!

VERDICT: If I knew a girl who wore a spiky bra, I would think she's kind of weird. For many men, however, they will think it's attractive, or even sexy. One thing's for sure: you'll definitely be unique if you decide to order one from this spike-selling site.

17

The Popcorn Fork
www.popcornfork.com

Do you need an eating utensil to eat popcorn? "Now you can say goodbye to greasy fingers and paper napkins. With new finger foods coming to market almost daily, the least I can do is help keep this delicious mess under control!" Well, why do you think they're called "finger foods"?

PRODUCTS: The popcorn fork is a chopsticks-like device that helps you eat popcorn without using your fingers. The popcorn fork doesn't have much in the way of practicality and ease, but at least your fingers stay clean. For those who are used to dispensable devices on their products, a built in salt shaker is included. However, be warned: "Ordering and using the POPCORN FORK will automatically cancel your membership in the FLAT WORLD SOCIETY! You may be ridiculed and put upon by the less enlightened. Your best friends may drop you like a dirty sock when they see you enjoying popcorn and other snacks with this instrument of cleanliness." Who wouldn't "drop" a person using this useless utensil? Give me a spork any day!

VERDICT: Exchanging common sense and practicality for clean hands isn't a good trade off. Greasy hands are an integral part of the experience in eating popcorn, in an odd, inessential kind of way. This site is a treat to visit if you're looking for something to lighten up your day, but don't expect finding anything cool. On second thought, the salt-shaker was pretty nifty...

18

Chia Pet
www.jeiusa.com/chia.html

With a catchy jingle (Ch-Ch-Ch-Chia!) and the promise of growing into a furry green plant, these putrid pottery pieces have become huge in the gift market. With Chia Pets, you supposedly can add water and seeds to the "pet," and it will grow green stuff. I say "stuff" because nobody seems to know what it really is. Is it fur? Hair? Leaves? "Chia"?

PRODUCTS: Various Chia products are available, such as a Scooby Doo Chia, or his counterpart, Shaggy Chia. Also available are various Chia animals, including Chia dinosaurs, pigs, and hippos. Looney Tunes Chias are here, with Taz, Bugs, Tweety (I thout I taw a Chia cat!), Daffy, and Elmer Fudd (Be vwary vwary quiet. I'm hunting Chia wabbits!), and, the best ones, Chia Homer and Chia Bart Simpson! D'oh!

VERDICT: Chias aren't the most reliable products; most times they grow mold instead of "Chia." I'd rather watch a marathon of *The Simple Life* with Paris Hilton and Nicole Ritchie than waste a single cent on this thing. Do yourself a favor and stay away from this sad store.

19   The Clapper

www.youcansave.com/clap.asp

"Clap on, clap off, clap on, clap off. The Clapper!" People just can't seem to resist clapping. This site offers the clapper, along with numerous other products, most of them straight off of TV infomercials, which is a sign that there's a 99.9 percent probability it won't work.

PRODUCTS: The Clapper is a device that allows you to activate and deactivate something by clapping. You plug the Clapper into an outlet, and then plug your light, TV, or whatever into the Clapper. After that, clap to your heart's content and watch your device magically turn on and off. Not merely convenient, the Clapper is also an anti-theft device! "The Clapper can be set up to activate the appliance when it hears any sound. If someone tries to enter your house, the Clapper can automatically turn on a TV or radio in your home." Cool, then the thief can listen to the radio AND steal my possessions.

VERDICT: The Clapper was made for two kinds of people: people who like to clap, and people who are lazy. Actually, it's for one person. The kind who are both lazy AND like to clap. The Clapper, along with other infomercial products, is little more than a novelty product that's a waste of your hard-earned money. Don't be surprised if your Clapper suddenly stops working and people stare at you when you're trying to "clap on" something.

20   Roadside America

www.roadsideamerica.com

The World's Largest Ball of Twine. The Big Lincoln Head. And the famous Muffler Men. All 100 percent American; all 100 percent weird. This site is your guide to America's stupidest, funniest, and downright weirdest destinations. From the Ben and Jerry's Factory Tour and Flavor Graveyard (flavors can die?), to the World's Largest Cat, these oddities are sure to delight any traveler who chooses to include them on a family road trip.

PRODUCTS: Don't forget to visit the Roadside America store, with the books *Roadside America* by Doug Kirby, Ken Smith, and Mike Wilkins (I wonder if writing it was easier or harder than writing alone?), *Mental Hygiene: Better Living Through Classroom Films 1945-1970* by Ken Smith (those old tacky educational movies), and *The Gallery of Regrettable Food*, by James Lileks (there must be a lot of flavorless food out there to make a book out of it).

VERDICT: Who would have ever thought that these strange sites could exist? I, for one, never heard of Mike the Headless Chicken. This site is proof of the saying, "Stranger things have happened." For information on a few extra stops you can make on that family drive down America's countryside, take a detour to Roadside America and check out what they have to offer.

21

Dog Nose Heaven
www.dognoses.com

"How many times have you wasted hours on end, scouring the Web searching for that perfect picture of a dog's cold, wet nose? Admit it, we all have." At Dog Nose Heaven, they'll stop at nothing to bring you pictures of dog noses. What good is a wet dog nose? "They're cold, wet, and <u>ready to sniff your ear</u>!"

PRODUCTS: You'll find "free samples" of numerous numbers of noses. Wait, did it say "free samples"? Does that mean that you can <u>pay</u> to get more? According to the site, you can. "With your paid membership to dognoses.com, you also get twenty-four hour a day, seven days a week access to our live webcams! Watch them sniff the camera lens! Watch their talented noses do tricks just for you!"

VERDICT: I'll admit, a dog's nose does feel a little nice on your skin, but it's nothing to obsess over. The mere thought of paying money to look at dog noses is just weird. Plus, some dogs may not like having cameras shoved in their faces. But, you gotta make a living somehow, right? Any normal person won't be captivated with these sniffing canines for very long.

22

Dehydrated Water
www.buydehydratedwater.com

"Stop drinking tap water. Stop drinking well water. Refuse to touch water from desalination plants." In other words, drink air. More questions about this fascinating phenomena? Check out the FAQ, with questions like, "How do I spit it out if I don't like it?" Answer: "Simply exhale and the dehydrated water will leave your body." One thing that drives this home as a stupid site is the question, "Are you serious? This site is a joke, right?" "This site is for real and we actually sell dehydrated water."

PRODUCTS: Dehydrated water is basically a fancy word for AIR. If you want to waste money buying air, dehydrated water is available to buy in fifty gallons ($4.95), and one thousand gallons (fifty bucks for one thousand gallons of air!) Don't forget the dehydrated water gear store, with dehydrated water T-shirts, baseball jerseys, and…thongs?! That is scary.

VERDICT: Words cannot describe how pitiful this site is. Pitiful as in the billy-goat-cursed Chicago Cubs baseball team. As in Gary Coleman running for California governor. Buy the clothes, if you want to be a walking advertisement for this pathetic product.

23

Pope Alien
www.popealien.com

Never believed that the words "pope" and "alien" would be used in the same sentence? Pope Alien is an assorted collection of comics and "advice," such as "What color is my pancreas?" They tell you, "Never, never be embarrassed about your pancreas…in answer to your question—it's a pukey, greenish-brownish red color." How informing. Also is the question, "I'm out of clean clothes. What should I do?" "Wait a while—eventually everyone else will be out of clean clothes as well, and you'll fit right in. Whatever you do, DON'T give in to the temptation to wash your clothing."

PRODUCTS: The Pope Alien shop feat
ers! The hat features the Pope Alien
and advice." The mugs have several
one of the T-shirts reads, "Well, m
with sticks you'd have more friend

VERDICT: My advice is that you
site. But the clothes are unique
friends about whether alien w
way to find out is find an alien world).

24

We Love the Iraqi
Information Minister
www.welovetheiraqiinformationminister.com

Let the world know this: We love the Iraqi information minister! The makers of this site adore, admire, and worship the ground that the Iraqi information minister walks on. His full name is Muhammed Saeed al-Sahaf, or, as they refer to him, "M.S.S." Old M.S.S. has sure said a lot of crazy things in his lifetime as the Iraqi information (or, more appropriately, misinformation) minister. The site is littered with such classic quotes as, "There are no American infidels in Baghdad. Never!" Or, "Our initial assessment is that they will all die." And, the best one of all, "The American press is all about lies! All they tell is lies, lies, and more lies!" Actually, I think that one is true.

PRODUCTS: Of course, what would an entry in this book be without a satisfying store? You can buy mugs that say, "No American will ever pour coffee into this mug! Never!" Or how about the Infidel Flying Disc, which says, "My feelings, as usual—we will slaughter them all." Right, and I've got a date with Jennifer Garner.

VERDICT: "No American infidel will ever read this book! Never! In fact, no American infidel will ever read ANY book!" Yep, that's the Iraqi information minister all right. Why anybody would think about loving this tyrant is beyond me. This page, however, is good for those with a twisted, and slightly demented sense of humor.

Weird NJ
www.weirdnj.com

...ought New Jersey could be so…weird? Weird NJ is your guide to ...n State's most bizarre, weird, and downright crazy attractions, myths, ...ends. Check out the "Only Go There at Night" section, where you can ...a virtual visit to the Devil's Tower, a tower with creepy legend that "if you ...lk around it backwards six times at midnight, the Devil himself will appear." ...Right, and if I walk around it twenty-two times, the tower will come to life and chase me.

PRODUCTS: And what site would be complete without a fittingly weird store? You can buy the *Weird NJ* book, subscriptions to the *Weird NJ* magazine, a Weird NJ embroidered sweatshirt, and even a Weird NJ bumper sticker. Put that thing on your car, and it'll make people think you're the weird one. The weirdest is the *Weird NJ Songs* CD: "Seventeen tracks by New Jersey artists performing original songs about our state's local legends and best kept secrets." Weird, indeed.

VERDICT: A fun site to visit to see a different side of New Jersey, as well as a great store with tons of, well, weird stuff. On a side note, one of the most famous legends on this site, the Jersey Devil (under "Unexplained Phenomena"), still is present today in the form of the New Jersey Devils NHL team. Weird origin for a name? Perhaps. Good hockey team? Definitely.

26 Who Would Buy That?
www.whowouldbuythat.com

Some of these products may leave you asking, "Who would buy that?" These items are all links to auction sites, mostly eBay. But there is some crazy stuff here. Each item has a funny description and a link to the said item.

PRODUCTS: One example of a past featured products is an item under the heading, "For the man who has everything…except a girlfriend": the Life-Size-Lady-in-Red-Leather Floor Lamp, a lamp with a leather-clad body of a woman for the base. How erotic! Or the Pet Bride Veil Dress Hat, with a picture of a rather sad St. Bernard wearing a pet-proportioned bridal hat. The appropriate description is, "Kill me. Kill me now." The obvious lesson out of this is that pets aren't meant to marry.

VERDICT: Who would buy these things? Someone, obviously. Some of these items have already been sold out. It's evidence that there are some crazy people in this world who want to find life partners for pets and have a leather-wearing woman in their living rooms. This is a great site for a laugh or two, and an opportunity to defy the name and say, "I would buy that."

27   Talk Like a Pirate Day
www.talklikeapirate.com/

Arrr! Avast mateys!! Watch for that thar day en Septemburrrrr, whear ye Talk Like a Pirate! This site proclaims that September 19 is International Talk Like A Pirate Day. It's quite simple, really: on September 19, you talk like a pirate whenever it's possible. This very unofficial holiday has actually become quite famous; you may have heard about it on a radio program on the 19, or in a news program. This site gives you hints on how to talk like a pirate. Start with the basics, where "ahoy" means "hello," "aye-aye" means "yes sir," "aye" (not to be confused with aye-aye) means "I agree," and "Arrr!" means just about anything. Graduate to Advanced Pirate Lingo, where "bilge rat" is a dirty insult, "beauty" means a woman, and, of course, the classic "lubber" or "land lubber," those that hate anything aquatic and prefer land.

PRODUCTS: Be sure to also board the Talk Like A Pirate "Booty" section (aka store), to find the "I've got Pirattitude" T-shirt, the "Arrr" sweatshirt, and the "Talk Like A Pirate" lunchbox. There's gear for the smaller set, like the pirate bib or toddler T-shirt. And of course, you can buy the "Dead Men Tell No Tales" shirt. True, since dead people can't talk, that is, unless it's on a soap opera.

VERDICT: What, may you ask is the point of all of this? The answer, as the site so elegantly puts it, "There is no point." This is the whole idea behind the fun and madness of Talk Like A Pirate Day. This site contains everything you need for this special day when it's in to talk like a pirate.

28

Fast Food Fever
www.jaybrewer.net/fastfoodfever

Fast Food Fever is "A site for people looking for a little more from fast food." This site has a ton of information on America's most popular type of restaurant. This site details fast food's world influence, such as an article on that tells you how Asian fast food is "delicious and nutritious" (only in Asia). Another crazy project is "the McDonald's adventure," which began April 1, 2004. For thirty days, Soso Whaley ate nothing but McDonald's. However, unlike the documentary movie *Supersize Me* (in which the filmmaker got fat and sick from a month of fast food), Whaley actually lost weight. Daily reports can be drawn up from the archives on this "exciting" project.

PRODUCTS: Once you're done carousing fast food facts, check out the online store, where you can buy fast food merchandise ranging from a FFF junior baby-doll T-shirt to a bib (best suited for eating fast food, of course). All products have the FFF logo: a fat guy with his stomach hanging out, eating a hamburger. What a positive role model.

VERDICT: How much fast food do the makers of this site really eat? I hope their zeal for fast food isn't as strong as their appetite for it, otherwise they'd have all sorts of health problems, not to mention being pretty fat. Anyhow, if you want to show off your pride in speedy cuisine, buy some Fast Food Fever gear and spread the word.

29

Squirrel Head
www.squirrelhead.com

This is one odd story for an organization. "It all started when a group of happy go lucky people rented a lake house from a realty company. After a nice relaxing weekend at the lake the group went home....Sixty days later they received a letter in the mail from the realty company with a laundry list of false claims of damages....[We almost sent] them a horse head to show them that [we meant] business. Of course, a horse head is not easy to come by nor is it cheap to ship. So I amended the plan to a squirrel head." After a nasty legal battle, the Squirrel Head organization now hosts lake trips and barroom parties.

PRODUCTS: Even though this is a hysterical story, the real attraction is the Squirrel Head store. Get Squirrel Head caps, mugs, and even a Squirrel Head calendar for those who want their devotion to be evident all year long. There's even a Squirrel Head infant creeper "for the squirrel pups."

VERDICT: I, for one, would be scared of people who sent me the head of some roadkill in retaliation for claiming money that rightfully belonged to me. And for all their troubles, all they got was part of a dead squirrel carcass. In any case, Squirrel Head sells a great line of products if you like squirrels, practical jokes, or both.

30 Indoor Wrestling
www.indoorwrestling.com

"Welcome to indoorwrestling.com—the premier site for stupid idiots." Indeed. This site has a ton of videos of guys acting like total, well, idiots. Most of the videos involve unnecessary violence, such as throwing a guy out a window, or smashing a keyboard over somebody's head after an extensive discussion about how computers don't work ("A computer should be like a toaster; you put the toast in, and it works."). Also included are forums where you can discuss the crazy antics of these insane indoor wrestlers, and profiles of all the "actors" that appear in the videos, with favorite movies, quotes, and the ever-so-necessary "BMW or Acura?"

PRODUCTS: Pay a visit to the Indoor Wrestling store, where you can buy products such as T-shirts, jerseys, hats, baby stuff, and even teddy bears. One logo shows a guy hitting the other with a box of fabric softener sheets. The other shows one of the "wrestlers" with a toaster in his hands, looking puzzled. How profound.

VERDICT: This indoor wrestling is even more stupid than "professional" wrestling. It does have one thing that the latter doesn't: it's real. (Or is it?) If you want to see a bunch of guys acting like total morons, this site will be a treat for you. Remember: do not try this at home. Seriously, don't. Unless you want to spend a week (or more) in the hospital.

31

Stupid Creatures
www.stupidcreatures.com

These are more like deformed sock puppets than "stupid creatures." Granted, they do look stupid, and they bear a slight resemblance to creatures. "Slight," however, is being generous. On this site, you can find a "Gallery" of stupid creatures, all of which look like they were made by five-year-olds. And yes, you can order every one of them.

PRODUCTS: Examples include Blinky, a gray, rabbit-like doll with a tail; Chickenhead, a red doll that bears no similarities to a chicken, Francine, who is entirely neon green and has eyes and nothing else, and many other stupid dolls. If you are compelled to do so, you can purchase a stupid creature of your own. The ordering section contains FAQs, with questions such as, "How much do the creatures cost?" Actually, they run "Minimum of $40, maximum of $65…The basic breakdown is $4.00 per inch…chances are you'll spend within the mid $40s to high $50s." And yes, they are made of socks.

VERDICT: This guy must make a huge profit off of these sock creatures…if people buy them. They look like they cost about one dollar to make. In a further cash-conniving aspect, the maker of these "creatures" wants you to send your own sock materials. But, you could take pity on him and buy one of them, if you desire a cheap sock puppet for a decoration, as this is his only job. Yes, I know. Sad.

32

The Angry Liberal
www.theangryliberal.com

This web pages give us more insight into those mysterious creatures known as liberals. The Angry Liberal is run by a liberal who is enraged at where politics stand today. "For more than twenty years, the decent people of America have stood idly by while conservatives transformed the term 'liberal' from a title of honor to a dirty word." How shocking! "America is about to find out that conservatives are exactly as they appear: Greedy, self-centered, uncaring bastards who will never get into Heaven!" I'm sure you know exactly who is and who isn't getting into Heaven, buddy.

PRODUCTS: Visit the Angry Liberal shop for a chance to purchase gear to flaunt your status as an angry liberal. Examples include stickers reading, "Kerry vs. Bush: Hero vs. Zero." Funny, who won the election again?

VERDICT: Why do politicians have to constantly bicker and argue? It seems as though there's no end to it. Perhaps one day, politicians will get along, and will be noble, honest, and dedicated to serving the hard-working people of America. Nah. The odds of that happening are slimmer than the chance that Michael Jackson will actually get his career (and his life) to be normal for the first time. The Angry Liberal is exclusively for just the people its name implies.

33 Duct Tape Fashion
www.ducttapefashion.com

This site sells accessories, only they're all made of…duct tape! You can buy dozens of products here made entirely of duct tape. Most of these look like they could be whipped up by people like you and me in less than ten minutes, but regardless, they're still charging a ton of money for these absurd accessories.

PRODUCTS: Duct tape wallets—such as the Tri-fold Wallet, the Duct Tape Mini-Wallet, and the Credit Card and Business Card Holder (how professional)—are available for you to store your money and cards in style. Why get a duct tape wallet? "Much more durable than most regular wallets…'Look what I've got' novelty increases popularity…[and] they are Super-Cool!" Super-cool, or super-stupid? Check out the Duct Tape Hats, with the "traditional color wrap-around brim style" hat, and the "camouflage ball-style hat." These hats run about ten to twenty dollars, all 100 percent duct tape. Duct tape belts, folders, visors, and even roses are available for purchase. I know girls love roses made of duct tape!

VERDICT: If you want to pay money for these ugly atrocities, that's up to you. Just remember that buying something that you could make at home for less is considered very, very, stupid. Of course, they do look a little cool…nah.

34

Cube Door
www.cubedoor.com

This square site caters to the productivity potential of the cubicle minions of corporate America. "Both David Vaughan and Bob Schmidt have spent a good percentage of their careers working in cubicles....Telling their coworkers to go away was not an alternative....The solution had to be attractive, affordable, and blend into the office landscape. What could solve this productivity problem?

PRODUCT: The result: the Cube Door, a retractable curtain that says "Busy" along with the Cube Door logo and website address. Takes just seconds to install, and starts working immediately. When in need of uninterrupted time, just pull the Classic shut. Think you can slack off with this thing? Think again. "Coworkers can still see you, but the 'BUSY' message is clear." Take that, slackers!

VERDICT: The Cube Door sounds like an ideal way to increase productivity by maintaining your privacy; in theory, that is. Just be sure to check with your boss before ordering the Cube Door. I claim no responsibility for offering a potential way to get you fired. Even with this clever curtain, though, it depends on you and your coworkers as to whether your office is a productive party or if you're the "Milton" of the office. And no, I'm not giving back your stapler.

35

Generally Awesome
www.generallyawesome.com

This site is "occasionally lame, but generally awesome." It features photos, comics, and other humor of the weird and the wacky. Like, "[MC] HAMMER COMES CLEAN: 'YOU CAN TOUCH THIS.'" In it, MC Hammer, who is now apparently a preacher (how that happened is beyond me), says that "I have maintained the façade for long enough. It was time to own up to the reality of the situation. All along it was easy for people, especially the ladies, to touch this." Comic strips include "Weasel Breath," "Cell-Phone Monster," and "Surf's Up."

PRODUCTS: In the store, you can buy Generally Awesome hats, "Fake University" accessories, and Generally Awesome T-shirts in the shape of McDonald's arches. McDonald's is generally awesome too, except when they screw up my order.

VERDICT: This site is exactly what it says it is: occasionally lame (sometimes a little too often) but generally awesome. By awesome, I mean a stupid, weird, twisted kind of awesome. Still, generally awesome. The store features nice products, and the jokes are enough to keep you drawn to this radically cool site.

36   Lunar Land Owner
www.lunarlandowner.com

Ever thought about purchasing lunar land for your mother, sibling, or significant other? Now's your chance! Lunar Land Owner can assist you in buying a piece of the moon. No more wanting puny moon rocks! "The UN Outer Space Treaty of 1967 stipulated that no government could own extraterrestrial property. However, it neglected to mention individuals and corporations." So, corporations are now the owners of the moon? If and when we colonize the moon, this is probably going to cause a lot of lawsuits.

PRODUCTS: The only product you can buy here is lunar real estate. Inside each ownership package is a "lunar deed," a "lunar constitution bill of rights" (to assist you in governing your moon land and its non-existent inhabitants), a "lunar plot map showing the location of your property" (as if you're ever going to visit it), and "a copy of the declaration of ownership filed with the United States, the USSR, and the United Nations." How can you file with the USSR if it don't exist anymore? The mind boggles.

VERDICT: Wouldn't a piece of moon land be a priceless gift to give your partner? Sure, it's cheesy (not green cheese), but you can own a part of the moon! Perhaps a mega-corporate icon will hunt down all of the two million (yes, two million) lunar-land owners and buy out the moon! Then they will be able to dictate a new lunar government! If you buy some lunar land and keep it, it could be valuable someday…in a thousand years.

37

Sugar Ray Dodge
www.sugarraydodge.com

Sugar Ray Dodge is the ranting of an opinionated guy who got the name from "a wrestler I created on *WWF No Mercy* for the Nintendo 64 back in 2001." Original origin for a name, isn't it? In the FAQ, questions arise such as: "You're A Jerk!" His reply: "This really isn't a question, but it's true. I am a jerk. What can I say?"

PRODUCTS: The core of this site is the Sugar Ray Dodge store, where you can buy shirts reading, "Don't Trust the Liberal Media!" "McCarthy: American Hero," and "I Hated France Before It Was Cool." Well, I wonder who he voted for last year? Don't forget the best line of products of out of all of them: the "Eat Cat" products. Like I say, "Two cats are three too many."

VERDICT: This guy is even more conservative than Ann Coulter! If he were president, he'd be egged by Democrats! Especially for thinking that Senator Joseph McCarthy was an "American hero." Well, someone had to stop those communists…right? If you're a staunch conservative, you'll love the products available at Sugar Ray Dodge. Liberals, you'd do well to stay away. Far, far, away.

38

Elftor
www.elftor.com

I've seen some weird comics before, but this one takes the cake. Elftor is about—what else—an elf, and his friend, Cheesetor, who is—you guessed it—a slice of cheese. Some strips include "Elftor Goes to a Bakery," "Elftor Can't Sleep," and "Elftor's Discourse in African American Vernacular." The last is actually quite clever. Elftor and Chessetor talk like gangstas, with lines like "home-theater system," "Home Depot," and "Home Owner's Insurance" replacing the common "homeboy" slang. Yo, yo, home shopping channel!

PRODUCTS: Buy Elftor T-shirts, buttons, lunchboxes, and, of course, thongs. The shirt has the Elftor title art, with Elftor staring at a solitary blue flower. The buttons have a small pixelized picture of Elftor, and the lunchbox has Elftor, Cheesetor, and three guest characters: a pothead Jamician reggae singer, a powerful Middle-Earth wizard, and a certain Public Enemy Number One that everybody wants dead. I wonder who these guys could be?

VERDICT: At times clever, at times stupid, and at other times totally insane, Elftor is an interesting comic strip that's worth a look. Whether your reaction is disgust, fascination, confusion, or a good chuckle, everybody will find something different with Elftor.

39

Ask Dr. Science
www.drscience.com

"There is a thin line between ignorance and arrogance…and only I have managed to erase that line." Dr. Science is the world's top authority on everything science, or so he says. The main feature is the "Question of the Day," where the unintelligent peons of the world (i.e., us) get to seek the grand knowledge of Dr. Science. One day's question was, "When is an atom neutral?" "When it's Swiss. Swiss atoms are hard to find, and when you do find one, they're terribly expensive." Aren't atoms free?

PRODUCTS: Stop by the Dr. Science store, where you can purchase a Personalized Dr. Science Greeting, where Dr. Science records an answering-machine message for you. Don't forget the Masters Degree in Science mouse pad, and the Dr. Science Techno Bundle ("for the nerd who has everything"), and a CD to load Dr. Science's senseless ramble onto your computer. But a must buy is the Smug Mug, which you can use to proclaim to the masses that "I Know More Than You Do."

VERDICT: This isn't science at all! He should be called Dr. Stupid! Actually, that title is most likely taken already, but who says there can't be two Dr. Stupids? If you value science, don't go here. If you value stupidity, then head on down to Dr. Science.

40

Veggie Van
www.veggievan.org

A car fueled by vegetable oil? Now I've seen everything... The Veggie Van, and its counterpart the Veggie Car, rival Scooby-Doo's Mystery Machine for genuine hippie design. The cars not only have giant flowers painted on them, they use vegetable oil for fuel! Mmmmm. French-fried fuel. That would require a lot of tubs of vegetable oil to keep it running.

PRODUCTS: Support the "biodiesel" movement by buying products from its catalog, such as *The Veggie Van Voyage* DVD, a twelve-minute video for $20! Talk about value! Don't forget to pick up the *Biodiesel Van Music* CD, a collection of music from Julia "Butterfly" Hill, Melissa Crabtree, and Julie Wolf! I've heard of all of them, haven't you?

VERDICT: Simply put, using vegetable oil for fuel sounds senseless. Vegetable oil for frying chickens, yes. Vegetable oil for fuel, no. I don't see this "revolution" picking up steam anytime soon.

41

I Love Peanut Butter
www.ilovepeanutbutter.com

Everybody loves peanut butter! This site is the online outlet for Peanut Butter & Co., selling high quality, "all natural peanut butter since 1998." Before you buy, check out "Fun Stuff," featuring the entry, "We Eat a Lot of Peanut Butter," with such facts as, "Americans eat about three pounds of peanut butter per person each year, totaling about five hundred million pounds...enough to cover the floor of the Grand Canyon." I can just imagine peanut butter covering the floor of the Grand Canyon, can't you?

PRODUCTS: Click your way on over to the I Love Peanut Butter store, where you can buy clothing and gifts, including a Peanut Butter Spreader, which is simply a large spoon. The peanut butter toys and books store features fun games for the young ones, featuring The Peanut Butter and Jelly Board Game, with "no reading required." I can imagine how deep that is.

VERDICT: If you want to sell peanut butter, that's fine, but do you really have to name your web domain Ilovepeanutbutter.com? If you salivate over a peanut butter and jelly, you can feed your love for peanut butter here.

42

Alien Technology
www.alien-technology.com

Aliens are invading! Well, they are on this site. Alien Technology sells all things alien. Be sure to play the *UFO Invasion* game (under "Alien Fun," "Alien Games"), where you try to blow up UFOs with missiles before they reach Earth. If movies are any indicator, our missiles will not stop a slew of alien invaders. Also check out the "Alien Glossary," the most amusing entry of which is "ALF," which of course stands for "Alien Life Form," although I don't think they're using it in the context of that lovable, furry, TV sitcom character.

PRODUCTS: You MUST buy something here, as the site's tagline is: "It is useless to resist our products." You may buy products that are serious and dedicated to real UFO studies (is there such a thing?). Others you may purchase are very off the wall, such as the "Alien Elvis" section: a line of products devoted exclusively to aliens in the King's garb, with shirts such as "Alien Elvis Strikes the Pose" and "Alien Elvis has left the galaxy." Not as easy as leaving a building, is it?

VERDICT: This site reminds me of a classic Christmas carol: "I Want an Alien for Christmas," by the Fountains of Wayne. One line is, "I want a little green guy, three feet high, has seventeen eyes and knows how to fly." Wouldn't you want an alien like that as a present? If you ask for one, you just might get it. Better yet, ask for a product from Alien Technology, a great place for everything about those little green men from the great beyond.

43

Men Who Look Like Kenny Rogers
www.menwholooklikekennyrogers.com

How many people look like Kenny Rogers? Apparently more than we think. Men Who Look Like Kenny Rogers (MWLLKR) puts it this way: "Have you noticed that a lot of men over a certain age look a lot like country-music superstar Kenny Rogers? This is certainly no knock on anyone…who wouldn't want to look like Kenny?" Well, me for one. And every other sane guy I know. Check out the photo gallery to see how many people look like this country king. Each photo is categorized by description, such as "Huggable Kenny," "Well-Lit Kenny," and "No-Neck Kenny."

PRODUCTS: Don't forget the official T-shirt, which has Kenny photos and reads, "Have You Seen Kenny?" Oh yeah, every day. The only bad part about the MWLLKR T-shirt is that it's "Available in large and extra-large only." What about the smaller and (much more importantly) larger Kenny Rogers fanatics? On behalf of the XXXXXL size Kenny clones, I protest!

VERDICT: These men do look a lot like Kenny Rogers. Perhaps there are others. Perhaps it's an alien cloning conspiracy! Even scarier is the thought that maybe there are other celebrity clones out there. Image the horror of another David Spade, or another Andy Dick. Or, heaven forbid, another Olsen twin. The last thing we need is another one of those.

44

Hunter Dan
www.hunterdan.com

"Create your own hunting scenarios!" Hunter Dan is a line of dolls with hunting gear, instead of swimsuits and tight shirts like Ken dolls. "Hunter Dan…action figures, with replica gear, big game figures, and hunting dogs offer unlimited possibilities for the young hunting enthusiast!" Now you can pretend to kill animals if you're too young to go Bambi-blasting.

PRODUCTS: There's the Hunter Dan Turkey Hunter and Hunter Dan Duck Hunter figures so you can bag your own plastic poultry. And don't forget Hunter Ann, a redheaded Barbie-look-a-like who doesn't appear to care as much about cosmetics and miniature plastic Ferraris as her trendy "cousin" does. The Big Game to go along with your hunting dreams is also a necessity, with items such as the Boss Tom Wild Turkey, the Beatty Buck, and his brother Hanson Buck.

VERDICT: What's the satisfaction in hunting with action figures when you miss out on the best parts of hunting? The mounted heads, the delicious venison and turkey, the thrill of the kill, the gutting and disemboweling? Whatever the reason for getting these demented dolls, be sure to give your young ones a reality check before you encourage them to act out their hunting fantasies.

45

MotoPets
www.worldwarone.com/motopets

It's a pet, on wheels! "Greetings come to you with hearts and flowers as you enjoy exciting and lovable world of MOTOPET!" Exciting. Lovable. Yeah. Isn't that nice? "MOTOPET is large hit of popularity, innovation of toy for childs of both boy and girl category! Boy child entrance to heart in Motopet's powerful motor and gears!! Ties the amusement facility of girl child with tender outer co-fur-ing!!" Boy and Girl category? Amusement facility? I guess crappy-wheeled products deserve crappy English translations.

PRODUCTS: Try out Motokitty, which is "talking politely and with grace! She say, 'Motokitty playful in wholesome and motorized fashion!'" Also try out Motopuppy, a Sheltie-looking dog who is "perfect for young child infected with tantrums!" Be sure to also take pity on "MotoGuinea," who is "least popular Motopet! No one buy him! We have ten thousand MotoGuinea in warehouse waiting for home!" Poor, poor, MotoGuinea.

VERDICT: Motopets is an interesting, albeit odd site, but one thing I couldn't figure out is how to order Motopet. As it says, "For the punctual and effectual delivery of Motopet, call Motopet, Inc. at 12-344-345-4545-55…Or fill out and, with mouse, be quickly clicking the 'Button!'" They make it a bit hard…don't they?

46

Pac Manhattan
pacmanhattan.com

Pac-Man, the arcade classic featuring a mouth eating dots, now is set in New York City! *Pac-Manhattan* "is a large-scale urban game that utilizes the New York City grid to recreate the 1980s video game sensation *Pac-Man*…in order to explore what happens when games are removed from their 'little world' of tabletops, televisions, and computers and placed in the larger 'real world' of street corners, and cities." So, they learn about city geography by playing video games? Pac-tastic!

PRODUCTS: All Pac-Manhattan goods have a Pac-Man icon sandwiched between "I" and "NY." I Pac-Man New York? T-shirts, mugs, stickers, and yes, Pac-Manhattan thongs, are all available. What a turn on, eh?

VERDICT: *Pac-Manhattan* is a very unusual application to real life learning. However, if you get to learn and play a fun video game at the same time, I'm all for it. Pac-Manhattan's store sells apparel that readily reminds people of the simpler times of clunky cell-phones, huge computers, bad fashion, and synthesized music. In short, a time we'd like to forget.

47

Balloon Hat
www.balloonhat.com

This site marks the first time balloons are fashionable! "In 1996, Addi Somekh and Charlie Eckert began traveling to different places in the world to make balloon hats for people and take photos of them." Sounds like one exciting trip! Photos and stories are available from all around the world, from America to China. I'm sure they had to bring a lot of balloon hats there!

PRODUCTS: Buy The Inflatable Crown balloon hat kit, where you can fashion your own helium headgear! I'm sure balloon hat style is very important!

VERDICT: The Balloon Hat kit was "seen on *Martha Stewart Living*," so you KNOW it has to be good! Seriously, though, balloon hats are a good gift for that person who has everything, and are unique enough to satisfy any tastes. Just don't let them float away!

48   Supreme Commanbear
www.worldwarone.com

All hail the Supreme Commanbear! Supreme Commanbear has a very unique story. "In 1857, a secret international consortium known only as the Choclatiers met in a secret base under Lake Geneva....This team of the world's top watchmakers, aeronautical engineers, and candy manufacturers created a hero to serve and protect mankind: the SUPREME COMMANBEAR." And what a delicious hero he is! And I thought the Swiss were neutral.

PRODUCTS: Buy Supreme Commanbear T-shirts, with the Supreme Commanbear on the front, and the words "History's Greatest Hero" on the back. Mouse pads are also available so you can be reminded of Commanbear's greatness while surfing the Internet. And don't forget the SC large mug, for a reminder of his power morning, day, and night. On second thought...maybe not.

VERDICT: The Supreme Commanbear, whoever he is, is anything but a hero. Not only is he a bear, he's also a confectionary treat! Would you rather hail the Commanbear as your leader, or eat him? I know I could go for some Commanbear chocolate.

49

Alcohol without Liquid Machine
www.awolmachine.com

In this case, AWOL doesn't stand for "absent without leave," it stands for "alcohol without liquid." That's right! The AWOL machine is "the brainchild of thirty-year-old Dominic Simler…who discovered that by mixing spirits with pure oxygen, a cloudy alcohol vapor can be created which can be inhaled." Aw, where's the fun in that? The AWOL machine's main draw is that it's "a solution to the two greatest problems today's drinkers have: hangovers and calories. This is the dieters dream."

PRODUCTS: The AWOL machine itself, of course! How does it work? "Once inhaled, the alcoholic gas goes straight into the bloodstream to give an instant buzz. The potent combination of oxygen and alcohol creates a feeling of well being, which intensifies the longer the vapor is inhaled." Of course, this "luxury" does not come without a price. It's only $2995.00! Three thousand bucks for alcohol you have to inhale?! Gimme a three-dollar bottle of Ripple anytime!!

VERDICT: Although you can buy this crazy gadget, nobody in their right mind would pay that much for something that is not only impractical, but not nearly as satisfying as the taste of a cold brew or cocktail!

50

My Name Is Phil
www.mynameisphil.com

This is the strangest thing I have ever seen. My Name is Phil is a story about aliens who like Kix, portals to other dimensions, and big, white, ball-shaped structures that pick up alien radio stations. "Every day, I receive many transmissions. I attempt to decode and translate all that I receive…Of those that I understand, I can only reveal to you a small percentage. The rest must be locked away until the second coming of Zaxon." Who is Zaxon, you ask? "Zaxon was born in 1450 AD somewhere near Constantinople. In 1452, in an attempt to escape persecution by the Turks, his family fled through the Northeast Portal into the unknown dimension…When Zaxon turned sixteen, and for reasons I cannot go into here, he was proclaimed leader of the land." Ok…right…

PRODUCTS: T-shirts, including the "My Name is Phil" and "Sir Gubb, The Flaming Bug Head Man" fitted T-shirt. On the back of another shirt is a guy, presumably Phil, holding an antenna, and wearing tinfoil and a funnel on his head, with the caption, "Always take time to listen to the aliens!" Simply unbelievable…

VERDICT: A site that is without a doubt the most senseless one I have ever seen (with the exception of The Leonard Nimoy Should Eat More Salsa Foundation from my first book). Phil definitely must either be insane, or must be on some sort of substance that he needs to stop doing. Now.

51

Yoga Kitty
www.yogakitty.com

"Higher Consciousness…it's not just for humans anymore." Now you can achieve enlightenment with your feline friends! "Our goal is to present a practical, step by step guide for humans and their cats to activate their fullest potential, allowing man, woman, and feline to dwell in the ecstasy of physical, mental, and spiritual health." You can view short Yoga Kitty videos online for FREE if you wish to sample the path to enlightenment with your cat. Check out "Clearing Past Karmas," where you can clear your head chakra by rubbing your cat "partner's" stomach over your head! Purr-fect for humiliating yourself and your cat.

PRODUCTS: Buy the Yoga Kitty T-shirt! "Impress your friends in yoga class! Pique the interest of animal lovers! Avoid doing laundry for another day!" What does doing laundry have to do with the path to enlightenment? Of course you'll want to buy full-length Yoga Kitty videos, featuring "three bonus added translation episodes." Now Spanish people can learn Yoga Kitty! Or, as they say in Spanish, "El Yoga Gato!"

VERDICT: Cats neither need nor deserve enlightenment. My mantra? "Oooom Two cats is three too many. Oooom." Yoga Kitty is definitely a waste of your money. The path to enlightenment is long and hard, and walking it with your cat will just be a burden. Take a deep breath, in and out, and chant, "I don't need to buy this. I don't need to buy this."

52

The Dog Island
www.thedogisland.com

What's the best thing you can do for your dog? Send him to an island! "Over twenty-five hundred dogs are already enjoying a better life at Dog Island. Separated from the anxieties of urban life, dogs on Dog Island are healthy dogs who live a natural, healthy, and happy life, free from the stress and hardship associated with daily live among humans." Stress and hardship? You call sleeping, getting your tummy rubbed, playing with chew toys, and getting free food hardship?

PRODUCTS: The Leather Empathy Training Leash is a leash that lets your dog walk you! "It's really quite simple. When you take your dog out for a walk, simply fasten one end to his/her collar, and fasten the other end to your collar." Don't forget sending YOUR dog to Dog Island will cost you absolutely nothing! Good, now I can say goodbye to my faithful companion forever at no cost!

VERDICT: Dog Island is an exercise in pain. Pain of humiliation explaining to your friends where your dog went, pain in saying goodbye to a faithful friend, and pain in simply thinking of this disgusting experiment. Forget about Dog Island, and keep your dog from going anywhere near it.

53

Mr. Breakfast
www.mrbreakfast.com

Finally, a mascot for breakfast itself! "Mr. Breakfast is committed to: 1) assisting breakfast lovers find the best possible breakfast, and 2) making breakfast lovers out of those who are not." Well, it is the most important meal of the day, right? Don't forget Mrs. Breakfast.com, where Mrs. Breakfast looks suspiciously like Mr. Breakfast with a wig on.

PRODUCTS: Movies. Yes, movies. *The Breakfast Club*, DUH! Also links to Amazon to buy breakfast products like wafflemakers, "Eggsessories," ramekins for soufflés, and even Mr. Breakfast clothing! You can get Mr. Breakfast's picture on a T-shirt or hat, mugs with the Mr. Breakfast logo, and T-shirts and sweatshirts that simply say, "breakfast." Ingenious!

VERDICT: Mr. Breakfast is a great breakfast resource with a hint of bizarre humor. All of its products remind you of waking up to a delicious meal to start off your day on the right foot. With a mascot who lives, breathes, and of course, eats breakfast, Mr. Breakfast is the perfect site for everything breakfast.

54   Tracie Austin
www.tracieaustin.com

Tracie Austin is the first talk show host dedicated exclusively to crazy people. Oops, I mean, the paranormal. "That's exactly what this unique TV talk show is all about: Conversation and exploration of other realities that reside on and off our planet!" Past guests include Karen Gonzales: Pet Psychic.

PRODUCTS: Tons of T-shirts, including a dog T-shirt for pet psychic enthusiasts like Ms. Gonzales! Mouse pads, mugs, caps, bumper stickers (I honk for ghost hunters!), lunchboxes (creates great lunch chatter like "My mommy's a psychic!"), and, of course, the obligatory Paranormal Flying Saucer! You could also call this a frisbee. All products have the Let's Talk Paranormal Logo, with the website's address at the bottom. Buy today and become a walking advertisement for a show about experiences with scary spirits and little green men from another galaxy.

VERDICT: If you're an avid fan of this show, these products are sure to delight you. If you're like me, however, and have never seen this show before, you're likely to form an immediate impression that this show is not about psychics, but psychos.

55

Corpses for Sale
www.distefano.com

If you've dreamed forever about owning your own corpse, now's your chance! "Each corpse is hand crafted and is very durable in construction. Total attention to detail is seen in certain features such as *nostril cavities* and *fingernails that are imbedded into the decaying skin.*" Ok, that's just gross. Check out the "Corpse Gallery," with several disturbing pictures of these "life-like" corpse creations, including one where a corpse is holding a baby in its dead arms. God help that poor child. God help you if you buy this schlock.

PRODUCTS: Buy Vampire Killing Stakes, "hand crafted from aged cedar wood with heavy twine wrapped around the handle for a sure grip. A leather cross is nailed into the stake for added protection." Protection from what? "Real" vampires? Glass Eyes are also here, as is the ever-popular Decayed Arm, "complete with fingernails, bracelet, and bone." I shiver at the very thought. Finally, there's the repulsively rotten Fetus in a Petri Dish. Now, that's just wrong. Don't forget the corpses themselves, which will run you about six hundred dollars, so you can have nightmares every single night thinking of these crazy cadavers.

VERDICT: This site tops the list for absolutely repulsive and sickening products. They're not only gross, they are not in the slightest sense worth paying for. You might get some value spending money on a particularly hideous Halloween display. But while these people excel at creating realistic looking corpses, they're not good for much else.

56

Despair, Inc.
www.despair.com

"Sometimes, you have to tell it like it isn't." Despair Inc. is a site that dares to declare "you have the potential to be so very much less." Funny, I thought it was the other way around. "Whether you're a pessimist, underachiever, or a chronic failure, I personally offer my unconditional guarantee that Demotivators will truly inspire you to new lows!" Sounds like a great idea, no?

PRODUCTS: Demotivators Sticky pads in the style of those self-motivational posters. Examples include Idiocy ("Never underestimate the power of stupid people in large groups."), Procrastination ("Hard work often pays off after time, but laziness always pays off now."), and of course, Mistakes ("It could be that the purpose of your life is only to serve as a warning to others."). Don't forget Despair Gear, with shirts that read "Unleash the Power of Mediocrity," "The Power to be your Worst," and "Insecurity."

VERDICT: Despair, Inc. is definitely NOT for people with low self-confidence. I have never seen so many products that inspire such depression about life. If you couldn't care less about your own image, though, Despair Inc. is a great way to remind you how being lazy, stupid, and ignorant is sometimes the best thing in the world.

57

Bowling Shirt
www.bowlingshirt.com

How can you make "the world a better place"? Do it "one bowling shirt at a time." That's right! Bowling shirts are this site's financial forte. "BowlingShirt.com offers the largest selection of retro-style, unisex bowling shirts available blank, theme-printed, hand-embroidered, and with personalized chainstitched names." What a great honor to be the top line of clothing for bowlers!

PRODUCTS: BowlingShirt.com offers various shirt styles, such as Classic Bowlers, Retro Bowlers (corny Sixties style shirts), Lounge Masters (shirts with an ugly colored stripe down the middle), Fifties Bowlers (button-up), and Swing Masters, which are nearly identical to Retro Bowlers. Remember to check out the Baddabing Mafia merchandise, including the "FUHGETABOUTIT" tank tops and panties! "Finally, you mob gals have something to wear during the summer!" Yes…the summer…

VERDICT: Bowling and retro enthusiasts alike will love the goods available at BowlingShirt.com. Whether you're a captain of a bowling team or a member of the Fifties Baby Boomer generation, BowlingShirt.com is sure to satisfy all of your needs for Fifties and Sixties merchandise.

58

Continental Sausage
www.continentalsausage.com

Take a trip through the exciting world of…sausages? "Continental Sausage has built a loyal customer base across the United States by producing 'All Natural' sausage products that are superior in taste and quality." Usually "All Natural" and "Quality" don't mix, like granola or oat bran muffins. You won't find just sausage here, though. "Continental Sausage also provides traditional domestic and imported European-style salamis, hams, breads, cheeses, and assorted grocery items." Talk about a wide range of expertise!

PRODUCTS: Start with the sausages themselves, including the delectable All Natural Chicken Sausages, which "contain no nitrites, MSG, or fillers [and] are made with All Natural ingredients!" Be sure to also take a look at their wide selection of cheeses from countries all around the world, including Sweden, Denmark, Holland, Germany, and of course, the good ol' USA. Tubs of Quark are also available, which is described as "A baker's cheese—often used for baking and desserts." Why don't they just call it Baker's Cheese instead of giving it name that sounds like a physics theory?

VERDICT: Unless you're patient and don't mind waiting days on end just for some "premium" sausages, Quark, or whatever you order, I'd suggest heading to your local supermarket for your sausage hankerings rather than ordering cross country from some strange sausage seller. It all depends on what value you put on your sausage.

59

Hidden Camera
www.hiddencamera.com

For all of your voyeuristic desires, it's HiddenCamera.com! "The Hidden Camera Store offers the finest in CCTV equipment and specializes in equipment of a covert or hidden nature. Normally used to monitor nannies/babysitters (popularly known in the press as 'Nanny Cams')…these miniature video cameras come already hidden inside smoke detectors, lighting, radios, clocks, etc." Isn't it possible this could be used for "something" other than security?

PRODUCTS: First, check out the DoorView B/W Door View Camera, which is "perfect for use in an apartment door peephole." What if you used it in a bathroom? Where's my privacy? Be sure to check out their "hottest seller," the EM100P B/W Pinhole Camera. "Install it…in a tissue box, behind a picture, behind a wall crack, or maybe in a flower arrangement." Do these perverted peeping aids ever end?

VERDICT: While hidden cameras may be good for cutting back on security system costs, the potential for them being misused is ridiculously high. Unless you want your house to be transformed into a Peeping Tom's paradise, stay away from HiddenCamera.com.

60   Big Fun Toys
www.bigfuntoys.com

They're big, they're fun, they're toys! They're Big Fun Toys! Shop different sections, such as "Big Fun Baby," "Big Fun Tots," "Big Fun Kids," "Big Fun Teens," and "Big Fun Adults." Big Fun for everyone!

PRODUCTS: For the babies, try Earlyears Earl. E. Bird! "With different fabrics in bright, engaging colors composing Earl E. Bird's arms, legs, and feet, this multicolored chicken is hard to resist." Babies find lots of things "hard to resist," like filling up diapers and spitting up all over, now don't they? For the toddlers in your house, try the Chicco Ball Pool Set, which features "two inflatable rings, each one with its own inflating valve. Also included are one hundred colorful plastic balls to add to your pool time fun!" Now you can play in the ball pit and the kiddie pool at the same time! For teens, there's Barney's Bowl-O-Rama Game, a game based on *The Simpsons* locale of the same name. Finally, for adults, there's the Rock 'em Sock 'em Puppets. "Here's what happens when a Nun, the Amish, and a Rabbi are pushed too far." I can just imagine…

VERDICT: Big Fun Toys offers loads of fun for kids and adults alike. The products are appropriately fitted for each age group, and they are, well, big fun! Whatever your fancy for fun may be, you'll find it at Big Fun Toys. "Be more popular. Have clear skin. Shop Big Fun Toys!"

61

Sizzix
www.sizzix.com

This company sells products that satisfy that itch you've always had…to die cut? "Crafting at home is now a whole lot easier and a lot more fun. The vision of Sizzix started as a personal die-cutting system and line of dies but has now evolved into a whole lot more." And, exactly what does "a whole lot more" mean? If you're confused, watch the demonstration video, which shows how, by pulling a lever, you can make shapes in materials such as cardstock, vellum, cork, sheet magnet, suede, paper, foil, self-adhesive rubber, poly foam, pop-up sponge, shrink film, paper wood, and more. Talk about versatility!

PRODUCTS: Try the Sizzlits Doodle Die Baby Set, with baby's head, safety pin, bottle, and the word "baby" die set! What about the dirty diapers die set? Also take a look at Sizzlits Doodle Die Party Set, with ice cream, cupcake, "party," and birthday present dies. Is it party, or "par-tay"? Be sure to take a gander at the Sizzlits Tote Bag, which allows you to carry around your Sizzix Sets, for a low price of fifty dollars! Talk about bargains to "die" for!

VERDICT: Sizzix may be an odd machine that seems to be able to cut through titanium with ease, but is nevertheless a fun product for your youngster that you might want to consider. Just be careful around the machine; it appears to be pretty powerful.

62

Killer Plants
www.killerplants.com

Watch out, *Attack of the Killer Tomatoes*, Killer Plants are in town! "Killer Plants is devoted to the mystery and excitement of botanical connections that make our lives, our civilizations possible." Plants, responsible for civilization? One factor, maybe, but what about the one million plus others? "Killer Plants is a new perspective of human knowledge stated in exciting twists and turns. After all, life is rarely simple." Life IS rarely simple, but everything else sounds a little too grand for a website about plants.

PRODUCTS: Buy AAA fruit baskets, with selections such as the Colossal Fruit Basket. Also check out the "Perfume and Cologne" section, with the masculine cologne by Dolce and Gabbana for Men, a cologne that combines "Skillfully blended notes of citrus, coriander, and lemon accented with cardamom, cedar, and vetiver." Great, so now I'll smell like a fruit tree.

VERDICT: Strangely, no deadly botanical organisms can be found on the site. Despite being a bit misleading, and considering plants don't sport the grandeur that this site portrays them as having, KillerPlants.com sells lots of things for your home and lifestyle that you can enjoy without images of deadly Venus Fly Traps and other mutant flora.

63

Wonder Magnet
www.wondermagnet.com

This site asserts "it is wise to invest in strong magnets." Wonder Magnet sells very, very, strong magnets. Confused? Check out the magnetism FAQ, with answers like, "Manufacturing: NdFeB magnets are complicated to manufacture. The powdered NdFeB material is packed in molds, then sintered. The non-magnetized 'magnets' are then shaped to the correct size and plated. To magnetize them, they are placed in a very expensive machine that generates an extremely high-powered magnetic field for an instant, using high-voltage capacitor discharge and coils." Yeah, now I'm not confused.

PRODUCTS: Check out the electricity section, for products such as the Anemometer Cup and Hub Assembly; " A windspeed meter is essential both for evaluating a site for wind-power potential, and for measuring the performance of your wind turbine." Well, doesn't everybody have a wind turbine? Also check out the mysterious "NdFeB Super Magnets: Grab Bag." "Perfect for the curious who are not quite sure what they want!" "Only catch is, what goes in the grab bag is completely up to us!" That doesn't sound good.

VERDICT: WonderMagnet.com is a completely complicated site with useless products, save for science nerds who have an insane understanding of what all of this stuff means. I would be more pleased with a gift from Barbie.com than I would be with a gift from Wonder Magnet.

64

Monster Trucks
www.monstertrucks-uk.com

Yee-haw! I'm goin' to the monster truck rally! Monster Trucks has everything for the truck fanatic. Wondering about the origins of this classic sport? Check out "How It All Began."

PRODUCTS: Check out the "Inside Monster Jam" video series, available in volumes one through five! Monster Jam must be really amazing if there's five volumes! Don't forget the monster-truck toy store, with Hot Wheels trucks including Spiderman, Wolverine, Predator, Bustin' Loose, and, of course, Wild Thang. "Thang" sounds more like a type of exotic underwear than a killer truck.

VERDICT: Perhaps the strangest thing about this site is that it's put together by a guy from England. Not Arkansas, England. Blimey, the Limey likes the trucks! Unless you're already a fan of these monster machines, and easily amused by seeing crappy cars being crushed under giant wheels, Monster Truck's line of products is definitely not for more refined tastes. Monster Trucks are interesting to a point, but not likely to capture your attention for very long.

65

Satire Wire
www.satirewire.com

Satire Wire's creators have stopped updating the site, but that doesn't mean it doesn't have a generous helping of humor for you. Browse the site's archives, with articles such as "Top Ten Party Preschools Named" (party on the playground, baby!), "Humans Mostly Not Dumber than Rice" (but they have more genes!), and "Men DO Talk about Relationships" (we're not ALL pigs).

PRODUCTS: Various T-shirts with catchy phrases such as, "Diplomas is for losers," and "There is no Global warming: I always wear T-shirts in winter" (well, doesn't everybody?). And, of course, "PR at work," with a construction-sign-style logo of a man shoveling a mound of manure. Various hats, mugs, and mousepads are also available with these slogans and the Satire Wire logo.

VERDIC : Ghile the Satire Wire site did stop updating in August 2002, their articles still are hidden treasures that offer loads of *Onion*-style humor. Whether you fancy original satire like "Nuke Treaty to be Signed, Ignored" (North Korea certainly is doing so), or want a T-shirt that degrades those sneaky PR representatives, Satire Wire has something for everybody.

66 Indignant Online
www.indignantonline.com

"Indignant Online: Because Attitude Matters." Indignant Online is another satire site with humor abounding. See the article "How to Get Cast by Quentin Tarantino," which reveals the secret: "So you want to get cast by Tarantino? Find a party he's going to be at, crash the gate, and make friends." Who knew it was that simple? See the "Indignant Sports" section with the article, "Mike Tyson in Trouble Again." No, he didn't bite another ear off, but he did cheat on his wife. Like Tyson says, "I hit her, she hit da campus."

PRODUCTS: Two classic books, *Email from Nigeria* and *Beware of the Club Girls*, both by Todd Allen. The first is described as "the new humor anthology from Todd Allen…Sociological observations run amok. Tales of relationships gone horribly wrong. The foibles of business and politics. Strange things defying categorization. It is Todd's lot in life to document such things, or at least make them up." Well, at least he's honest. Don't forget the best line of clothing, ever: "PETA: People Eat Tasty Animals." It's funny because it's true!

VERDICT: Any site that has "People Eat Tasty Animals" clothing is a winner. With two witty books and hilarious topics, Indignant Online is a great place for eccentric humor, with a twist.

67

Jedi Master
www.jedimaster.net

Watch out, Luke Skywalker: The Star Wars Kid is in town! Who exactly is the Star Wars Kid? "Back in November 2002, Ghyslain (the SWK) was goofing off at a school video studio and recorded himself fighting a mock battle with a golf ball retriever that he used like a Lightsaber. His friends found the tape and uploaded it to KaZaA as a joke. Within two weeks, someone had added full *Star Wars* special effects and sound effects to the tape. Currently, new clone videos are being created at the rate of one per day!" And I thought I was embarrassed often enough.

PRODUCTS: Various T-shirts featuring the SWK, including a "Feel the Power" shirt with a cartoon of the kid holding a yellow Lightsaber. Also one with the letters "SWK" in Star Wars style writing with a silhouette of the kid, Lightsaber in hand, with the caption, "He is the one that will bring balance to the force." Don't forget the "Put Ghyslain in Episode III" petition T-shirt. After all, if George Lucas was able to put in Jar Jar Binks, putting in the SWK is a more that feasible feat.

VERDICT: Whether you're a Star Wars fanboy or a fan of this chubby mind-trick master, Jedi Master is a look into the maybe humiliating, but certainly hilarious world of the phenomena that is the Star Wars Kid. The force will be with you…always.

68

Fried Social Worker
www.friedsocialworker.com

Fried Social Workers, unite! Why are these dedicated servants so tired out? "Too many of our employers fail to empower us with the ability to perform effectively, doing so in a multitude of ways." A long explanation about the errors in social worker management follows, including "mismanagement," "schedule imbalance," "intense work days," and "chronic fear of downsizing." Sounds like any corporate workplace these days. What makes fried social workers so special?

PRODUCTS: Many products are available for purchase, including coasters, posters, license plate frames, T-shirts, coffee mugs, baseball caps, mousepads, tote bags, and even clocks to count down to the end of the hectic day in the life of a social worker. The most memorable ones include a poster with an administrator holding a sign saying "Merry Christmas…now get back to work." Isn't that the truth?

VERDICT: Whether you're a fried social worker yourself or a fan of government employee humor, Fried Social Worker is a great resource for fun, witty commentary. The products aren't bad either, and are great for weary workers with wit, or anyone else who enjoys catchy commentary.

69

Pimp Hats
www.pimphats.com

Yo, yo, fa shizzle! Pimp Hats iz here! This site is a seller of headgear for all you ballas out there! "We pimp clothes all over the world! The only producers of real pimp suits!" What's the difference between a real Pimp Suit and a fake one? Don't forget the shopping promise, "We look forward to serving your pimp needs." Yo! They fo' real!

PRODUCTS: Check out the aforementioned "real" Pimp Suits. Choose from the Black Valboa with Zebra, a black suit with zebra fur lining or the White Valboa with Snow Leopard. How many poor animals did they have to slaughter to get these sick suits? Or perhaps, how many little polyesters met their doom? The suits, which include the coat and pants, cost $149.99. No wonder they're "real"; the prices are outrageous! Don't forget the hats themselves, with selections including not just white and black "suga daddy" hats, but also purple, red, and pink hats! So, with the cane, suit, hat, and "bling" (jewelry), it would cost you over two hundred dollars to look like a pimp. Ridiculous, I tell you!

VERDICT: Buying a Pimp Hat will ultimately lead to ridicule and shame; nobody likes a wannabe. Like going to see a bad Ben Stiller movie like *Dodgeball: A True Underdog Story*, Pimp Hats is just a desperate attempt to touch the world that few of us see (or want to see).

70

Penguin Magic
www.penguinmagic.com

Do you believe in magic? Penguin Magic is a resource for "serious" magicians everywhere. Their products reveal everything you need to know to discover the secrets of magic tricks. "Magic is different [from] other hobbies and even other performance arts. Magic has a very strong and wonderful community aspect to it. We're proud to be a part of that community, and we welcome you and look forward to sharing our love of magic with you." A community dedicated to impressing gullible fools and making skeptics ponder what the "logical explanation" is.

PRODUCTS: Start with the *Magic Tricks Anybody Can Do* DVD. "Magic for beginners, taught by a world-renowned master! Hands down the best beginner's guide to magic out there." Now, let's see, how do I make that card disappear again? Move up to the Time Machine trick, which is "one of the very best effects in all of magic. The power of this effect on a group of spectators is beyond description. You will literally scare them!" With what? The resurrection of Jeffrey Dahmer? Or maybe the resurrection of the career of Vanilla Ice? Now I am really scared.

VERDICT: Penguin Magic may have nothing to do with penguins, but it has everything to do with magic. The magic may be real, like Anna Nicole Smith's weight loss (thank you Trimspa!) or, it may not be real, like Bill Clinton's autobiography. Real or not, it's an interesting entertainment medium that has some interesting products to match here on Penguin Magic.

71

Jolene's Trailer Park
www.jolenestrailerpark.com

Visit the official site of Jolene Sugarbaker, the Trailer Park Queen! "The Jolene Sugarbaker Company is your source for fun, witty, quirky original T-shirts and gifts by comedian Jolene Sugarbaker! You may have seen our products on ABC, CBS, Fox, *Good Morning America*, or one of several newspapers and magazines!" No actually, I haven't, and I'm not sure I want to.

PRODUCTS: Start with the Cicada Invasion line, T-shirts featuring those pesky bugs native to all fine trailer parks. Buy a coaster that says, "I Ate Me a Cicada." Even with proper grammar, that would still be gross. The best line of products is the White Trash line, featuring such classic slogans as, "Don't Make me Slap You with my Flip-Flop," "Trailer Park Princess," and, of course, "White Trash with Class!" Three words: Fab-U-Lous!

VERDICT: Jolene may be the queen of trailer parks, but these products are, without a doubt, overly offensive. If you're the type that likes your apparel outspoken and outrageous, much like Hugh Hefner's *Little Black Book* (no, really, it's a real book), Jolene Sugarbaker is the gal for you.

72

Holokits
www.holokits.com

Beam me up, Scotty! Holokits is "your one-stop shop for holographic film and plates, instructions, and resources, so you can make holograms and teach holography." Holography classes? Weird. "The wonders of technology!

PRODUCTS: If you need a specific part, browse the "Holographic film and plates" section. 30 2.5" X 2.5" plates are ninety-five dollars. Think that's expensive? Try a roll of 39" X 33" film, which will run you about $1,385! If you're not sure what you're looking for, buy a kit. One standard Holokit with recording material, developer trays, instruction materials, a chemical processing kit and a Holography Diode Laser is $160! What can I do with all of this junk? Make a three-dimensional stick figure?

VERDICT: Holograms may sound like they belong on Star Trek, but now even you can make your own holographic doctor, or something like it. If you have the money to spare, or if you have some "practical" use for it (that's beyond my comprehension), go for it. But, much like a Cadillac Escalade, it's too expensive, too gaudy, and too useless for my tastes.

73

Global Spot
www.globalspot.com

The mission of Global Spot is a dire one. Millions of dollars have been dedicated to fighting various plagues that afflict our modern civilizations, however, not one cent, nada, nothing, zip, has been put aside to fight the most dastardly of all: BOREDOM! Finally, someone who understands! This is a collection of satirical stories, jolly jokes, quizzical quotes, and more humor that is dedicated to "curing boredom on the Internet." Isn't that the most important thing?

PRODUCTS: Buy T-shirts with various popular catch phrases and humorous concepts. Buy the "You're Fired" T-shirt, to convey what Donald Trump says on his hit show *The Apprentice* to everybody who sees it! Or, get a shirt with a shocked yellow face on it that reads, "Much to Bob's horror, he discovered too late that his date Jane was really JOHN!" My worst nightmare, on a shirt. A shirt is also available with the now-stale Nineties catch phrase, "Talk to the Hand." That got old years ago. Stop trying to say it now.

VERDICT: Whether you like bizarre articles such as "Friendly Dog Prevents Killing Spree," or products like the "Shut Up" T-shirt, GlobalSpot.com has plenty of satirical humor and satirical products to match. True to its name, this is a great "spot" for humor on the "global" wide web.

74

Vynsane
www.vynsane.com

This is not just Vynsane, it's insane. On the main page, there's a brain with branches sticking out that link to various parts of the page, with the phrase "Vynsane 4.0" at the bottom. I'm confused already. You'll be even more confused when you click on "design," with various pieces of album covers and posters grouped under the headings "Hetradyne," "Hemenway," and "Fantastic Toyage." The deeper you go, the more you wonder what the heck this is all about.

PRODUCTS: The Vynsane shop features more appropriately weird apparel. Products include underwear that reads, "Do Not Enter." Talk about an obvious statement. Also browse the bacon selection, products with a picture of a piece of bacon on the cover, and an appropriate description to the line, "mmm...bacon shirt..." Other products include Sloths (with photos of sloths on the shirts), "Kung Fu Master," "Don't Tell Jesus," and the "Vynsane" section, with "other random stuff that doesn't fit anywhere else." Doesn't that describe this site in general?

VERDICT: With a bizarre "theme" that seems to be as weird as Cher's selection of outfits, Vynsane sells products that are even weirder. Unless you like confusing people, Vynsane's products are not recommended for the reasonable, logical type. Think carefully about this one.

75

World Kickball
www.worldkickball.com

It's America's least favorite sport! Next to professional outdoor soccer, at least. "Welcome to WAKA—the preeminent adult kickball organization and the world governing body of kickball. In its seventh straight year, WAKA continues to help tens of thousands of players across the United States and the world experience the joy of kickball." I prefer the Joy of Pepsi, thank you very much.

PRODUCTS: Buy the WAKA "Play Kickball" shirt, and flaunt your love for kickball. That is, if you love kickball, which you probably don't. If you're missing equipment for the sport, simply get the "official kickball" to complete your requirements! "WAKA big red kickball with WAKA logo—the only official ball of kickball." It's official, so it must be quality construction! And of course, everyone needs an Official Kickball Scorebook for those all important statistics.

VERDICT: Kickball isn't the most recognizable sport in the world, and you wearing World Kickball clothing won't help. Unless you're a fanatic of the sport, buying this site's dorky duds will do nothing to inspire you or your friends to take steps to promote this square sport.

76

Liquid Medication
www.liquidmedication.com

This site is home to a comic known as *Liquid Medication*, presumably another one of the hundreds of phrases describing alcohol. "Liquid Medication is the brain child/comic release created by Andy King. That would be me." Really? We didn't know. "I realized I make people laugh every day so there is no shortage of ideas, and as for the artwork…I apologize in advance." Apology accepted.

PRODUCT: T-shirts, stickers, and baby crawlers are available with the Liquid Medication logo: a martini glass. What a nice thing for a baby to wear; a crawler with an alcoholic drink on it. What will the parents tell them when they get older? Also is a T-shirt with American colors reading "Andy for President" along with a drawing saying, "I'll get s*** done." Such a tactful statement, no?

VERDICT: It's plain to see that the comic strips in Liquid Medication are uninspired, as are the petty products. The artwork is even worse, and looks like something out of a children's coloring book. Like watching an episode of the tragically cancelled *Method and Red*, wearing Liquid Medication clothing is not something you want to be seen doing.

77

Just Toilet Paper
www.justtoiletpaper.com

This page sells toilet paper. But, it's not just any toilet paper: the rolls have humorous designs on them! Going to the bathroom is fun again! Wait, was it ever?

PRODUCTS: The current "hot items" are the Saddam and Osama rolls. Just where those two belong! Or perhaps you'd like the Camouflage roll; your toilet paper now can blend into the jungle landscape! Toilet paper with hearts, kisses, shamrocks, flowers, balloons, and even angels are also here for your hygienic pleasure.

VERDICT: While toilet paper may not need fancy designs, (seeing where it will end up), Just Toilet Paper is an interesting prospect. If you're into saving money, however, this site is not recommended; individual rolls are eight bucks. If you've got money to blow, however, Just Toilet Paper is a quirky, odd way to add variety to your bathroom.

78

Money Factory
www.moneyfactory.com

This site is actually the home to the US Bureau of Engraving and Printing, a division of the US Treasury. If you wish to learn more about our official currency, see the FAQ, with questions like, "What is the weight of a currency note?" The answer? "The approximate weight of a currency note, regardless of denomination, is one gram. There are 454 grams in one U.S. pound, therefore, there should be 454 notes in one pound." How considerate for those of us who don't know simple mathematics.

PRODUCTS: Buy pieces of U.S. history, like an engraved copy of the Declaration of Independence, so it may "serve as a reminder of the freedom that all Americans possess and the foundation on which it stands!" Unfortunately, some Americans don't understand that well enough (cough, celebrities, cough). But the real attraction is Uncut Currency Sheets, real sheets of money that can be used for, what else: wrapping paper! The wrapping is more expensive than the present; a sheet of thirty-two dollar bills only costs $50! What better way to give a gift? What a bargain!

VERDICT: Wrapping paper made out of real money may not be very economical, but as the site so aptly puts it, "They make an especially unique gift for that 'hard-to-buy-for' person." Hard to buy for, as in a rich snob? In any case, money factory has some great gifts for people who want something a bit different.

79

Creative Chocolates of Vermont
www.creativechocolatesofvt.com

"Creative Chocolates of Vermont, Inc. is where your imagination creates the only boundaries in our Chocolate World." The world of chocolate. Ahhhh, I can see it now. Creative Chocolates of Vermont "pride ourselves on the ability to adapt just about anything into chocolate. As the years have progressed we've moved into more exciting territory." Exciting meaning weird?

PRODUCTS: Don't want to wait for dessert? Make the whole meal a chocolate treat! Products include a burger made out of different kinds of chocolate, a chocolate TV dinner, and a chocolate pizza. Hey, Ma! What's for dinner? Chocolate! The best of the bunch, however, is the chocolate toilet. Now toilets can be used during a meal, not after!

VERDICT: I would tend to think that "creative" would mean artwork, like Picasso, or DaVinci, or Warhol (soup cans, art?). According to this company, however, food is art. While chocolate may not be the most recognizable form of art, it certainly is the most delicious. Mmm…chocolate.

80

Flamingo Surprise
www.flamingosurprise.com

"Just think of how surprised that special someone will be to wake up to a yard full of pink flamingos cavorting on the lawn or to any of our many other yard displays." I can't imagine. Really, I can't. Flamingo Surprise is a service that sets up lawn displays secretly for birthdays, anniversaries, and other special occasions. "Your special surprise is guaranteed to be delivered between midnight and six o'clock in the morning and picked up that same evening between 5:30 and 8:30 p.m.!" What if they're early risers? Wouldn't be much of a surprise then. More like "what the **** are you doing on my lawn?"

PRODUCTS: You can opt to select the traditional Flamingo Surprise. You can select by a type of display, including animals, with examples such as blue, pink, and rainbow flamingos (perfect if you're not sure of their favorite color…or something like that). Or select by occasion, each with a sample phrase. The birthday option for thirty, forty, fifty, and sixty year celebrations has an example reading, "Oh no! Bob hit the big 4-0!" What if Bob didn't want the neighbors to know he was forty? Look out for Bob tomorrow. Finally, you can purchase flamingo apparel and individual lawn ornaments.

VERDICT: I find it interesting that flamingos are pink. Not many things come in pink, except for Barbie's latest line of fashion. Pink, green, or blue flamingos make interesting lawn ornaments, and flamingo Surprise is the place to buy them, along with a few other surprises (who can resist a cow lawn ornament?).

81

Nunsense

www.nunsense.com

Nunsense is a live theater musical series about nuns. Shows include *Nunsense, Nunsense 2, Nuncrackers*, and a few more strange shows having to do with frightening little old ladies in penguin costumes. What exactly is the show that started it all about? "The Little Sisters of Hoboken…went unnoticed until one day their cook, Sister Julia…unwittingly served some tainted vichyssoise soup and fifty-two sisters died of botulism."

PRODUCTS: The line of nonsensical Nunsense products include magnets, key rings, CDs, DVDs and videos of the productions, and T-shirts and other apparel, such as the T-shirt with the phrase "Holier than Thou" on the chest. Holier than thou, because…?

VERDICT: Nunsense may sound a lot like "nonsense," and for good reason. Nuns are supposed to be respected religious figures, not objects of ridicule. Nevertheless, Nunsense has managed to make nuns into just that: stupid and ridiculous.

82

Amish Mart
www.amishmart.com

As weird as it sounds, you can buy Amish products over the Internet! No, the Amish have not decided to go high-tech; they sell them through a modern company. "Our facility is located in the small town of Geneva, Indiana, which is right in the heart of the Amish community here in northeastern Indiana." Do they know you're using unholy electricity to sell their work?

PRODUCTS: A variety of handcrafted Amish products are available, including baskets, bookends, desktop organizers, and coat hangers. The rooster bookend features a colorful wooden rooster, now only forty dollars! Those Amish sure charge an arm and a leg for their projects! And who said Amish food was all gruel and vegetables? Buy Amish candy, fudge, jellies and jams, pies, and more. They've even caught up with the health food craze, offering sugar-free caramel, chocolate, and peanut-butter bars! Order them by the case, or individually (why would you want to wait for days to get one sugar-free candy bar?)

VERDICT: Why are Amish people so against electricity? Their beliefs may be different from today's world of computers and cell phones that take pictures (read: useless), but they sure can craft some good furniture and tasty food, as this site so readily demonstrates.

83

Glow, Inc.
www.glowinc.com

Remember how fascinating glow-in-the-dark products were when they first came out? Now there's a whole online store for them! "Ultra glow products are fourteen times brighter than those available in retail stores." This site has project ideas, technical notes, and instructions available for every aspect of glow in the dark. Glow in the dark projects? What kind, a glow in the dark bookcase?

PRODUCTS: Buy Glow in the Dark paint or powder. Which one should you choose? Fifty pounds of white Glow in the Dark powder will set you back about $6,782.00. No joke. The paint appears more reasonable at $1,302.00 for five gallons of paint. Five gallons of "special" paint will cost you about as much as a good computer. Hmm...a computer, or glow in the dark paint? Decisions, decisions.

VERDICT: Things that glow in the dark are in the same league as professional wrestling, fart jokes, and shiny objects. The simple mind is easily amused. You can see it in the dark, big deal. You can see TV screens in the dark too. Glow, Inc. sells products that are uninteresting and unreasonable. Who would pay $300 for one can of glow in the dark paint? I rest my case.

84

The American Sumo Association
www.sumoamerica.com

Sumo Wrestling isn't a sport reserved to the Japanese anymore; now it's waddled over to America! "Today the sport boasts unprecedented popularity in Japan and is rapidly gaining followers throughout the world. This increasing acceptance can be attributed to a number of factors, including the beauty of this one-to-one sport which combines strength, agility, and balance." Balance? Agility? Agility is the last thing I'd associate with these blubbery behemoths.

PRODUCTS: You can buy Sumo books, including *Dynamic Sumo* by Clyde Newton. "It is all here starting from the basics, including the rules of competition, daily life in a sumo stable, and the rituals that mark each transition point in a wrestler's career" Sumo stable? Well, like horses in a stable, Sumo wrestlers require mountains of food and large sleeping accomodations, hence, the "stable." You can also buy American Sumo T-shirts, available in small, medium, extra large, and double extra. That's it. No bigger. Seriously.

VERDICT: The most repulsive aspect of this site is that shirt sizes only go to XXL, not XXXXXXXXXXXXXXL. This is unexcusable! This is an outrage! What good are Sumo wrestling shirts if they don't fit Sumo wrestlers? This makes these products ultimately useless.

85

The Beer Store
www.thebeerstore.ca

Gee, I wonder what they sell here? As the site so frankly puts it, "It would be difficult to find a larger selection of beer anywhere in the world than at The Beer Store." The name certainly suggests that, doesn't it? "Currently, The Beer Store offers more than three hundred brands from over seventy brewers from around the world—and the selection continues to grow." Three hundred different tastes. And I thought there were enough varieties of weight loss books!

PRODUCTS: Think their online store sells beer? Unfortunately, no. You Canadians will have to visit your local Beer Store, or, if you live in America, you can take a road trip up to Canada to buy beer, just like those underage college students! Anybody can buy their Beer Gear, though. Depending on whom you're buying for, check out "Beer Gear for Him" and "Beer Gear for Her." There are T-shirts, hats, and jerseys featuring different brands of beer, including Budweiser, Coors Light, Labatt Blue, Molson Canadian, and various other brands. There's a little problem, however; NO MILLER GEAR! The Beer Store hates Milwaukee! Shame, shame!

VERDICT: The Beer Store (or as they say in Canada dere, "Da Beer Store") may have a simple name, but it's for good reason: they're all about the beer.

86

American Nuclear Society
www.ans.org

It's pronounced "nuk-ulur." The ANS is a company raising awareness about nuclear energy in the United States. Their mission is to "serve its members in their efforts to develop and safely apply nuclear science and technology for public benefit through knowledge exchange, professional development, and enhanced public understanding." Most of the "public understanding" about the word "nuclear" is that it's a huge type of explosion.

PRODUCTS: Choose from a wide variety of nuclear research materials, including handbooks like the "2004 World Directory of Nuclear Utility Management," available now with CD-ROM for $825. If you're normal, however, and you just want the word "nuclear" on your chest, check out their clothing line, including sports shirts, fleeces, briefcases, and more. Each piece of clothing comes with the ANS logo, a blue atom with the organization's name.

VERDICT: Two types of people will enjoy the products on the ANS web page: real nuclear scientists, and science geeks. If you're either of these, now's your chance to wear the ANS logo with pride. Whether you're chatting about nuclear physics, getting beat up by dim-witted jocks, or both, ANS has the apparel for you.

87   Sea Monkeys
www.sea-monkeys.com

Sea Monkeys are the "world's only instant pets." Just mix a couple of dry packets of ingredients together, and you've got little, almost-invisible creatures swimming around in your water. They look sort of like small tadpoles, but it's hard to see them unless you're really close to the tank. Even tiny goldfish can be seen easily, and they're more decoration than a pet.

PRODUCTS: You can begin with the Sea Monkey Starter Kit, which is "all you need to start your own colony of sea monkeys." It includes Water Purifier, Growth Food, a Calibrated Feeding Spoon, and Instant Live Eggs, which are described as "the <u>mysterious</u> ingredients that (when combined with Packet 1, Water Purifier) hatches instant LIVE baby Sea Monkeys." Mysterious translates into "a word we're using to get you to buy this junk."

VERDICT: I don't like the idea of a pet you can't even see very well. How do you know they're not dead? How do you know they're there at all? Can they fetch a ball? How do you know you didn't get a big batch of nothing with it? Sea Monkeys may be "the world's only instant pets," but "instant" is no substitute for fun and interesting.

88   Spudgun Technology Center
www.spudtech.com

It's kinda like paintball, with potatoes! What exactly is a Spudgun? "A Spudgun is a simple device made usually from plastic water pipe, designed to launch/shoot/lob a potato or similar object a long way, farther than you could probably throw it, to distances exceeding three hundred yards." Why would I want to shoot potatoes three hundred yards when I could eat them from a distance of zero yards? This site sells products for "what is fast becoming a favorite weekend past time for people of all ages." People of all ages like potatoes being shot at them?

PRODUCTS: So many models to choose from! The PVC Combustion Spudgun is the basic model, which is a barrel attached to a barbeque lighter. Upgrades include making the barrel longer and detachable, and buying a tennis ball barrel. But it's supposed to shoot potatoes! If you like your Spudguns large, buy the SGTC Mega-Launcher, which "weighs seventy pounds," "shoots twenty-four ounce soda bottles as 'ammuniton,'" and looks like a plastic cannon.

VERDICT: Using a gun to shoot potatoes at people is an extreme waste of good food! There are starving people in China and India who would thank the heavens for being able to eat your abundant "ammo" source! Poverty consideration aside, Spudgun is still quite a useless product. If you want to play with non-lethal guns, do paintball, not potatoes.

89   Spy World
www.spyworld.com

This site must be where James Bond shops! Spy World is "dedicated to helping protect your privacy, assets, and your personal safety with our latest Spy equipment, tools, and gear." Spy World sounds like it should be called "Paranoia World."

PRODUCTS: You can buy the Cellular Voice Encryption if you think those crazy crime lords are listening in on your conversations. How much for this complicated cellular tool? Only $2,200! You can't put a price on your safety! Or, you can purchase the Soviet Spy Monocular if you wish to do the spying. "[This] prismatic lens system magnifies an amazing eight times, and fully-coated optics provide extraordinarily clear, stable image when viewing distant objects like sporting events, concerts, or spying on someone!" In other words, a lawsuit waiting to happen!

VERDICT: Spy World is not a place for cool spy gear like I originally thought. It's for paranoid freaks who think people are out to kill them. With wire taps, bug detectors, and other gear for detecting those non-existent people who are out to get you, only political figures and other VIPs should even consider Spy World gear.

90

Feng Shui Store
www.fengshuistore.com

Good for karma, good for life, man! You may have heard of Feng Shui and have a vague idea of what it is. The exact definition is "a way of understanding and focusing attention on the energy that permeates the spaces in which we live and work." Groovy, man. Groovy. Feng Shui "shows you how to transform those areas into places of peace and harmony through the placement of furniture, mirrors, plants, crystals, wind chimes, and colors." Does anybody realize how crazy this sounds? Center your couch for enlightenment, paint your poodle for peace. Yeah, sure.

PRODUCTS: In the extremely descriptive "Bright Objects" category, you can find peace-inducing products such as the 50mm Baroque Crystal. "Used for meditation; help create freedom from worry; hang in cluttered area to 'unstick' energy; or hang over your bed to ease financial worries while you sleep." A crystal is going to take away my financial worries? Maybe, but it doesn't pay the bills!

VERDICT: I've never been one to believe in fake mind-altering stuff like Chi, Karma, Aura, and the like. Leave that stuff to Miss Cleo and her cheating cohorts; The Feng Shui Store is no different. Unless you're "hip" and want to cash in on this "cool" new trend while you're at it, fine, but otherwise, don't bother.

91   Richard Simmons Store
www.richardsimmons.com

No! Please, God, no! The Richard Simmons store is by far the weirdest, stupidest, and downright most DISGUSTING store in this book. This spandex-clad exercise guru was huge back in the eighties when the aerobics craze was at its apex. Now, he appears like more of a deranged lunatic.

PRODUCTS: For those who are stuck in the time when disco was actually cool, you can (CAN is the key word; you should NOT) buy the *Disco Sweat* DVD. "This workout is complete with lighted dance floor and the most fantastic '70s tunes that'll make you want to *Shake Your Booty* and drop those inches for good." I never, never want to hear the words "shake your booty" and "Richard Simmons" in the same sentence.

VERDICT: As Mr. Simmons once said himself, "The first word in diet, is DIE." In other words, you're going to die, go crazy, or both if you listen to this deranged diet guru. Richard may have been cool back in the eighties, when tight exercise suits for men were in, but he's just plain weird now. Run. Run far, far, away.

92   William Shatner Store
www.williamshatner.com

THE official web SITE of WILL—I-AM SHATNER! That's right! The superstar of such successful series as *Star Trek* and *TJ Hooker* has a stunning site, along with an equally stunning store! Bill's site features news on his daily activities, along with occasional blurbs from his daughter Lisabeth. Hopefully, she does not share the eccentric speech patterns of her father. You can view the fan club page, blurble about Bill in the forums, and, of course, visit his store.

PRODUCTS: You can peruse Mr. Shatner's wide selection of movies, including *William Shatner's Spplat Attack!* In it, "William Shatner leads the forces of earth to resist the alien hordes led by national radio personality Mancow, and the cyborg warriors led by paintball icon Tom Kaye." Bill, Mancow, cyborg warriors, and paintball? What an irresistible combination! Also available is a collection of autographed merchandise, with dozens of pieces of memorabilia autographed by the sci-fi idol himself! And what Shatner site would be complete without a music masterpiece by the man himself? *Has Been*, William Shatner's new album, features an equal mix of solo songs and songs with very, uh, notable guests.

VERDICT: I can rest in peace knowing that I have finally found a website where I can purchase William Shatner's unbelievable music. Sarcasm aside, Shatner's site is your one-stop shop for Shatner merchandise. Whether your fancy is the William Shatner Priceline Bobblehead doll (what about his fellow spokesman, Leonard Nimoy?), or products from his failed *Tekwar* series, Shatner is still all the rage. In the geek universe, that is. Oh, and if you see Bill around, tell him to remind his friend Mr. Nimoy to eat more salsa. (see LNSEMSF.com)

93

Levitron
www.levitron.com

Levitron: a really expensive toy flying saucer! "Spin the top—and watch it float! The Levitron spins and surfs on magnetic waves! Pass your hand above, underneath, and around the top. It will continue to spin and float only touching air!" And the best part: "no batteries required!" As Captain Obvious says, though, that doesn't mean "no power required."

PRODUCT: The Perpetuator is what makes the Levitron, well, levitate. "This special electromagnetic drive device works with the Levitron, allowing the top to remain levitated indefinitely in space. The Perpetuator creates magnetic waves which silently and invisibly spin the floating top at a rate of over 2.5 million revolutions per day!" So it spins. Big deal. If you want to buy this terrific trinket, you can buy it online from Innovatoys.com or Hippygift.com. Hippygift.com? Figures…

VERDICT: Like holograms, Levitron may be out of the realm of science fiction, but once again, truth is sometimes stranger than fiction (just look at Michael Jackson). Levitron may make an interesting gift, but its practical applications are slim to none. Good for an expensive thrill, bad for anything meaningful.

94

Wishing Fish
www.wishingfish.com

Here's another funky gift store for you to buy the best new "trendy" stuff. "Our collection includes an eclectic mixture of styles: vintage and modern, funky and sophisticated, East meets West. Our products are practical enough to use every day, yet beautiful enough to save for a special occasion. Use them to create your own unique environment, your own (life)style." Lifestyle, or just…style?

PRODUCTS: The "Living" section offers such interesting trinkets as Bloom Flowers in a Can. "Simply crack 'em open, add some water, place them in a sunny windowsill, and watch the flowers grow!" They're not just flowers, they're flowers in a can. In the "Fun and Games" section, you can sample more of this site's "avant-garde" style selection with Coal Bubble Gum, in a stylish, simple black box. "The outside of the box features phrases like "because you've been very bad" and "it's all you get—sure to send any guilty conscience into overdrive." And don't forget the Oral Fixation Mints. The innuendo meter in this product is in overdrive as well.

VERDICT: Wishing Fish offers a lot of nifty new age gadgets and organizing tools, as well as a good selection of retro gifts. Whether you're looking for flowers in a can, insect nail clippers, vitamin C bath cubes, or a chocolate voodoo doll (eat it to torture your jerky ex-boyfriend!), Wishing Fish has a little something for everybody.

95

Robot Shop
www.robotshop.ca

The future is here, but the future sure is expensive. "Here you will find robot toys, robot kits, and robot parts to build your own robots. If you need a sonar, a motor, or just an intelligent vacuum like Roomba or Karcher; this site is for you."

PRODUCTS: All are expensive; this site is also for people with big wallets. Take the Robocleaner RC 3000 for example. "Take the drudgery out of boring vacuuming chores"… for $2,000! That seems like an awful lot to take the boredom out of cleaning your house. Or, how about the Arm Trainer, a "remote-controlled robotic arm"? "Built by OWI, this robotic arm has been selected by Dr. Toy as one of the one hundred best children's products and ten best educational products in 1998." How much will this "educational" toy run you? About $120. Robotic slaves for everybody? Yeah, in about one hundred years.

VERDICT: There seems to be a common theme among most futuristic technologies that are becoming reality: they're amazing examples of technology, but horrid examples of value. Running about $50 for just an average robot part and as much as $2,000 for the actual robots, Robot Shop is extremely expensive. It'll be another few years before this overpriced junk becomes both practical and affordable.

96 Swords and Armor
www.swordsandarmor.com

Now you, too, can be a real-life Knight of the Round Table! This site sells replica and authentic versions of medieval armor and weaponry. "The edged fantasy weapons, shields, plate armour, suits of chain mail armor, medieval knight helmets , arms, and weapons are available at the lowest prices anywhere." How does this site define low?

PRODUCTS: They define it as ridiculously high. Want a reproduction of an armored breastplate? It'll set you back about $170. How about chain mail, which is advertised here as the "best price on the planet-guaranteed"? Two hundred sixty dollars for a chain mail shirt. It's not all triple-digit prices though; you can buy a Sword of Carlos V for $90. I guess it costs less to chop off heads than it does to keep yours on.

VERDICT: If you want to be King Arthur for a day or have a medieval museum in your home, Swords and Armor can give you a taste of the "knights in shining armor" of centuries past. But, like anything it's going to cost you, a lot. And no, you shouldn't swing swords at people. It's dangerously dumb, kind of like Paris Hilton.

97 Crazy Aaron's Putty World
www.puttyworld.com

Silly Putty: bad food, good fun! Don't think that Silly Putty is fun? Take a testimonial from "Desk Toy Deprived #783." "This was the MOST FUN experience I've had internet shopping. The putty arrived super fast and is gorgeous…it's a lot more useful than doodling because my hands get exercise." Finally, some fun, wholesome hand exercise!

PRODUCTS: You could try the newest putty rage, the Heat Sensitive Hypercolors putty. "Hypercolor Thinking Putty is thermochromic— just a touch from your hands or a warm coffee mug will reveal a new, 'hot' color." It changes colors, dude! Sure, the TV does that too, but, it changes colors! There's also a groovy trick with your microwave you can do with this putty. "Use your microwave with Hypercolor Thinking Putty and verify the speed of light!" Really, it's just finding the hot and cold spots in your microwave…but, "verifying the speed of light" sounds so much cooler! Glow in the Dark Putty, Primary (regular) Putty, and many other types of putty are also available.

VERDICT: Silly Putty was never something I liked; the idea of playing with goo never interested me. Some people might view putty as a chance for artistic expression. While I can't imagine what "art" you'd create with silly putty, with "modern art" being the way it is, you never know when you'll create the next masterpiece. Good for the little ones (as long as it's not eaten), bad for anybody else.

98 Montana Diaper Store
www.mtdiaperstore.com

Designer diapers from Montana! "Cloth diapering is not what it used to be. Our store sells products that make cloth diapering easy, cost effective, and healthy for your baby and our environment." Cost effective, maybe. But what about when you need diapers NOW? Be sure to check out the "Getting Started" section for all the info you need about diapers, including the type of diapers you'll need. There's also info on alternative diapers, like hemp diapers, which sport "natural anti-microbial properties." Can babies get sick by wearing diapers? What's the purpose?

PRODUCTS: A featured product is the Wonderoos One Size Pocket Diaper, which appears to be a very versatile diaper. "Wonderoos are a one size pocket diaper that will fit most babies from eight to thirty-five pounds." Talk about flexible! Or how about the very colorful Fuzzi Bunz, which "feature super soft microfleece inners and colorful outers." Now babies can be dry AND stylish!

VERDICT: Ordering designer diapers makes about as much sense as about listening to *She Bangs*, or any other Ricky Martin song for that matter. Go to the store for your diapers—Pampers or Huggies will do better than any of these bad baby-butt covers.

99

Apron Store
www.apronstore.com

Ah, the apron: the preferred clothing accessory of cooks everywhere! The Apron Store sells...you guessed it, aprons! The Apron Store is run by Howard Uniforms, "A manufacturer of aprons since 1950." Making aprons for fifty-four years? What an accomplishment!

PRODUCTS: So many aprons, so few that we need! The Waist Apron comes in twelve colors and is "our best value in the traditional food service apron." If you're looking for an apron for protection from other kinds of stains, try the Garden Aprons. Remember, "Cultivating a green thumb takes practice, patience, and a few handy accessories—like this personalized apron." I just gotta have an apron for gardening! And don't forget that all aprons can be customized with "screen printing and embroidery!" Now your apron can have witty one-liners, or even offensive jokes. Wouldn't you just love to see your chef wearing an "I spit in your food, hope you like it" apron?

VERDICT: For the neat freak who doesn't like dirty clothes while gardening or cooking, the Apron Store offers some convenient ways to keep clean. And, with custom embroidering for restaurant owners, creative cooks or epicurean wise guys the possibilities are endless.

100

Talking Presents
www.talkingpresents.com

Talking Presents: "Sensory shopping for the ears!" All of the presents on TalkingPresents.com make noises when you want them to! From animals to calculators to clocks, everything here can talk to you, in some way or another.

PRODUCTS: Check out the celebrities section to find the disturbing Singing Dancing Ricky Martin bear. "Sing along as this cool character moves to the beat and sings the sensational 'Livin' La Vida Loca.'" Sensational? More like sickening. Amazingly, this site offers twenty-six talking cookie jars, in the form of alligators, barns, bees, cops, lighthouses, knights, and rappers. A rapping cookie jar? I think I just lost my appetite. There are even educational talking gifts, such as the Phonics Firefly.

VERDICT: Talking can be a good thing, or a bad thing. Good if it's funny, witty, or insightful; bad if it's about unintelligent, stupid topics. In this case, talking is, much like the real thing, a mixed blessing. Good for the Talking Toucan Parrot, bad for the Fart Machine. Good or bad, the choice is up to you.

101

Fluns
www.fluns.com

Welcome to the site that has "the largest selection of creations by Karen Rossi, Messages from the Heart by Sandra Magsamen, and Ruby Lips by Phyllis Vaughn on the Internet!" For those without a clue as to who those people are, this store is full of aged accessories identical to the goodies at cheap thrift shops everywhere.

PRODUCTS: Start with the "Fanciful Flights" section, full of such absolute delights as the Aerobic Instructress, whose description is a cute little poem. "Feeling the burn/It's firmness I seek. Tight arms and abs/Five times a week!" What a creative advertising tactic! The "Oh, You Doll" section has a ton of creative characters like Louise the

Chocolate Lover ("give me chocolate and nobody gets hurt"), Marcie the Garage Sale Queen (why buy here when you could find her at an actual garage sale?), and Georgie the Biker Mama (old ladies in leather biker gear…sexy!). What an eclectic cast of characters, huh?

VERDICT: Fluns may be full of interesting goodies, but everything you see here can be found at your local junk shop. You can get any of these old-styled oddities, in some form or another, for half the price at a rummage sale, Goodwill store, craft fair, etc. Unless you find a great gift that really grabs your attention, I'd advise against this overpriced site.

102

Wicked Cool Stuff
www.wickedcoolstuff.com

Wicked cool, man! Wicked Cool Stuff has many cool products aimed to please any taste. From older comedies like *I Dream of Jeannie* to modern "marvels" like Spider-Man, there's a large variety of great gifts here, including action figures, bobbleheads, toys, T-shirts, posters, and a whole lot more. While some products may be less attractive to you (I didn't care for the *Merman: Masters of the Universe* collectible bust for obvious reasons), something else will definitely catch your eye here.

PRODUCTS: Take a trip back to the '70s and the beginnings of the Kool-Aid Man with the Kool-Aid Red Wacky Wobbler Bobblehead, where "The classic Red Kool-Aid pitcher makes his bobblehead debut as an oversized Funko Wacky Wobbler!" And what, exactly, is a Funko Wacky Wobbler? The one section that didn't float my boat was the traitorous "Political T-shirts," with such shirts as the Red Chinese Star on Green T-shirt, the Fidel Castro Green T-shirt, and the Soviet Union Hammer and Sickle Red T-shirt! Try wearing something like that fifty years ago, you commie traitors, and you'd be tossed in the clink!

VERDICT: For the most part, Wicked Cool Stuff is full of, well, wicked cool stuff! Whether you're looking for superhero action figures like the Barbie as Wonder Woman collectible doll (fighting crime with great hair!), or bobbleheads from TV classics, Wicked Cool Stuff has a ton of stuff suited to fit anybody's tastes. And anyplace that has a talking Homer Simpson clock is okay by me.

103

The Lighter Side Co.
www.lighterside.com

Join the light side, Luke! The Lighter Side Co. is "famous for its collection of licensed and nostalgic collectible merchandise, like Betty Boop, *Wizard of Oz*, Coca-Cola, Looney Tunes and more, the catalog offer gift-givers some amazing choices that they won't find anywhere else." Lots of copy-right protection, isn't there?

PRODUCTS: There's the Solar Frog White T-shirt, a T-shirt with an assortment of colored frogs on it. Let's encourage diversity with rainbow colored frogs! Another featured item is the Bustier Bag, a purse with a bust on the top of it. Gives a new meaning to "carry-ing my bust with pride." Finally, there's the Mr. Wonderful Talking Doll; hear him coo, "I love you;" "Will you marry me?" "You've been on my mind all day—that's why I bought you these flowers!" and thirteen other endearing phrases that will win your heart. What a great idea. Finally, a doll who will be sensitive for us, so we don't have to be!

VERDICT: Like Wicked Cool Stuff, Lighter Side is chock full of neat nostalgia and modern merchandise alike. From Elvis and *I Love Lucy* to the *Simpsons* and the Pillsbury Doughboy, there's a respectable selection of collectables that are perfect for older folks and the younger generations alike.

104

Adventures in Crime and Space
www.crimeandspace.com

Adventures in Crime and Space (ACS) specializes in "mystery, science fic-tion, and horror books." You can check for future releases, join a reading group, and learn about conventions, such as Armadillo Con26, a "literary science fiction convention." What does a sci-fi nerd convention have to do with armadillos? I shudder to guess.

PRODUCTS: If the plots are as weird as the titles, then the authors of these books are unusual individuals. The site features titles like *The Empress of Mars* by Kage Baker, and *Blood Will Tell* by Jean Lorrah. The latter's plot is summed up by Amazon.com: "Kentucky police detective and Olympic gold-medal marksman Brandy Mather is intrigued by the smiling, aged body found in the office of a heretofore missing professor, who now is deemed to have died of old age. When other corpses, including Brandy's best friend, turn up with the same expression, she is determined to solve their cases." A serial killer who puts smiles on his victim's faces. What a happy peppy plot!

VERDICT: The novels on ACS may be a bit far out, but they certainly do look interesting. The authors of these books sound very imaginative, albeit eccentric (I proudly count myself in that category). Not as interesting as bathtub racing (Number 424 from my first book), but nevertheless, interesting.

105   Mike the Headless Chicken for President
www.miketheheadlesschicken.org

Mike the Headless Chicken: "When a clear lack of direction is the obvious choice!" Mike's story began when a farmer chopped off his head to have him for dinner. Mike was found the next morning, alive because the "ax blade had missed the jugular vein and a clot had prevented Mike from bleeding to death."

PRODUCTS: Their official campaign store features a T-shirt with Mike's logo, reading, "MIKE: Celebrating a long history of open minds." Apparently, "open-minded" means no mind at all. A second T-shirt features the phrase: "Chicken lives for 2 years with no head," followed by the slogan, "Only in Fruita, Colorado!" If a chicken can live without a head there, Fruita must be one freakishly scary city.

VERDICT: I'd rather go to a Ludacris concert and sit next to the speakers than place a vote for Mike the Headless Chicken. Chickens do not make good presidents, especially when headless (although if you'll turn to the left, you will spot some chickens who appear to be headless).

106

Mothers Against Peeing Standing Up

www.mapsu.org

First, moms want us to go shopping with them, and now this? The mission of this "organization" is self explanatory. They supposedly have proof against common "myths." The "myth" forming the MAPSU foundation is "Myth 1: Men can pee standing up." "The reality is men cannot pee standing up without getting as much as a stray drop on the seat or the outside surface of the toilet. Fragmentation of the urine stream causes particles of urine to dissipate. The larger the distance urine has to travel, the bigger the dissipation radius gets." Such a scientific explanation on the physics of urinating!

PRODUCTS: Their first line is a selection of products like T-shirts, hats, boxers (wouldn't males who pee standing up wear those?), sweatshirts, and jerseys with the MAPSU logo: a male stick figure standing up, urinating into a toilet, with the red "no" circle over it.

VERDICT: Why be against something that's so natural? This page is nothing but the rantings of fanatical feminists. I'd rather vote for Lyndon LaRouche than recommend MAPSU. This page is for anti-man radicals; and their products are even worse. Get away from this page. Get far, far, away.

107

Jockey's Room

www.jockeysroom.com

It's not just about the horses anymore! "From Asmussen to Velazquez, you can find biographies, photos, stats, news, links, jockeys' diaries, birthdays, photo galleries, chat rooms and message boards, voting panels, online email, advertising, jockeys' classification, UK betting websites, UK racecourse maps, and lots more on this site." That's a lot of junk on jockeys!

PRODUCTS: Buy Jockey apparel, such as the Thierry Thulliez Fan Top, the Oscar Urbina Baseball Jersey, and the Kieren Fallon AND

Thierry Thulliez Hooded Sweatshirt. Not just one, but TWO jockeys! Any other jockey product imaginable is here, including baby and toddler gear, mugs, beer steins, coasters, mousepads, lunchboxes, clocks, and a whole section of posters, books, and videos. Does this site ever stop with the jockeys?

VERDICT: It's ironic that most of the attention on horse racing is featured on the horses. They don't talk, and they'd rather eat grass than be stars. And yet, little credit goes to the humans that actually ride them (the jockeys), train them, and even the people who own them. Secretariat won the triple crown, and few people even know who his owner was, much less his jockey. Jockey's Room helps remedy that problem. Actually, no. These vertically challenged horse riders will forever remain a joke.

108

Soap on a Rope
www.soaponarope.com

SoaponaRope.com: "Your online source for the world's best and most unusual bath products!" The site's signature product is just as it says: soap, on a rope. The soaps are in a amazing variety of different shapes, ranging from clever to crazy.

PRODUCTS: Tons of different soaps on ropes, such as the Musgo Real S.O.A.R. "please give a big bathtub splash to the granddaddy of soap-on-a-rope! Claus & Schweder has been making Musgo Real since way back in 1887." The concept of soap on a rope has been around since 1887? Fascinating…this SOAR also has "stylish packaging [which] makes a great presentation when you give it as a gift for that special guy in your life!" How many guys like soap as a gift, especially if it's on a rope? And if you give someone soap, isn't it just a subtle way of saying "wash up, you stink"?

VERDICT: Putting soap on a rope doesn't make soap any more special or useful than it already is, not to mention that soap wasn't very special to begin with. The novelty SOAR products are good gifts though; Homer Simpson is as glorious in soap form as he is anywhere else.

109

The Tango Store
www.tangostore.com

The tannnnnnngo! The Tango Store sells music that's a perfect backdrop for the dance of the same name. There's a huge selection of tango music here, by tons of different artists from around the world, as well as an equally impressive selection of movies. And you've probably never heard of any of them!

PRODUCTS: Some new releases included the *Adios Nonino-1966* album, by Anibal Trolio, with songs like "Sombras Nada Mas," "Payadora," and "Buenos-Aires-Tokyo." Tango in Tokyo? I never knew Japanese people liked to tango so much! There's also tango DVDs, like the exciting *El Fondo Del Mar*, which translates into "The Bottom of the Sea" and features a scuba diver on the cover. What do scuba diving and tango have to do with each other?

VERDICT: Many people think of the tango as an exotic, quirky dance. Apparently, that combination has swept thousands of fans off their feet as fast as the dance does it. Now that I've discovered the tango genre, it's opened up a whole new world to me! Actually, no. Only hardcore fans of the dance need apply at this site.

110

Buttons 4 U
www.buttons4u.com

Want some custom buttons for your clothing? As stupid as that sounds, this is the place to get them! "We are your complete source for bulk wholesale priced items for the sewing, crafting, and scrapbooking industry. We have the hottest items on the market!" I didn't know that buttons were in such demand. I've met a lot of pinheads, maybe it's time to meet some buttonheads.

PRODUCTS: Check out the "Product Spotlight" for goodies like the Pewter Sun 1 1/8 Inch Wide button, a half a dozen for $9.48, or a gross (144 buttons) for $75.60. That's a lot of money, but a lot of buttons! They also have buttons made out of rhinestone, one dozen for eight dollars!

Even buttons made out of precious metals, like gold and platinum. We need these, because…? This site also sells beads, Chinese Frogs (a type of button that looks nothing like a frog), fringe, and more.

VERDICT: I need extra buttons just about as much as I need another John Tesh album. Only businesses or compulsive fashion hounds need these grossly expensive clothing fasteners. You would do better buying buttons from a local craft store. This store does have it uses sometimes, but more often than not, it's just plain useless.

111   Nature's Platform
www.naturesplatform.com

"Two-thirds of humanity use the squatting position to answer the call of nature…" If it's good for peasants in China, why shouldn't it be good for us? "In those cultures, appendicitis, diverticulosis, hemorrhoids, colitis, prostate disorders, and colon cancer are virtually unknown." They DO know starvation and poverty, however. I'll take "unnatural" elimination and a cushy American lifestyle anyday.

PRODUCTS: Nature's Platform is a device that allows you to go the bathroom in a "squatting position," ie: standing on top of the toilet and dropping your butt way below your knees. To use it, follow these four steps: "[1] Stand with your back to the platform. [2] Set one foot on the platform. [3] Lean back, placing both hands on the platform. [4] Raise the other foot." Sound complicated? Be reassured, "It's much easier done than said!" Most things are the other way around. How much will it cost you to buy this insane apparatus? Only "$119 plus $13 shipping and handling"! And, don't forget, Nature's Platform "Has been endorsed by Yoga teachers"! Ooooom, Breath, Relax, Poop.

VERDICT: I don't really care if two-thirds of humanity go to the bathroom like this. In the West, we don't go to the bathroom that way, unless we're deep in the woods and really have to go. If you buy this defecating aid, people won't just think you're weird, they'll think you're a total moron, because you spent money to help you answer nature's call by putting a platform atop a perfectly usable toilet.

112

Jib Jab
www.jibjab.com

Jib Jab is a comedy site that shows humorous videos, mainly about politics and popular celebrities. Examples include "Cooking with Clinton," an innuendo-packed cooking show featuring the former president. Another example is the "Vote Ahnuld" video, made during the California recall where Arnold Schwarzenegger outlines his "plan" for California (terminate illegal aliens, blast away the federal deficit, etc.).

PRODUCTS: Frisbees, T-shirts, doggie T-shirts, magnets, mugs, and mousepads with two designs: the Jib Jab logo with two men with old, turn-of-the-century haircuts and outfits (where they got this loony logo, I don't know), and the This Land gear, a parody of Woody Guthrie's "This Land" starring none other than George W. Bush and John Kerry where they sing, insult, and brag their way into our hearts.

VERDICT: Quit yo' jibba jabba, fool! Jib Jab is full of some strange stuff. It's pretty clever though; you have to admit their campaign ad for Ahnuld really was headed in the right direction. He could have just "terminated" Gray Davis and taken over California with no resistance. Oh, wait, he DID do that. Jib Jab is twisted humor, but twisted in a good way. Much like the game Twister.

113

Making Fiends
www.makingfiends.com

Making Fiends is a site with flash animation movies. In the first episode, a blue girl named Charlotte (her face, clothing, and legs are all blue) meets a giant red cat that swipes away a boy she just met. Inside the school, the teachers and the students are forced to do what the "green girl" (Vendetta) says because she has a giant, scary hamster, although the blue girl is oblivious to this fact, acting very nice and carefree. The episodes get weirder and weirder as the series continues.

PRODUCTS: You can buy the Vendetta T-shirt (A green Vendetta on a black shirt), the Charlotte T-shirt (A cheery Charlotte in a blue T-shirt) the Giant Cat T-shirt (A Mad Kitty on a gray T-shirt), and the Muffin Films T-shirt (A friendly singing muffin on a brown T-shirt). You can also buy original art prints from this psychotic series.

VERDICT: Making Fiends is stranger than anything in recent memory. Perhaps not as strange as Marilyn Manson, but almost as strange, and that is saying a lot. The products are the kind that make people think you're a social outcast. And if you wear their demented shirts, you probably will be. Perfect, however, for dark senses of humor. Very dark.

114   Degree Confluence
www.confluence.org

It's a real-life *Around the World in 80 Days* with Degree Confluence! "The goal of the project is to visit each of the latitude and longitude integer degree intersections in the world, and to take pictures at each location. The pictures and stories will then be posted here." What a daunting task! So far, the team has found 3,242 "successful primary confluences," and has taken 33,141 photographs. That's a lot of film for taking pictures of a statistic.

PRODUCTS: There are various products with a mosaic of various locations on the front and back, and the words "Degree Confluence Project." The shirt has text reading, "No minutes…no seconds," and "Photographing latitude and longitude integer degree intersections throughout the world." Now you have the option of explaining the shirt yourself or making people stare at it, trying to figure it out!

VERDICT: These locations are nothing more than numbers! Still, it's interesting to see where this insane quest takes these coordinate-crazy researchers. Most of them appear to be in the middle of nowhere, but you have to wonder whether one could be on the private property of some crazy hermit (git off ma confluence or I'll hav to git ol' Bessie and pump you full of lead!). But, in the name of science, the search must continue!

115

Going Bridal
www.goingbridal.com

Going Bridal is a site full of wedding horror stories. You can confess your bridal sins at the "Bridezilla Confession Booth," or click on the link that puts it best: "I don't have anything to confess, but I want to read everyone else's!" There are scary stories about "passive-agressive social-phobic mother[s]," as well as a bride who "slept with [the] best man [the] night before [the] wedding." What is wrong with these people?

PRODUCTS: Don't let the kids visit this store; with apparel lines like "Please shut up about your f***ing wedding," and the Greedy Bride line of clothes, these products have attitude. The latter features an old-fashioned, sarcastic-looking picture of a bride with the line, "Thank you for the completely inadequate wedding gift." There's also a simple selection of clothes with the phrase "Going Bridal" on them. "It's like going postal, but with tulle."

VERDICT: Getting married is supposed to be a happy time, but as this site so elegantly points out with its Bridezilla confession stories, sometimes it doesn't work out that way. It sure didn't work out for Darva Conger of *Who Wants to Marry a Multi-Millionaire* and for almost every couple on ABC's *Bachelor* series. Going Bridal is a treasure trove of weddings gone wrong, with products as a testament to these marital disasters.

116

Cannon-Mania
www.cannon-mania.com

This store sells reproductions of civil war and other historical cannons! Now you, too, can own your own cannon to impress your friends and frighten your foes. They make "great gifts" and good "awards for speakers." Thanks for speaking at my party; here's a cannon! I mean, everyone needs a large piece of artillery to use on those nasty annoying neighbors.

PRODUCTS: All cannons, with all the necessary accessories. Over one hundred fifty cannons are here for you to buy, including the 1/3 Scale Golf Ball Firing Cannon, available in twenty-four-inch and thirty-inch barrels. Even though it fires golf balls, it still looks like it was made in 1860. Weird, huh? There are also decorative cannons, black powder cannons, and cannon ammo. If you're asking, "Do I need a license to buy or shoot a cannon?" The answer: "NO!" Yay! Let's go cannon crazy!

VERDICT: Cannon Mania? More like Cannon Maniacs. I'd be scared if my neighbor bought a cannon. I'd have a strong suspicion that someday I'd find a hole in the side of my house. Cannons should only be purchased by museums and Civil War re-creation committees, not by people like you and me. At least not by people like you.

117

Monkee Mania
www.monkee-mania.com

Hey, hey, we're the Monkees! Monkee Mania is dedicated to one of the USA's first "boy bands," before sex-filled videos and bling-bling rappers started to dominate music. "They're the band that wasn't a band that became a band!" So, wait. Are they a band, or aren't they? Pictures, song lyrics, and downloads are available, as well as a full-fledged shop.

PRODUCTS: You can buy T-shirts, sweatshirts, jerseys, tanktops, mugs, coasters, mousepads, and more with groovy slogans like "Love is the ultimate trip" and "Phantasmagoric Splendor" on a groovy flower, tie-dye, hippy-style background. Links to Monkee auctions on eBay, as well as a link to Rhino Records where you can buy their CDs, are also included.

VERDICT: The Monkees may be a basically extinct band, but, as the site points out, they're still going strong today. The Monkee Mania store is a must-see for fans of the band, and even though finding a fan site may be odd nearly forty years after they began, you'll be hard-pressed to find someone who can doubt the influence of both monkeys (look how many bad movies resort to live monkeys to get appeal), and Monkees.

118

Mr. Zed
www.mrzed.com

Mr. Zed is one crazy guy. He claims to have been around since the times of the Ancient Egyptians. He appears to be made of a tough plastic polymer, so this is a reasonable explanation. Wait, nobody knew about plastic six thousand years ago!

PRODUCTS: Mr. Zed's videos are available for purchase, including the first one: *Mr. Zed Show Volume 1: From Outer Space, Into Your Face!* "Join the affable android Mr. Zed high above the earth aboard his own private satellite, Zedsat1…You'll meet the Zedsat's computer Mona…And Big Al Unpronounceable, the 'legitimate' businessman from the horse head nebula!" What an epic cast! Also available is *Splooty's Revenge*, where you can meet Mrs. Al (Big Al Unpronouceable's mom) and his evil twin brother Bob. Gotta have an evil twin brother. Absolutely gotta have one. These are certainly "the videos you can't afford to be without."

VERDICT: This guy looks more like a really happy, older version of Barbie's ex, Ken (really, they broke up; a Mattel spokesman announced it in 2004). If Mr. Zed is as weird as he sounds, I want to stay away from him. Plus, anybody who has that unnatural shine in his eye (look at the graphic on the home page…it's scary) can't be trustworthy.

119

Don't Be Stupid
www.dontbestupid.com

It's not an insult; it's a positive message! "Don't Be Stupid is a positive based company. Be it our slogans, clothing line, athletes, skaters, boarders, BMXers, surfers, etc.—you name it, we're there to help make a difference in the way you look at life and how life looks at you!" Intellectual giants like skaters, snowboarders, and surfers can make a positive impact on my life? Who knew?

PRODUCTS: Buy various "positive" shirts, with phrases like, "You miss 100% of the chances you don't take!" True, but remember, you also miss out on 100 percent of the consequences, too. There's also the words "Impossible, Never, Fear, Can't, Loser," followed by "Not in my vocabulary." A positive message, until you see the words, "Don't be Stupid." There's also "university shirts" with the slogan, "University of DBS (Don't Be Stupid)." Well, isn't that supposed to true of EVERY institution of higher learning?

VERDICT: I would think that "don't be stupid" is more of an offensive threat than a positive message. If somebody told you "don't be stupid," would you take it as a positive message meant to make you a smarter person? Or would you assume you ARE stupid and are being warned to stop? Such a quandary. Don't be stupid by buying products that say "don't be stupid."

120 Hamster Liberation Front
www.hamsterliberationfront.com

It's time to liberate rodents everywhere, according to the Hamster Liberation Front. "The Hamster Liberation Front was founded in 1989 by Damond X and…it went forth into the world, proudly proclaiming its motto, 'Be nice or we'll kill you!' to the world." Okay…I'll be nice…

PRODUCTS: The HLF offers a wide variety of T-shirts, including one with "Che Hamstera," who is, according to the home website, "the symbol of our revolutionary front and is spoken of with great amounts of pride and awe." He appears to be little more than a hamster with a Fidel Castro-style beret. But remember, "pistols and cheese are the only tools necessary for revolution." There's also the politically incorrect Gerbil Jihad T-shirt, which is depicting a gerbil as a Middle Eastern terrorist.

VERDICT: It's hard to tell what "rights" the Hamster Liberation Front is fighting for. This site makes it sound like they have rodent revolutionaries everywhere. Who's to say we won't wake up to a gerbil as our ruler? In all seriousness, though, the Hamster Liberation Front joins the ranks of the Penguin Conspiracy (www.thepenguinconspiracy.com from my first book) in the realm of the weird and wacky.

121 Rocky the Mustang
www.rockythemustang.com

It's "the only mustang in the world with its own website!" Rocky the Mustang's site is a big story about the perils and adventures of Rocky the Mustang Boy. "See what people are saying…" What are they saying exactly? "A world first…daring…provocative! -*The Buckethead*, July 2001.""It changed the way I look at mustangs…" -Monty Montagne, author of *What's Wrong With That Horse?* Random Hoof,1999"

PRODUCTS: There's Rocky Cowboy hats, Rocky T-shirts, Rocky Home Furnishings, Rocky Equine supplies, Rocky Limited Edition Ford Explorer, Rocky Beermug, and books. Click on the link to each and you'll get a picture of the product…with no place to buy it. Another one of those deceptive, but strangely entertaining, sites that claim to have a store, but are really spoofs.

VERDICT: While this mad mustang may not actually sell what it claims to, the site is another site with a "what the heck is this all about" feel to it. And, while I doubt this site was made by a mustang (more likely a crazy human who thinks he's a mustang), it is an appropriately wild story.

122 Beer Can Bob
www.beercanbob.com

The premise behind Beer Can Bob is to take a picture of yourself holding a beer can with "Bob" on it. How do you get a Bob beer can? Simply print or draw a picture of Bob's face on a piece of paper, put it over your beer, and take a picture. This site has cartoons of Bob, a game called *Roadkill Bob Bingo*, the ever-so-necessary "Beer Can Bob for President" section, a "Support Thong Awareness Month," and much more.

PRODUCTS: Tons of types of T-shirts are available, including the "Support Thong Awareness Month" line, as well as T-shirts reading, "My Name's Bob...What's Your Excuse?" My excuse? My name's Dan. And of course, who can resist the appeal of a "Nuke 'Em and Move On. Simple Solutions for Today's Problems. Beer Can Bob for President" shirt? Also available are Bob Coozies (if you're too lazy to print out the downloaded template or draw Bob on your beer) and Bumper Stickers including the popular "Got Milk" parody, which is of course, "Got Beer?"

VERDICT: It's interesting to see what kinds of pictures are taken of this strange persona. If you're bored beyond belief and need to do something with your friends that'll get attention, take a picture of Bob and it just might make it to this wild website.

123

Derds
www.derds.com

What exactly is a Derd? "Good derds like trucks with tanky accessories, like skid plates, winches, rollbars, etc., and old sports cars with tweaked engines. The choice of music is key: pounding out the '80s rock including AC/DC, Metallica, GNR at all times." In other words, Derds are rock and roll fans stuck in the '80s. Mullets, big trucks, and leather pants will help you identify the quintessential derd.

PRODUCTS: There's the Derd-essential music, like Metallica's *Black Album*, Guns 'N Roses' *Appetite for Destruction*, and, of course, AC/DC's *Back in Black*. By now, any confusion you may have about these dirty Derds is gone, now isn't it? There are also mousepads, mugs, T-shirts, and hats with the "Derds.com" logo. Rock on!

VERDICT: Whether you are a Derd, know a Derd, or couldn't care less about this rare breed, the Derds website is a humorous look into the world of an age past; the world of torn jeans, long puffy hair, when rock and roll was what it should be: a bunch of crazed, drug-addled guys screaming at the top of their lungs.

124

Cheeseland
www.cheeseland.net

"Ahh...the power of cheese!" Cheeseland is home to "The Federated States of Cheeseland." The history describes the Cheeseland religion, based on Uddera, the Cow Goddess, who has "the five stomachs of the afterlife." People who pass on Go a different stomach depending on how good or bad they've been. Wow...and I thought the Church of Spongebob Squarepants and the Church of the Blind Chihuahua were weird.

PRODUCTS: The usual assortment of shirts, hats, mugs, etc. with different logos and slogans, including "Got Cheese" (haven't we got enough "got" slogans already?), and the Federated States of Cheeseland logo, with the world map made of cheese. There's also a calendar with various Cheeseland images, a bumper sticker reading "Proud Citizen" with the FSC logo (doesn't that also stand for the Forest Stewardship Council?), and a bib with the slightly clever phrase, "Don't Spill the Cheese."

VERDICT: Worshiping food is not my idea of a good religion. I don't worship bread (unlike the folks at the "White Bread Power" website), I don't worship pie (unlike the Holy Church of the Pie, another church not included here), and I definitely don't worship broccoli (unlike Broccoli.com...at least, it seems that way). If you must join a crazy church, join the Church of Shatnerology. You can't go wrong with "toupee and girth" worship.

125

International Center for Bathroom Etiquette
www.icbe.org

Have trouble observing proper bathroom behavior? Here's the place to get help. "Our mission is simple and our goals are clear: to educate everyone on proper conduct in the bathroom, and in so doing make the bathroom experience more enjoyable for everyone." Enjoyable? We go in, we go, we get out. Why does it need to be enjoyable? And, as for me, I'd rather avoid bathroom "experiences."

PRODUCTS: There are T-shirts, mugs, and tote bags with the ICBE logo: a no-smoking style sign showing two stick figure men using a urinal next to each other. The "proper" way is represented by a green circle surrounding two stick figure men using the urinals, with one empty one in between them. I don't think we need to be told to do that.

VERDICT: Half the stuff on this site is just common sense; the other parts are just weird. When somebody advises peeing in the sink instead of using a trough ("since they do after all look just like funny little urinals on a bench"), that's just weird. Still, this site is much like a train wreck: repulsive, yet compelling and impossible to resist looking at.

126

Mad Martian
www.madmartian.com

Mad Martian is touted as "The Museum of Modern Madness," "madness" with a mass of material on eyeballs, as well as pseudo-crappy sci-fi movies, broccoli men, etc. Be careful to avoid being sucked into the "Interactive Toilet of Terror, the most frightening virtual commode on the Web." Visit the "Eyeball Museum," which contains a sightings section of pictures or paintings of large eyes. Fascinating, in a creepy, "what the heck is this" kind of way.

PRODUCTS: The gift shop has various eyeball related categories, like toys, balls, inflatable décor, lightup and glow toys (are we seeing a trend with bad products and glowing?), and much more. From the "Realistic" section are eerily authentic eyeballs, including glass eyeballs and "mountable" eyeballs. Be sure to consider the "Giant Inflatable Eyeball Hammer," an inflatable hammer covered with pictures of eyes. Weird, but awesome, too.

VERDICT: If you're the type that wishes Halloween were every day of the year, Mad Martian is definitely for you. Shopping at the gift shop is an eye-catching experience (pun intended). Buying eyeballs is a sure-fire way to freak out your friends. For horror and sci-fi fans alike, Mad Martian is a must-see.

127

Drinking Gadgets
www.drinkinggadgets.com

Here are items to help you get drunk as a dog! "Building a home bar? Want a pool table to impress your mates?" Mates? Romantic or casual mates? Such a vague definition. So much booze.

PRODUCTS: There are ashtrays for you smokers out there (how to avoid this suicidal habit? Don't start), as well as bar towels, glassware, and the obligatory neon signs. Buy such neon classics as the Budweiser Lizard, Hot Food, Cappuccino (I suppose drinking coffee is "drinking," but it doesn't quite fit the theme), the Rolling Stones neon sign, and more. Also available are tons of Coca-Cola accessories, gambling equipment, and more. And don't forget the "Booze Tube," an ingenious tower that holds six pints of "beer, wine, cocktails, or spirits depending on your intentions, or, if the latter, whether a compatible liver donor can be found."

VERDICT: Drinking Gadgets has a lot of accessories that can spice up your home bar, as well as some cool décor to make your bar have a more authentic look to it. There's tons of high-caliber collectibles to found here, with a few pleasant surprises as well. This site a must for bar-hopping guys and gals everywhere.

128

Freakatorium
www.freakatorium.com

The Freakatorium. It vaguely sounds low class, but is actually a very high-class museum. "The Freakatorium offers contemporary visitors a unique educational experience in an environment of wonder. Come visit our museum and PREPARE TO BE AMAZED!" Who wouldn't be amazed by freaks?

PRODUCTS: There are T-shirts in various sizes offering some of the prime exhibits of the Freakatorium. There's the Lobster Boy tee, with a picture of a girl frightened by a lobster with a human face. There's also the Monkey Boy, with an ape body and a boy face. The Shrunken Head is another good tee, as is the Two-Headed Skeleton and Zoma the Cannibal. These people CAN'T be real…can they?

VERDICT: These people truly are freaks! It's obvious they are just examples of circus myths that have spread throughout the world over the last century. The history section talks in great detail about the evolution of these "exceptional people," yet still refers to them as "freaks." There's tons of fun to be had at the Freakatorium if you're a fan of those odd circus sideshows, or just plain weird stuff.

129

NeoPaws
www.neopaws.com

Are you done with Designer Doggie Wear, but still crave more canine clothing? NeoPaws is another store designed to satisfy your desire for designer dog apparel. These clothes, however, are more than just fashionable; they make your dog safer! NeoPaws's creators have designed "a full line of high quality, innovative, and easy to use products with the animal's safety, comfort, and performance in mind." Easy to use, but are they easy on the wallet?

PRODUCTS: Apparently not! A good example of the "value" of these products is shown in the dog life vests. These life vests are designed to protect your dog on boating trips, by swimming pools, and in larger bodies of water. Sounds like a good idea, but before you go credit card crazy, keep in mind that these vests range in price from twenty-six to fifty-two dollars. If you think that's bad, wait until you see the Pet Step Ramp, a ramp designed to help your dog get up onto beds, cars, and grooming tables—for one hundred fifty bucks. Never mind that they're fully capable of doing it themselves (at least, my ten-pound Bichon can); let's spend money on a useless plastic ramp!

VERDICT: And I thought that the Popcorn Fork was useless! Sometimes I wonder who buys this stuff! Hopefully, you're not foolish enough to go on a spending spree of stupid, overpriced, useless dog products. While some of these products may have their uses (the life vest, MAYBE), you'd have to be pretty stupid to buy a pair of dog shoes for fifty-two dollars. Heck, you'd be pretty stupid to buy dog shoes at any price!

130 **Reality TV Hall of Shame**
www.realitytvhallofshame.com

This is reality TV at its lowest. "If there is a reality TV participant who has done something extraordinarily stupid, shameful, or painful to watch, they will be inducted. If there is an entire show that likewise deserves it, they will be inducted as well." Wow, with that definition, 95 percent of the reality TV shows out there must be in the Hall of Shame.

PRODUCTS: Buy various reality TV DVDs featuring their fair share of shameful moments. *The Simple Life* full season DVD is one whole season of shame. Add Paris Hilton to anything and you've got an automatic shame inductee right there. There's a similar theme with the *Anna Nicole Show* season one DVD. It was the same thing as *Anna Nicole's Caribbean Vacation*, except that she made a magical transformation back into a supermodel, a big change from being a cow in season one. The spaced-out look and behavior is still there, though.

VERDICT: Once again, it's like a bad car accident, or a child throwing a temper tantrum in public; you have to watch, you can't look away. Watching Paris Hilton and Nicole Richie sleaze their way into the hearts of rural America, or watching Donald Trump fire Omarosa Manigault is such a disgusting guilty pleasure that you have to indulge in once in a while. The Reality TV Hall of Shame can help you do just that.

· ·

131 **Drift Day**
www.driftday.com

What do Tarzan and a strange form of auto racing have in common? Everything, of course! But not Tarzan, king of the jungle; Tarzan Yamada. He is a racer featured on the Drift Day website. What is Drift Day, you ask? "Drift Association LLC. is an organization that hosts Drift Day for drivers who would like to learn the art of drifting." OK…

PRODUCTS: You can buy DVDs, apparel, and...car parts! 4 Links, Lateral Rods, Tension Rods, and more are available for you to beef up your ride. You'd better have some cash, though; the cheapest part is $150. If you're not interesting in turning your car into a racing car that goes sideways, you can buy DVDs featuring racers, including *Tarzan Time Attack*.

VERDICT: Watching cars slide around in circles isn't my idea of fun. The idea of a day dedicated to improving "drifting" skills isn't very exciting to me, either. Whether you want to invest in this racing craze is up to you.

132

S-P-O-N-G-E

www.s-p-o-n-g-e.com

Ghosts, the occult, anything else that's made up to get attention; that's what SPONGE is all about. "Welcome to S-P-O-N-G-E, an organization dedicated to exposing and uprooting the unspeakable horrors that exist on the fringes of our awareness. You can join and help to defeat the slimy doers of evil!" You mean the government? Or those non-existent paranormal demons you speak of?

PRODUCTS: "Show off your Historian Status with SPONGE Merchandise! Fight the Evil! Support the Cause! Eat Fiber!" I'll consider that last part, but I'd rather not. The shirt features the Elder Sign logo on the front (which really looks more like a tree) and the site address and the words, "Fight the Evil," on the back. "Make people say 'What the hell's that thing on your shirt?'" Well, at least they're honest. SPONGE Elder Sign Temporary Tattoos let you have the tree-like elder sign on your body (where you put is up to you) for a day or two. Also available are weird (and just plain ugly) sculptures and posters.

VERDICT: This site is obviously a joke, and the products are a joke as well. Nobody's going to understand what "SPONGE" is. So, unless you're willing to explain the whole premise of this nutty site time and time again to your friends, you'd be better off without these products. If you like explaining your taste for the unusual, however, be my guest.

133

Cars in Barns
www.carsinbarns.com

We've all seen them. Cars abandoned on the side of the road, some near barns. This site is dedicated to pictures of abandoned cars—in barns and other unusual, out-of-the-way places. There are three separate galleries: the "Bowties in Barns," with Chevrolet and General Motors vehicles; "Mopars in Barns"; and "Blue Ovals in Barns" for Fords. All the galleries have a TON of pictures.

PRODUCTS: The Cars in Barns T-shirt has a design showing two cars with cracked windows in a field by a barn, along with the phrase "Rotting American Muscle." There is also the Cars in Barns calendar, with a different picture of rotting American muscle for every month of the year. You can also download CIB wallpapers and screen savers.

VERDICT: Great site, but why cars in barns? Why not cars in junkyards, or cars on front lawns? Where are the cars on fire, or cars from car crashes? And what about the most original idea of all: cars in garages! We may not have all the essential locations for abandoned, rusting cars, but we've got cars in barns.

134

Celebrity Battles
www.celebritybattles.com

The premise behind Celebrity Battles is simple. You choose a question like, "Who Would Win in a Fight?" or "Who is More Likely to be Arrested?" You're presented with two choices. In the case of the latter, it might be Geraldo Rivera and Captain America, George Lucas and Robert Blake, or even George Lucas and God! Nobody can arrest God! The site has full statistics for the battles, including the top ten leaders and the bottom ten as well. For "Which Girl is the Best Singer?" Faith Hill was number one, while Ru Paul and Whoopi Goldberg were the two worst (Whoopi Goldberg? You mean Caryn Johnson?).

PRODUCTS: Buy mugs, T-shirts, and underwear with the Celebrity Battles logo: a crazy person hitting himself with two clubs. What does that have to do with celebrities? Well, I can think of a few celebrities who should be clubbed violently whenever they open their mouths.

VERDICT: This site isn't just fun; it's downright addictive. You find yourself clicking for your favorite celebrities until the cows come home. This site is like Pringles: "Once you pop, you can't stop." A must see for anybody who has an opinion on a celebrity.

135   Tech Comedy
www.techcomedy.com

Ever heard those customer service horror stories from friends and family in that department? This site is full of them. "Tech Support Comedy, or TSC, is a website dedicated to providing comic relief for those of us working in the tech support field…it also provides a much-needed forum to vent frustrations from a very aggravating job." How about aggravating for the customers when our electronics aren't working?

PRODUCTS: The Tech Comedy store "contains products that are of particular interest to people that work in the area of technical support." What do they mean by this? Headsets and staplers, of course! On the main store page is a link to Red Swingline Stapler.com, a site reminiscent of the Virtual Stapler site (first site in my original 505 book). If you prefer more casual gear, check out the T-shirts section, with witty phrases like, "I worked in tech support and all I got was this stupid t-shirt…" on the front, and "…and your credit card number" on the back. Who knew that tech support employees work as con artists in their spare time? Another memorable shirt reads, "I get paid for tech support…" on the front. "…I don't get paid to care" is on the back. Well, everybody with a job can relate to that.

VERDICT: Tech Comedy is obviously a must-see for tech support and customer service employees, but there's some humor for everybody else here too. Whether you're a big-wig executive or a lowly janitor, you're sure to find something to like at Tech Comedy.

136

Turtle TV
www.turtletvnetwork.com

Turtle TV is a humor website with turtle games, poorly made and extremely cliché turtle movies, and a "philosophical" "Ask Granny" feature where you ask Granny Turtle a question and she responds. When I asked her what I should put in this book about her, she said, "Who cares? We're all gonna burn in hell anyways." Well, Granny, I DO care, and I was kind enough to convey your message to my readers. You're welcome!

PRODUCTS: For pure ingenuity, try the Fitted Brief Tanks, a tank top that is "Men's underwear made into girls tanks!!" As long as they're not used underwear! The real attraction, though, are the Turtle TV DVDs, which feature "live turtles starring in parodies of movies, television, and pop-culture including *American Beauty*, *CSI*, *Jaws*, *Matrix*, *Blazing Saddles*, and much more!" Don't we have an overload of those parodies already?

VERDICT: Turtle TV's biggest weakness is that everything it's done has been before; many, many times before. I've seen a full load of *Psycho* parodies, a million *Matrix* parodies, a slew of *CSI* parodies, and a ton of any other parodies that Turtle TV attempts. Unless you can't get enough of those spoofs of popular TV and movies, Turtle TV is just another little fish, er, turtle, in the big Internet pond.

137

Bar Code Art
www.barcodeart.com

Have you ever seen those photomosaics, where they take very small pictures and put them together to make one image? This is the same thing—with bar codes. This site offers tons of bar code, with images of everyone from Jesus and Elvis to Oprah and Bill Gates. You can even get yourself bar coded by entering information about yourself. There's also a Bar Code Wind Chimes video, a bar code clock, distorted bar codes, and Datascapes—"Collages made with found bar codes to depict flowers." Very, very strange.

PRODUCTS: You can buy the Jesus Bar Code T-shirt, which depicts a very lifelike image of the Lord himself. Or, you can buy a bar-code flipbook, which, when flipped rapidly, zooms down from the Jesus image to one of the millions of individual bar codes that makes the image up. Jesus seems to be a popular image for this site…good choice. There are also bar code tattoos, with words like "slave," "scan me," and "for sale," which can project that creepy notion that you've been "manufactured" by someone. Very disturbing.

VERDICT: I never knew bar codes could make up such complex images. If you're interested in the kind of unique art that this site features, check it out; they're not just mass-produced portraits.

138

Curse of Jethro
www.curseofjethro.com

Like a lot of sites in this book, "The purpose of this site is to make you laugh." The difference? "If you do not have Jethro or know someone with Jethro, this won't be funny. But if you do, laugh out loud, have fun, and enjoy your visit." If you read the story, however, it becomes much funnier. "When I was growing up I realized I had this affliction. If I could trip on it, break it, fall and hurt myself, I would. One day, out of the blue, this affliction became 'Jethro'. Jethro started taking the heat for everything that I screwed up. In the end it made me a much better person because Jethro gave me someone to blame without hurting anyone else." The twenty-three "Laws of Jethro" contain basic ground rules for Jethro, such as, "It's gotta be the truth," "It's unexpected," "It's sometimes painful," "It can happen when you're by yourself, but you'll probably be in a crowd," and, "It's like Murphy's, but cooler."

PRODUCTS: There are shirts, visors, beanie caps, regular caps, and stickers with a basic, stick-figure-like man slipping and falling, suspended in mid-air, with the phrase, "Got Jethro?"

VERDICT: Jethro is funny once you realize that he's a fictional entity you can blame when you make a mistake and end up hurting yourself, humiliating yourself, or both. This site's apparel is a great way to laugh off the painful mistakes in life. Got Jethro? Everybody does.

139 8-Legged Entertainment
www.8legged.com

This is an Internet show about an octopus named Tako who cooks. The show is called *Deep Fried Live*. "The only cooking show hosted by an appetizer." And he's a cute little appetizer, too! You can click the "What's New?" button to see what's new with the site. There's also a *Deep Fried Live* archive, chronicling "Tako's origin and the details of his sketchy beginnings." What lies inside this archive? You'll have to see for yourself!

PRODUCTS: There's a holiday store, where you can buy ornaments and apparel. Unfortunately, the ornament store apparently opens only around Christmas. Smart marketing, Tako! The holiday apparel store allows you to buy shirts with Santa Tako for Christmas, turkey shirts for Thanksgiving, and Tako in a pumpkin for Halloween. The funniest Halloween shirt, however, is the Zombie Clambakes store, which has the catchy phrase, "Deep Fried…Dead or Alive." Anything deep fried should be dead already. Regular T-shirts, posters, eight-legged university gear for the college kids out there, and Tako's kitchen gear are also available for purchase.

VERDICT: An octopus doesn't appear as a very tasty appetizer to me. I'd rather have some mozzarella sticks or nachos. But Tako is too cute to eat anyway! The animation show is full of inventive humor and actually teaches you how to cook a few delicious recipes. So, cook with Tako, and catch a laugh or two along the way.

140 Funny Box
www.funnybox.com

"We couldn't afford a farm so we got a box." Funny Box is a humor website with pictures, jokes, a "lukewarm psychic jar," and a "one-liner library." The pictures section features several hilarious pictures featuring Bill Clinton (fake ones, of course), and the "Confucius Say" one-liners section, with witty lines like, "Confucius say man who shoot off mouth must expect to lose face," and "Confucius say man with one chopstick go hungry." So true.

PRODUCTS: T-shirts, teddy bears, hats, and more with various phrases. Be sure to check them out, as many are very funny. "Again backwards is shirt stupid my. It dang!" Another fun one is, "Think less. Smile more. Kiss butt. Be popular." Eighty percent of the U.S. population should wear this shirt! There are tons of others, like, "I may be on an elevator to hell, but I'm pushing every button on the way down," "I think my reality check bounced," and, the best one of all, "Yes. I am fat." Brutal honesty can be a good thing.

VERDICT: This site is another valuable opportunity to lose countless hours discovering all the worthless knowledge this site has to offer. But, you can rest assured that you'll lose those hours laughing your head off.

141 Revenge Lady
www.revengelady.com

Anybody with a bone to pick will be at home with Revenge Lady. "Revenge Lady gives advice on using the ancient art of revenge to bring humor and happiness back to your life." Don't get mad, get even!

PRODUCTS: You can order yellow Revenge Lady stickers with a woman holding a briefcase and a flag. Is that flag supposed to represent freedom? Feminist liberation? What? You can order a "personalized breakup/get lost letter or phone call" script; just provide Revenge Lady with the details. Wow, what a concept. There are also quintessential books like, *The Woman's Book of Revenge*, and *The Woman's Book of Divorce*. Such positive books, aren't they? You can also buy supplies for a Divorce/Breakup Party. What better way to celebrate losing the love of your life with a party?

VERDICT: They say revenge is bittersweet. In my experience, it's just plain sweet—except when it happens to you. But, if someone wants revenge on you, you screwed up anyways, so you deserve it. Seriously, however, this site is a great site that shows the humorous side of getting even.

142

Mutton Bone
www.muttonbone.com

Mutton Bone is home to a most disturbing product: Inflatable Love Sheep. Yes, you read right. This site sells an inflatable sheep with fishnet leggings, as well as a few other goodies as well. Just remember: "No actual sheep were harmed (or even consulted) during the research and development of this product."

PRODUCTS: Buy the Love Ewe, the original Inflatable Love Sheep. "Get one for your boss, your best buddy, or that guy in the next cubicle who only bathes before Star Trek conventions. Of course, you could also get a Love Ewe because you are lonely and pathetic." Well, at least they're honest. There are also T-shirts and mousepads featuring the Love Ewe, including the "Don't Get Arrested" T-shirt.

VERDICT: This site is sadder than the *Guys Gone Wild* DVD series (nobody likes to see fat, drunk, naked guys, thank you very much). Who in the world would turn to an inflatable sheep to satisfy their desires? Like the site says, only get this sick sheep blowup if you're "lonely and pathetic."

143

Watch Me Eat a Hot Dog
www.watchmeeatahotdog.com

The name says it all. "Watchmeeatahotdog.com is an independent media conglomerate located in beautiful New Orleans, Louisiana. It started as the drunken brainchild of three friends, and was conceived one evening at local landmark Mid City Lanes Rock 'n' Bowl. Since that fateful evening, it has grown into the international phenomenon that we know today." How come I've never heard of it?

PRODUCTS: There are various hot dog inspired products, including a bib saying, "**** baby food, I want a hot dog." Actually, you'd probably want to keep babies—and kids and general—away from that one. Another product is an apron that reads, "For Those About to Eat…We Salute You," with a picture of a hot dog in between the two phrases. There's also a Watch Me Eat a Hot Dog calendar, with a mysterious black-and-white picture of an eye on the cover, and guys stuffing their faces inside. So cryptic…

VERDICT: If you like hot dogs, visit this site. If you don't like hot dogs, visit this site. If you're an environmentalist vegetarian, visit this site. If you're anybody who has the Internet, visit this site. The humor and the products are perfect for everyone.

144 Friday the 13th Films
www.fridaythe13thfilms.com

It's everybody's favorite masked serial killer! This site has everything you could ever want to know about Jason and all of the *Friday the 13th* films, from number one to number 2,179. Or were there more? I lost track around number eight. This site has information on the cast and crew of all of the movies, as well as scripts, storyboards, bloopers, and a *Friday the 13th* timeline. So, was *Friday the 13th* Part Three before or after *Friday the 13th* Part Four? Hmm…

PRODUCTS: Buy the *Friday the 13th* boxed set for only $59.95! It includes the first eight movies, along with extras and deleted scenes. Some film subtitles include *The Final Chapter* (which was actually Part Four), *A New Beginning* (of what, mediocrity?), and of course, *Jason Takes Manhattan*, in which the hockey-masked chainsaw murderer takes on a cruise ship full of moronic teenagers. That must have been an Oscar winner!

VERDICT: I still say the best *Friday the 13th* movie—not to mention the best movie ever—is *Freddy vs. Jason*. The concept was genius: put two psychotic serial killers together and stick a bunch of stupid, stereotypical teenagers between them while they battle it out! The only film that came close was *Aliens vs. Predator*. Is there a connection between mergers of fictional universes and absolute crappiness? I say there is.

145

Bunny Heaven
www.bunnyheaven.com

Bunny Heaven: "Gifts for People who (heart) rabbits." What's with this substituting a heart for the word love? Do they think we can't read? The best part about Bunny Heaven, though? "Because we love rabbits, Bunny Heaven generously supports rabbit rescue efforts throughout the country." Rescue them from what? Aren't most already free, hopping happily and pillaging our gardens? Or maybe rescue them from some delicious rabbit stew.

PRODUCTS: Various pieces of gold, silver, artisan, and casual jewelry, bunny ceramics, and bunny wear. For the "low" price of $40, you can buy the Cosmic Bunny Pin. "You've heard of the cow jumping over the moon? Well this is a sterling silver bunny jumping over the Earth!" For forty bucks, I get a little pin with some crazy astral rabbit scenario? Another must-have is the Home is Where the Rabbit Is pillow, a pillow with a rabbit lying on a carpet by a door. Rabbits aren't dogs. You shouldn't let them run around in your house. If you want to, good luck catching the hopping critters.

VERDICT: Not everybody may like rabbits (farmers and vegetable garden owners come to mind), but if you don't like rabbits, there are always alternatives. On the main page, there's Kitty Cat Heaven, Sun, Moon, and Stars Heaven, and Daisy Heaven. If you like any one of these beautiful products of nature (wait, cats aren't beautiful at all; they're useless), visit BunnyHeaven.com and take your pick.

146

Extreme Ironing
www.extremeironing.com

Ironing to the EXTREME! Extreme Ironing is "the latest danger sport that combines the thrills of an extreme outdoor activity with the satisfaction of a well-pressed shirt." Participating in Extreme Ironing "involves taking an iron and board (if possible) to remote locations and ironing a few items of laundry."

PRODUCTS: You can get a more in-depth look at extreme ironing with the *Extreme Ironing* book. Or, you could get the *Extreme Ironing* DVD, a documentary with "more outdoor ironing action from around the world than any other documentary." Actually, I think it's the ONLY documentary with outdoor ironing. Can't decide between the two? You can get BOTH! The Extreme Ironing Double Pack comes with both the *Extreme Ironing* book and the *Extreme Ironing* DVD. Double the ironing, double the fun! You can also buy Extreme Ironing: The Calendar, "covering sixteen months from October 2004 to March 2006." Between this and the double pack, that's a lot of ironing!

VERDICT: Ironing in exotic locations is a stronger indicator of insanity than if you attended a ouija board party. But then again, there's nothing quite like wearing a freshly pressed shirt while climbing one of the world's tallest mountains. Too bad you'd freeze if you were only wearing a dress shirt. Extreme Ironing is an extremely strange sport, and that alone makes it worth checking out.

147 The Bald Truth
www.thebaldtruth.com

There's an old saying that goes, "God only made so many perfect heads, the rest He covered with hair." The Bald Truth makers don't seem to follow this mantra; they're a radio show focusing on restoring hair. "The Bald Truth is the only radio program devoted entirely to the prevention and treatment of hair loss. If you or someone you know is losing their hair, you can't afford to miss The Bald Truth." Well, I guess I can afford to miss it!

PRODUCTS: Buy books on hair loss, including *The Bald Truth* by the host of the show, Spencer David Kobren. There's help for women as well, with *The Truth About Women's Hair Loss*, also by Spencer David Kobren. Hey, anything that helps us have less bald women is fine by me.

VERDICT: If you're losing your hair, you may do well to visit the Bald Truth. On the other hand, if you're confident in your self-image, or, if you're NOT losing hair, you don't need to visit the Bald Truth, unless you like laughing at people losing hair, you sicko.

148

Unique Box Shop
www.uniqueboxshop.com

Boxes are usually for storing items, but these beautiful boxes are different. "We started our business in 1997 with our Costa Rican Puzzle Boxes and gift items. Until October of 2001, we only sold them in local arts and craft shows. Our customers were so fascinated with the boxes that we started getting calls to make local deliveries and mailings to their out-of-town friends and relatives." Expanding is the key to success! With the Internet anyone can sell any crap to a world wide market.

PRODUCTS: You could start with Puzzle Boxes of the World, each with its own difficulty level. The Japanese Puzzle Boxes are described as "beautiful, functional, and intriguing." They come with instructions, but remember that "Sometimes these are in Japanese, but they are illustrated and easy to follow." So, just because you were too lazy to include English instructions, we have to rely on pictures? Shame, shame. Russian Collectible Boxes, India's Mango Wood Boxes, Moroccan Thuya Boxes, and many more boxes with odd names are available for your purchasing pleasure.

VERDICT: Most of these boxes aren't even storage devices. Some of them are games, and others are for decoration. The Russian Nesting Dolls (those wooden dolls with smaller ones inside each one) aren't even boxes; they're, well, dolls. Still, if you're looking for the gift for the person who has everything, you're sure to find a good gift at the Unique Box Shop.

149

The Pet Casket Shop
www.thepetcasketshop.com

The Pet Casket Shop: "High Quality Pet Caskets at an Affordable Price!" Way to market something for such a tragic time. "At the Pet Casket Shop our goal is to provide the public with an Earth friendly, affordable option for pet burial." That's right! They're BIODEGRADABLE! Finally, a pet burial option for those who are paranoid about ruining the environment!

PRODUCTS: Choose from either the Earth-friendly biodegradable pet casket, or the permanent pet casket that will ensure your pet has a place in eternity. Both can "accommodate pets up to ten pounds in size." Is your pet a bit bigger? For ten dollars more, you can a larger pet casket. "This casket will hold the largest of cats...Dogs up to twenty-five pounds will fit easily in this one." What if my dog is bigger? Can I not give my pitbull or German Shepard a proper burial?

VERDICT: It's a little funny to see such happy-go-lucky advertising for pet burial. Granted, the death of a pet isn't a HUGE tragedy, but some people are really attached to their pets. I know I couldn't live without my crazy fluffy puppy. If you have a small, deceased dog or cat that needs a proper goodbye, you can find a casket here. Or, you could just visit for humor purposes.

150   Fossils for Sale
www.fossilsforsale.com

Own a piece of history! For those of you who have been living in a cave for the past one hundred years, fossils are "the remains of prehistoric life or some other direct evidence that such life existed." They're the petrified remains of creatures that lived millions of years ago. Fossils can be big, like dinosaur footprints, or they can be small, like seashells. You can find both here, available to purchase.

PRODUCTS: Various dinosaur remains are available, such as teeth, claws, eggs (for those interested in that crazy *Jurassic Park* scenario), tracks (footprints), and bones. You can buy a real Tyrannosaurus Rex tooth, but the authenticity will cost you about $1,800. There's also exciting Coprolite fossils available, which is, in layman's terms, dried-out dinosaur poop. How much will these fossilized feces cost you? About $70. What an exquisite artifact!

VERDICT: It may be interesting owning a piece of history, but unless you have a big, fat wallet, or are a serious scientist, these artifacts are too expensive for the average Joe. You may be able to afford some dinosaur dung, but do you really want that?

151 Pole Vault World
www.polevault.com

You probably know about pole vaulting. It's an Olympic sport where people use big, flexible poles to jump over another pole propped up by two other poles. Pole Vault World, whose motto is "Altitude with Attitude," sells anything and everything pole vaulting.

PRODUCTS: If you want to host this high-flying sport in your back yard, you can buy pole vaulting equipment, like Perimeter Pads, which allow the pole vaulters to land without breaking bones or smashing something. There are also special poles for jumping, including Carbon FX Poles.

VERDICT: Unless you're serious about competing in this wacky sport (serious as in going for the Olympics serious), Pole Vault World doesn't have many practical uses. If you like leaping into the air for five seconds and landing on a soft pad, however, you might want to consider entering the "exciting" world of pole vaulting. I'll keep my feet firmly planted on the ground, thank you.

152 Soap Opera Store
www.soapoperastore.com

"I slept with your sister, who's actually my sister and came back from the dead two months ago, who's having a baby that could be yours, or mine, or maybe a midget alien who is possessed by Satan!" That's a standard soap opera plot in a nutshell. Soap Opera Store offers products that are as senseless as the plots to these demented dramas.

PRODUCTS: You can browse products by your favorite soaps, such as *One Life to Live*, *Days of our Lives*, *The Bold and the Beautiful*, and *The Young and the Restless*. I've got a good name: *The Jealous and the Sleazy*. Each soap offers its own unique products. *All My Children* fans can get an "Erica Kane" fleece throw for their couch. *As the*

World Turns has such products as oven mitts, baseball caps, mugs, and beach towels. Nothing says "I like sleazy programs" more than a soap opera baseball cap. The most disturbing product, however, is the *All My Children* Collectable Card Game. What grown person would want to participate in such nonsense?

VERDICT: I have been scarred for life after being forced to watch soap operas by my mother and sister. As much as I love those two, I will carry the scars of watching countless love-making scenes, schemes to steal babies, and other atrocities from the world of soap operas for the rest of my life. While some women will adore this site, men should not visit this site, under any circumstances whatsoever. None. Seriously. Don't.

153

El Chupacabra
www.elchupacabra.com

It's Bigfoot, only two feet tall and in Puerto Rico! "First spotted in Puerto Rico in 1994…the Chupacabra has reportedly attacked and devoured the blood of a wide variety of animals including dogs and sheep." Right, and I've seen the Tooth Fairy and an honest politician. What does this creature look like? "The Chupacabra has had many sightings where its height was reported to be anywhere from three to six feet tall. Some say it walks, some say it flies, and some say it has a kangaroo hop." Maybe there's multiple Chupacabra species! Or, maybe it doesn't exist at all.

PRODUCTS: Shirts, hats, mousepads, mugs, stickers, and anything else you can think of. The products have one of two logos: the crossing sign "El Chupacabra X-ing" logo, and a crude drawing with the Chupacabra's various body parts on it. Bigfoot, the Loch Ness Monster, a normal Michael Jackson…what's next?

VERDICT: "Believers" in UFOs, Bigfoot, Nessie, government conspiracies, Roswell, alien abductions, and anything else without a shred of solid evidence to it will all find El Chupacabra products attractive. However, the products are humorous enough that believers and skeptics alike will enjoy having this creepy creature on their chest.

154

Submarine Store
www.submarinestore.com

"A few beers and many sea stories among ourselves and our submarine brothers guided us to the conclusions that: 1) the submarine community remains small, specialized, and elite; 2) a sincere and honest demand for submarine memorabilia exists; 3) no central, specialized outlet for these items existed, and; 4) between us, we had the knowledge, resources, and commitment to supply these kind of products to our brothers and sisters in the submarine community. Thus, the Submarine Store was born." A few beers and some stories led you to sell submarine memorabilia? What an interesting origin!

PRODUCTS: You can buy submarine art, models, patches, and books. Of course, there's the obviously needed "Subwear" section, including hats, T-shirts, jackets, workout wear, and (gasp!) lingerie! That's right! Who says submarine crewmen can't have some fun? Black Bikini-Cut U.S. Submarine Force Certified Panties are available to purchase for your girl. I'm sure she needs to know they're "certified." I wonder exactly who does the "certification." I'd volunteer!

VERDICT: Even if you're not a submarine crew member, you could buy this gear and say you are. It'll certainly impress some people, especially the ladies. If you're looking to lie about having military experience and bragging about your fictional adventures under the sea, the Submarine Store is for you!

- -

155

Accident Reconstruction
www.accidentreconstruction.com

When there's a car accident and nobody quite knows what happened, police use sophisticated equipment and software to reconstruct the accident. Now, you can get those same tools for your own personal use!

PRODUCTS: You can buy a DBD Crush Reformation Jig to figure out exactly how a car got crushed, or a laser to measure skid marks. Various books on car accidents are here for you, like the three volumes of *Accident Investigation in the Private Sector*, by Jack Murray, M.B.A, C.L.I, C.F.E. That's a lot of qualification! There's also *Forensic Analysis of Seatbelts*, by Don J. Felicella. *"Forensic Analysis of Seat Belts*...is the new book release from Kinetic Energy Press that will answer your questions when you really need to know something important about seat belts." I know I need information on seatbelts all the time! Like why does that little bell keep ringing and those lights keep flashing when I'm not wearing a seat belt?

VERDICT: While this site may be useful for forensic analysts, law enforcement, and other officials involved in traffic investigation, anybody else will be ultimately confused by this site. Unless you have serious business here, or are interested in learning the intricacies of accident reconstruction, you'd best stay away from this site.

156

Great Big Stuff
www.greatbigstuff.com

In this case, bigger is definitely better. "Many years ago, I was delighted to find a store called 'Think BIG!' in my local mall...However, I was dismayed when their retail stores shut their doors...I took that as a call to action to fill the void—and a BIG void it was!" Ha, ha, ha, "big void." Not funny.

PRODUCTS: Grossly oversized versions of just about anything can be found here. There's the mammoth Giant Big Lips Lamp, a novelty lamp featuring a pair of luscious lips. There's also a Great Big (fake) Diamond Ring, the sixty dollar, ten pound Great Big Candy Bar (for those with really, REALLY big appetites), a Great Big Chess Set, where two hands are required to play chess, and much more.

VERDICT: Sometimes, you just gotta think big. A lot of these products are irresistible! Who wouldn't want a giant candy bar that allows you to gain ten pounds in one day? Who can say no to a giant pair of underwear? And, who can resist what is perhaps the best one of all, that indispensable item that maintains "an erect stack of papers": a giant paperweight in the shape of a Viagra pill? I rest my case.

157

Texas Bigfoot Research Center
www.texasbigfoot.com

It's Texas's headquarters for the original monster legend! But, wait, he's not a monster, according to this site. "We are dealing with a primate, an elusive primate, not a monster; the 'missing link,' a shape-shifter from another dimension, or an extra-terrestrial being." Nobody's ever produced a reliable photograph of this thing! How do you know he's not a supernatural zombie or something?!

PRODUCTS: You could start with a subscription to the Texas Bigfoot Research Center newsletter; $15 for four issues a year. Fifteen dollars for four issues of rumors and gossip about a monster! Such a deal! There are also tons of shirts, mugs, bags, lunchboxes, and almost anything else Bigfoot you can imagine. Books on this elusive entity are also available through the site.

VERDICT: If Bigfoot is real, how come nobody has ever captured the beast? Maybe they have captured one, and there's a government conspiracy against revealing it. At least, that's according to paranoid science geeks with nothing else to do besides dream up cover-ups and research things that have not a shred of evidence to them. But, then again, he could be out there, and that's exactly what the TBRC is here for.

158

Buy a Kite
www.buyakite.com

Buy a kite, fly a kite! "High Flyers Flight Company is one of the East Coast's largest full-service kite stores. Since 1993, HFFC has been supporting the kiting sport in all ways possible." I didn't know there was such a thing as competitive kiting—now I know. Have doubts about the expertise of these high-flying retailers? Well, their staff "consists entirely of kiting fanatics; these people know kites, and can capably assist you." Anybody who admits that probably knows kites very well.

PRODUCTS: Kites, kites, and more kites. If you're into competitive kiting, try the "Sport Kites," with models like the Adrenaline Prism kite, a stealth-bomber-shaped black, red, and purple kite for $49. Think that's outrageous? Visit the "Specialty Kites" section to find the Giant Lobster kite, for the insane price of $450! I'm not paying that much for a giant flying lobster!

VERDICT: Kiting is fun once in a while, but I can't imagine anyone who likes to compete in this mockery of a sport, not to mention willing to spend over $400 on buying a kite. Some of the kites are reasonably priced at below $50, they have creative designs, and look nice. If you're looking for a good kite beyond something you'd find at the dollar store, you can find it here, but unless you're a serious, "competitive" kite flyer, watch your wallet while browsing. If someone tells you to "go fly a kite," this is the store for you.

159

k-Bee Leotards
www.k-beeleos.com

This is a site for gymnasts, ballet dancers, and strange men who like to prance around in skin-tight clothes. "For gymnastic leotards designed to withstand repeated training sessions while still looking good and at an affordable price, look no further than k-Bee Leotards." That being said, if you wear them just to "look good," something's not right with you.

PRODUCTS: Print Leotards, such as the Think Pink leotard, with a "Very pretty pink floral print with matching straps." Matching straps! How stylish! For colder weather, there's Long Sleeve Leotards, including suits with holograms and glitter! If you want something other than leotards, check out the "Shorts and Pants" section. All pants have the word "glitter" in them. Usually, anything with "glitter" is bad, as Mariah Carey so expertly proved.

VERDICT: Once again, this site appeals to a limited audience. This seems to be the case with all of the sites in this book. If you have a need or desire to wear skimpy, form-fitting costumes, buy from this site.

160 Insane for the Chains
www.insaneforthechains.com

This site is about something insane, but not in the way you think. This site is about disc golfing! Insane for the Chains specializes in humor for the sport of disc golfing, or Frisbee golfing, as it's also known. There's even a cartoon called "Basketcases" about the mishaps and misadventures of disc golfing. Humor at its finest!

PRODUCTS: There are golf towels, bumper stickers, calendars, and water bottles. (Boy, I really worked up a sweat tossing that disc, I need a drink.) This site is so confident in its customers that it offers gift certificates! Twenty-five and fifty dollar gift certificates are available for that special disc golfer in your life. Who would want to spend $50 on clothing for this freaky Frisbee sport? The shirts themselves include one with an Absolut Vodka-style layout reading, "Absolut Basketcase," with the words "100% Disc Golf" and "Insane for the Chains" at the bottom. I've seen better spoofs of the trendy alcoholic drink.

VERDICT: If you like throwing a Frisbee to your dog for hours on end, Frisbee golf may be the sport for you. It's much cheaper than regular golf (spending $150 or more on one club is not my idea of money well spent), and it is kind of fun (I've played before; I didn't do so well). If you're a regular on the course, Insane for the Chains is recommended.

161 Lumberjack Shows
www.lumberjackshows.com

"Experience the excitement of Lumberjack Sports today!" I'll opt to pass on that one, but that doesn't mean you have to! On this site, you can get tickets to shows, and learn more about events like the Ironjack and Ironjill series (Lumberjack sports doesn't discriminate!), and the Great Alaskan Lumberjack Show (only in Alaska).

PRODUCTS: You can purchase tickets to the exciting Great Alaskan Lumberjack Show! "Hardy lumberjacks would gather once each summer in the sawmill town of Ketchikan to compete against rival logging camps. These fit, rugged men fought hard to take home the bragging rights of becoming the 'King of the Woods!'" Lumberjack clothing, like the obligatory plaid vest and suspenders, and gifts like the Bobblehead Moose and Wooden Double-Bit Axe are also available.

VERDICT: Chopping down trees sounds more like work to me than a sport. Backbreaking, monotonous work at that. On the other hand, maybe you're interested in the senseless destruction of natural resources? Let's play "Who Wants to Cut Down Trees for Fun"! Anyone? Oh, guess not.

162   Aardvark Store
www.aardvarkstore.com

Of all the animals in the world to name a company "dedicated to the finer things in life," this site had to choose aardvarks. It offers a diverse cigar selection (most of which are not surprisingly from corrupt South American countries), as well as an "eclectic" wine selection. Accessories for both of these indulgent luxuries are also available for purchase.

PRODUCTS: This site offers an exotic variety of cigars from all over the world. Since the cigar market is so, um, "diverse," they're separated into two categories: Cuban, and Non-Cuban. Well, now we know how communism manages to work in Cuba! Choices range from the Rafael Gonzales collection (any relation to that cute little Elian who got kidnapped by Janet Reno?), to the very expensive Coronas Extra, now available in a box of twenty-five for Aardvark's price of 220£, including VAT (value-added tax). For us Americans, don't worry; there's a conversion tool inside the site to help translate those silly British monetary units. There's also a nice collection of wines, as well.

VERDICT: While one person's definition of "the finer things in life" may differ from the others (my personal definition is good restaurant pizza), the Aardvark Store offers the more, shall we say, stereotypical selection of these things. Whether or not you have the money to blow on these unnecessary amenities (hear that, credit card addicts?), go ahead. I'm nobody to stop you from wasting your money.

163

Lazy Dog Linens
www.lazydoglinens.com

Doesn't your faithful companion deserve the best bed possible? "Easier to clean than standard zippered dog bed covers, our sheets can be thrown in with your everyday laundry. Your dog can enjoy a nice fresh bed everyday." Does my dog NEED to enjoy a fresh bed everyday? Does it WANT to enjoy a fresh bed? It's a dog. It eats food from the garbage and sniffs other dogs' butts. What does it care about clean linens?

PRODUCTS: Various luxury sheets are available in colorful designs that your dog won't notice at all. Print sheets are available in patterns such as Country Plaid, Doggie Want a Bone (a pattern with various colored bones on it), and Raining Cats and Dogs (with cats and dogs spread throughout the pattern). Think that's fancy? Check out the two holiday patterns: Be My Valentine and Lucky Four-Leaf Clover. Where are the Christmas and Thanksgiving patterns? My dog deserves a bed cover for every holiday!

VERDICT: If your dog has to have custom covers for his or her bed, then that's a sign of being pampered too much, which inevitably leads to laziness. Oh wait, I'm thinking of human children. Dogs more likely couldn't care less if they had a dirty brown bathroom towel to sleep on. But, if you like doggie bed covers for your own tastes, then you have every reason in the world to shop here.

164

Polka-Store
www.polka-store.com

It's the world's coolest dance! The Polka Store has the self-proclaimed title of "the most fun and exciting polka site on the web!" Neither "fun" nor "exciting" are words that come to mind when thinking of polka.

PRODUCTS: Polka, polka, and more polka! Buy polka videos or DVDs, with videos seemingly covering every polka artist imaginable. Documentaries, music videos (I know I love polka music videos to dance to!), and other types of programs are available for artists like Les Bondi, a Concertina Hall of Famer (whatever that means); Louis Bashell, the Polka King of Milwaukee (my hometown); and Walter Ostanek, "Canada's Polka King." There seem to be a lot of polka monarchs around, huh? Don't forget that if you buy five videos or DVDs, you get one FREE! Why would I need six polka videos? Tapes and CDs, sheet music, dance instruction videos, a "Polka Botique" with T-shirts and hats, a traffic sign reading "Accordian Player Parking Only" and much, much more are also available on this wacky website.

VERDICT: Polka is music for older folks and people stuck in the past. I can understand how the elderly would like this (back in their time, this music was hip and cool, believe it or not), but why would anybody else think THIS is cool? If you find yourself liking this stuff, and you're under the age of sixty, there's something very wrong with you.

165

Troll Forest
www.trollforest.com

"Trolls of trolldom welcome you! Read our troll stories, go troll-shopping in our troll catalog, and read about our troll history!" That's a lot of troll! Despite their claim, there really is no troll history; just a bunch of weird children's stories.

PRODUCTS: Different colored troll T-shirts in red, bright blue, lime, and yellow. There are two different designs: a fat troll with crazy hair saying, "I Love the Beach! Wilmington, NC," and the same fat troll with sunglasses saying "Surfs up; Let's go!" These trolls seem to like warm, ocean climates. Funny, I thought they lived under bridges. Sizes are offered in youth extra small, small, medium, and large, as well as adult small, medium, and large. Adult XL and XXL sizes are three additional dollars. That's unfair to fat people! Unfair!

VERDICT: The stories on Troll Forest are standard children's story fare, and the drawings are substandard compared to better children's stories like Dr. Seuss. There are no rhymes, either, which made Dr. Seuss's books so memorable. The shirts are good for kids who like this type of thing, but there's no reason to buy adult shirts from this sub-par story site.

166

Mexican Sugar Skull
www.mexicansugarskull.com

Mexican Sugar Skull sells Day of the Dead merchandise. Day of the Dead is a Halloween-like holiday from Mexico where loved ones who have passed on are remembered. It's a very festive holiday. However, despite the sweet name of sugar skulls, these seemingly tasty treats are not for eating, but for decoration. Weird, huh? This site was also "featured on the Food Network *Food Finds* program! We hope you saw it." Unfortunately, no...

PRODUCTS: Plain pre-made sugar skulls are available to buy, with a "fifteen percent discount for dozens." Even if you buy one dozen, it's gonna cost you; one medium skull is four bucks. There's also strange skeleton folk art, with various ceramics, paintings, and fabrics featuring skeletons dressed up in human clothes, dancing, playing music, and basically throwing huge parties, for skeletons. Strange...but cool.

VERDICT: This holiday sounds like it's got the right spirit; celebrating death rather than mourning it. Most religions say that death is the beginning of a new life, but for those who don't have a religion, um, good for you. Anyway, MexicanSugarSkull.com sells everything you may need for this unusual, but fun, holiday.

167

Johnny Utah
www.johnnyutah.com

Yet another crazy site for a fittingly crazy sport: base jumping! There are loads of pictures of people parachuting and jumping from mountains, bridges, buildings, and other high places. The best part of this site, though, is the "Ex-Presidents" section, showing a photo of what appears to be George Washington, Abraham Lincoln, Richard Nixon, and Ronald Reagan preparing to jump from platforms in the air. Very, very, awesome!

PRODUCTS: Buy great videos like the *Official Bridge Day Safety* video, an "educational video [that] shows many examples of problems that can occur while BASE jumping. The examples shown are from eight years of Bridge Days." Eight years, a whole video of mistakes. Who do they let in to these competitions? You can also buy the *Johnny Utah Packing Video*, a video which "demonstrates my packing method...It includes techniques on how to pack neatly without clamps and the Super Mushroom PC packing technique." That sounds more like packing an illegal substance than a parachute.

VERDICT: What do the revolutionary war, the civil war, the Watergate Scandal, and the fall of Communism in Russia all have in common? Well, presidents were involved in all of them, and all of these presidents have base-jumped, too! If you like thrills, danger, and famous presidents, Johnny Utah's site is for you!

168

Cajun Chess
www.cajunchess.com

This site has nothing to do with gumbo, jumbalaya, New Orleans, or a giant mish-mash of cultures in one melting pot of corruption. But, it has everything to do with chess! "Enjoy unbeatable wholesale pricing on our extensive inventory of chess products...The CajunChess.com online chess supply store is the one-stop shop for all of your chess equipment needs." What about our voodoo, tarot card, adult entertainment, and cooking needs?

PRODUCTS: There are demo boards for players serious about chess. Demo boards are outlines of chess boards used for strategy purposes. Actual chess sets and boards are a necessity for any chess player, and you can find them here, including wooden and plastic pieces and wooden and vinyl boards. Where are the specialty chess sets, though? There's also software and games, for those who like sophisticated AI to play against, although you won't get anything close to Deep Blue.

VERDICT: While most chess players will find this a good resource, I'd like a little variety in my chess sets. What about the sets from your favorite TV shows? What if we want *Star Wars* sets, or *Simpsons* sets, or *Sopranos* sets (must...have...Sopranos!), or those really expensive crystal sets? They say variety is the spice of life. You'd think that with the "Cajun" part of the name, we could have some of that tasty spice, but this site is way too bland for my tastes.

169

Weasel Balls
www.weaselballs.com

Talk about a specialty store! "At the Weaselballs.com Store, we have a pretty niche business. We sell weasel balls, and that's all. We don't sell underwear, lawncare supplies, or automatic weapons…anymore—just a weasel and a ball, inextricably linked, forever and ever…the weasel desires the ball, yet the ball is indifferent…it flees. The weasel pursues. It is comedy and tragedy all rolled into one." Such a change from black-market weapons to the philosophical properties of weasel balls!

PRODUCTS: Why, weasel balls, of course! What else would this super-cool site sell? However, if you want a Weasel Ball, you must get both the weasel and the ball. Why? "The weasel's love for the ball is too strong. It transcends definition. That's why." Who knew Weasel Balls were so deep? The weasel balls are available for the low price of $7.00 (plus S&H…sneaky, huh?). And remember, AA batteries are not included.

VERDICT: While weasel balls may be fun toys for toddlers and even for some simple-minded adults, this site's promotional puffery makes them into something from a Shakespearean epic. Weasel Balls are electrically rolled balls with a little stuffed rodent attached to them. Nothing more. If you think this site has hit the mark on the "complexity" of weasel balls, you MUST be crazy.

170

Totally Britney
www.totallybritney.com

Totally Britney is "your ultimate online source for everything Britney Spears." (What, like quickie Vegas marriage annulments and swapping spit with other female singers?) Pictures, song lyrics, quizzes, downloads, chat rooms, forums, and much more are all available in worship of this super-sleazy singer.

PRODUCTS: Toxic: her song is also the way to discuss the repulsive, tainted nature of her products. Her *In the Zone* CD is available, with horrible "hits" like "Toxic," "Me Against the Music (featuring Madonna)" (we all know how much Britney "likes" Madonna…ugh), and "(I got that) Boom Boom (featuring Ying Yang Twins)." I don't know who they are, but I hate them already. Obsessive teenage girls can also buy the Barbie Sing With Me Karaoke Machine with twenty-four songs, featuring a number of tracks by Britney. Barbie and Britney: together, they're pressuring young girls to achieve that "perfect image"! Such role models!

VERDICT: Oops, she did it again! Set a new low for celebrities, that is. With every new song and publicity stunt, Britney becomes more of a "slave" to the pop culture world that's given her so much. I look forward to the day when her seemingly endless fifteen minutes of fame are up.

171 Awesome Tuxedo
www.awesometuxedo.com

For awesome tuxedos, visit Awesome Tuxedos! "We have been in the formal wear business for over fifteen years. We have been doing business on the Internet with the Awesome Tuxedo website for over four years." Recently they have expanded to what they like to call a "brick and mortar storefront" (they use the term twice in two paragraphs). "Brick and mortar storefront," for those who aren't familiar with this term, means a local retail location, i.e., a store. Wow.

PRODUCTS: Tuxedos galore! Every brand of tuxedo, from the generic Classic Tuxedos, to famous retailers like Perry Ellis, Chaps Ralph Lauren, Super 120s, Geoffrey Beene, Lubiam, and Fumagalli's! I've heard of the first two, but "Super 120s" sounds more like a gas station. If you're pinching pennies, check out the "Bargain Tuxedo" section, "Bargain" being in the mid-hundred-dollar price range.

VERDICT: If you're having a wedding or big party soon, Awesome Tuxedo is a must-see. If not, you should keep this one in mind. Why is it weird, then? Well, "Awesome" is not a word I'd use to describe formal wear, and I'll leave it at that.

172

Over the Hill Gifts
www.overthehillgifts.com

Over the Hill Gifts is dedicated to making getting old a little less miserable. "We have over-the-hill birthday gifts, thirtieth-birthday gifts, fortieth-birthday gifts, fiftieth-birthday gifts, sixtieth-birthday gifts, sixty-fifth-birthday gifts, seventieth-birthday gifts, seventy-fifth-birthday gifts, eightieth-birthday gifts, ninetieth-birthday gifts and one-hundredth-birthday gift ideas. We have over-the-hill party supplies for your over-the-hill birthday friend!" One-hundredth birthday? Would a one-hundred-year-old person even know what's going on? How many people even live that long?

PRODUCTS: There are gift ideas for every monumental birthday after thirty. The standard gifts for all birthdays include buying newspapers from the day you were born, party supplies with the age number on it, and dolls and mugs with the age. For fifty, forty, and thirty year olds, there are board games with trivia from the '50s, '60s, and '70s respectively. There are also supplies for theme parties like Cinco de Mayo, Mardi Gras, and luau parties. One great gift from the latter is the Hawaiian Grass Hula Skirt, perfect for putting the "aloha" back in your tropical bash.

VERDICT: This site is great to keep in mind, as there's always one person in the family who's beginning to go "over the hill." There are some great ideas for younger people, too. Next time you want to help that special someone feel a little younger (or probably older) on their birthday, head over to Over the Hill Gifts.

173

The Funk Store
www.thefunkstore.com

The Funk Store is "The Internet and the world's foremost authority on independent raw funk music." What's the different between raw funk and regular funk? "Although you can now purchase all styles of music at the funk store, our mode of operation will remain hard-edged and raw funky!" I didn't know "raw funky" was a mode of operation…

PRODUCTS: Check out the discs available. Past selections included *Invasion of the Booty Snatchers,* which is "straight to the dance floor" with hits like "Riding High," "No Rump to Bump," "Huff n' Puff" (a takeoff on the Three Little Pigs story), and of course, "Booty Snatchers." The rest of the site is full of albums by artists like George Clinton, Jimi Hendrix, Funkadelic, and Parliament.

VERDICT: I'm not one to judge this site, because I'm definitely not funky, and absolutely not raw funky. For those who do like these tunes, however, you'll be pleased with the massive magnitude of fabulous funk available here. This site's target audience is selective, but it will take pleasure in shopping at this funky site.

174

Pretty Ugly
www.pretty-ugly.com

What a name for a writer's group! "Welcome to the official website of Australia's Pretty Ugly Collective. We are a group of writers, artists, and zinesters with a feminist bent, keen to see more Aussie gals turn on to the power of pen pushing!" You like art and you think you're ugly…is there a connection?

PRODUCTS: Buy issues of the *Pretty Ugly* magazine. The covers of the magazines are shown with three designs: the face of a woman with a pretty ugly, slicked-back, old-schoolteacher-style haircut, a woman's restroom figure holding a guitar, and a woman putting her hand out with *Pretty Ugly* on her palm. Gives a new meaning to "Talk to the hand!"

VERDICT: Most of the pictures of women on this site aren't that ugly, so why is that what they name their site? Is it supposed to mean they're ugly on the inside? Does it have some kind of other philosophical meaning? Are the actual women behind the site pretty ugly? Pretty Ugly is a very cryptic message, and the site is fittingly hard to decipher.

175

Forbidden Planet
www.forbiddenplanetstore.com

Forbidden Planet is a site selling products from sci-fi, fantasy, and comedy series, including *Lord of the Rings*, *The Simpsons*, *Star Trek*, *Star Wars*, *Buffy the Vampire Slayer*, and other shows with large nerd fanbases.

PRODUCTS: The current hot item is the Bleeding Edge Goths seven-inch series three. "Series three is a very sexy series indeed; there's classic goth attire in red and black, then there's the nurse in blue PVC and the house maid in suspenders and frillys!" They look more like something from *The Munsters* or *The Addams Family* rather than "sexy." You can also buy stage prop replicas from the shows, and even *Star Trek* uniforms! I find them highly illogical, captain...

VERDICT: While this site does have some valuable items for the average Joe, most of these products cater to the hardcore geek crowd: the kind that like to argue on Internet forums endlessly about whether *Star Wars* or *Star Trek* is better; about whether Batman or Spider-Man would win in a fight, or about whether Buffy Summers or Princess Leia is hotter. In short, if you're obsessed with comics, sci-fi, and fantasy stories, you'll love these products. If you have any form of life, however, stay away.

176

Primate Store
www.primatestore.com

It's more fun than a barrel of monkeys! The Primate Store is your source for "everything for primate lovers." There's tons of information on these highly intelligent and highly humorous creatures, with sections like "Diet," "Housing," and "Primate Species." There is also is a section with the answer to the demand that everybody has voiced: "I want a monkey!" Well? "Primates are one of the most attractive animals in our animal kingdom. But they are unpredictable, destructive, expensive, and they need a lot of care and attention. Since some of them can live for over forty years, they truly are a life-time commitment. Are you the person that is willing to spend most of his free time with his monkey?" Now that you put it THAT way, no.

PRODUCTS: Despite the strong warning against buying a monkey, this site offers supplies to aid in caring for one. Toys, supplements, treat holders, diet foods, and gifts are available, but perhaps the best is what appears to be primate cereal called Primate-Os. Like Captain Crunch! Mmmm…sugar-coated, calorie-laden, delicious Captain Crunch. "Stays crispy even in milk!"

VERDICT: If only everything were like the movies, where everybody falls in love, and where school is all play and no work, and where monkeys are the perfect pet. Where it's possible to win the lottery, have psychic abilities, and, of course, own a monkey that can play pranks and do tricks. The reality of getting a primate is much harsher, apparently. In the movies, it's possible to raise a monkey with ease, but in real life, it's a lifetime responsibility. Still, the Primate Store is your source if you're crazy enough to take on this tough task.

177

Glowing Pets
www.glowingpets.com

Look what the wonders of science have brought us this time. "In 2003 scientists created the ultimate pet: genetically modified fish that glow in the dark. In the future, more pets will be added to the list. Take a look at what may be possible." There are then three pictures of bright green fish, a bright yellow baboon, and a bright green elephant. I didn't know elephants and baboons could be pets! And I don't think you'd need to make an elephant glow in the dark to be able to find it.

PRODUCTS: T-shirts and sweatshirts with different designs, like the "Hung Elephant," the word "hung" on the front and a picture of an elephant on the back. What does this have to do with glowing? There are also shirts with various brightly colored animals, including the Glow Lemur, Glow Sloth, Glow Chameleon, Glow Zebra, and another picture of a glowing elephant.

VERDICT: What's the public fascination with glow in the dark products? You can see them in the dark. Who cares? I can see the moon in the dark; why aren't there more moon products? Glowing is getting old. Don't buy into this quick cash scheme.

178

Groovy Juice
www.groovyjuice.com

Groovy Juice is "The virtual store and nostalgic center specializing in '60s and '70s fashion and popular culture." Sixties and Seventies nostalgia center? Does that mean this site will have protests and drug use on it? Or in the spirit of Abbie Hoffman, can we just "steal this store"?

PRODUCTS: New products include the Early '60s Black Two-piece Sequin Silver Burst. "This petite two-piece mini dress is sleeveless and sparkles in the front with a pointed silver burst design created from sewn sequins." It looks more like a tacky dress that went out of style forty years ago. The same is true of the Black and White Psychedelic Art Shirt, and the Blue Travolta-Style Disco Shirt, a style made popular by John Travolta in *Saturday Night Fever*. Good luck "staying alive" in this shirt. This site also sells "'70s disco, pimp [clothing]…bell bottoms, hot pants, granny dresses, jumpsuits, '60s go-go girl, Mod, mini skirts, hippie, and psychedelic wear."

VERDICT: Disco is dead, and so is everything else on this site. The clothes may be good for theme parties and other events held in memory of these times, but wearing them around regularly will make people think you fell through some kind of time warp. As they said back then, don't be square by buying from this strange, "psychedelic" site.

179

Rainbow Symphony
www.rainbowsymphony.com

Rainbow Symphony has nothing to do with the natural light phenomena, nor with classical music. It has everything to do with 3D glasses! "Rainbow Symphony Inc., a leading manufacturer of 3D glasses, has been supplying quality paper eyewear and specialty optical products for over twenty-five years." Quality paper eyewear, huh?

PRODUCTS: Buy 3D glasses and 3D Fireworks Glasses, including the Cash in with Coupons 3D glasses. "It's simple to attach one or two redeemable coupons to our 3D Fireworks Glasses. Use them to increase customer traffic and sales at any business." Now I can see multicolored 3D images AND aggressive advertising! Wow, man, I'm having a bad trip! You can also try out the 3D glasses for FREE! Click on "Free Stuff" (a phrase with hypnotic qualities…FREE…STUFF), and you can learn how you can get glasses for free. Plus a SASE inside another envelope, for a total of seventy-four cents plus the envelopes. That's not free! How deceptive!

VERDICT: I've always viewed 3D glasses as cheap and cheesy. The presentation of this site does nothing to contradict that image. The "quality paper eyewear" this site sells is anything but quality. If you must insist on watching things in 3D, however, by all means buy these ghastly glasses.

180   Golf Cart Tire Store
golfcarttirestore.com

As if a Golf Cart part site wasn't sad enough…golf cart tires? With "Over seven thousand tires in stock," you're sure to find what you need here, if what you need is tires for golf course transportation.

PRODUCTS: It's a golf cart tire treasure trove! Eight-inch, nine-inch, ten-, twelve-, eighteen-inch tires; all here and begging to be bought! Be sure to ride your cart in style with golf-cart-tire hubcaps. Silver, chrome, and gold hubcaps are available for eight- and ten-inch tires. Puts the "bling bling" back into your golf ride! Was it ever there to begin with? Don't forget the lift kits for golf carts, as well as lug nuts, center caps, and valve stems. Talk about a hole in one!

VERDICT: Golf-cart enthusiasts will be in paradise here. What's more, the uses for golf carts are expanding! Senior citizen communities, along with hunters and other outdoorsmen, are having a ball with these crazy carts! Avid golfers and outdoorsmen will find this site somewhat useful, but for most others it's just another crazy store.

181

Tail of the Dragon
www.tailofthedragon.com

Once again, the name is misleading. "Legend says a Dragon lives in the mountains of western North Carolina. He tests your skills on US-129 with 318 curves in 11 miles. Everyone who comes to ride the Dragon will always remember it." The dragon is actually a road that sports car and motorcycle enthusiasts frequent. Sorry, delusional mythical creature hunters!

PRODUCTS: T-shirts, tank tops, hats, stickers, and pins and patches with many different logos. Most having a dragon, a car, and/or a map of US-129. Books, videos, and DVDs telling the story of the Dragon are here as well. But remember, "This video is not intended to be instructional, or to show you safe riding. We are providing it as entertainment only and encourage everyone to ride responsibly within their abilities." Do as I say, not as I do.

VERDICT: Tail of the Dragon is great for racing and road vehicle fanatics. Bikers should consider this winding road as somewhere to go wild with their hogs. The site also provides quite a story about the history of this twisting throughway. Anybody looking to learn more about the history of a famous American roadway will find it at Tail of the Dragon.

182

Kazoo Store
www.kazoos.com

It's the great Kazoo! I always loved that little green alien pal of Fred Flintstone. No, wait, that's the Great Gazoo. Whether you're a *Flintstones* fan of not, you can't deny that the Kazoo Store is a unique, albeit strange store. "In his shows around the country, Rick (the owner of the store) gives each audience member a kazoo, and forms a giant kazoo band. Over the years Rick has given away nearly a million kazoos. He has become known as "The King of Kazoo." Sounds like this King is the generous, misguided ruler of a very large, very annoying band!

PRODUCTS: Products like the Kazoobie Plastic Kazoo, "a high-quality plastic kazoo made from nearly unbreakable plastic." "Nearly unbreakable" actually translates into "cheap and easy to break." "These kazoos come in a variety of bright colors and make a very good sound." A very good sound? How descriptive! Don't forget the Wedding Kazoos next time you have a wedding. They even offer gold and silver imprints on the kazoos with phrases like, "Thanks for coming to our wedding." This cheap frill will cost you $16 for twenty-five of them, three dollars more than the regular plastic kazoos.

VERDICT: Fortunately, these cheap plastic instruments come in bulk, so you won't have to worry about the inevitable breakage of these molded musicmakers. If you're looking for an incredibly annoying way to make some noise at your next party, look no further than the Kazoo Store.

183

Angry Alien
www.angryalien.com

Angry Alien is a site with thirty-second cartoons featuring famous Hollywood flicks. Only these movies are acted out by animated bunny rabbits. Parodies of *Titanic*, *The Shining*, *The Exorcist*, and *Alien* are here for your viewing pleasure. Under "Other Stuff," you can also find *The Pigeon Kam*, a cartoon drawn from the point of view of a pigeon. Why the name "Angry Alien," then? "When I first started my little biz, I needed a logo. I had sketched some sample ideas with ridiculous names (such as this one), and the image of a testy alien standing next to a rotary phone tapping his foot just spoke to me. I figured, 'eh, why not' and it just stuck." Some of my best ideas have been found this way.

PRODUCTS: The usual assortment of hats, shirts, tote bags, and other apparel with logos featuring camera crew bunnies, director bunnies, and a bunny troupe. The Angry Alien line has a blue-headed alien with an angry face. How original! Don't forget the *Pigeon Kam* T-shirts as well, along with other miscellaneous logos.

VERDICT: For only being thirty seconds, these cartoons sum up the plots of the movies pretty accurately. The sheer speed of the enactments is an element of what makes the cartoons so appealing. Angry Alien is really about bunnies making fun of movies, but it's still extremely entertaining.

184

Designer Doggie Wear
www.designerdoggiewear.com

It's as humiliating as wearing that ugly cardigan sweater from your aunt; only it's your dog that's feeling embarrassment. Designer Doggie Wear sells sweaters, vests, and shirts designed specifically with canines in mind. "Tired of those knit sweaters, the ones with legs that your dog hates? We came up with a unique design and method of fastening that we think you'll love." We might love it, but the dogs certainly won't.

PRODUCTS: This site sells fleece coats, raincoats, and cooling coats for dogs. Cooling coats are "to be soaked in water, then wrung out slightly and put on your dog. The evaporating water will cool your dog down on hot days. Very useful for active dogs." That, or a dish of water and a hose. For owners of dachshunds (weiner dogs), there's "designer doxie wear," coats "made to fit the long, lean, low, doxie body!" (Almost sounds like a doggie lingerie ad, and that is really unnerving!) Well, it's good to know we can buy these ridiculous coats for ANY dog.

VERDICT: While these coats aren't necessary for your dog, I've got to say that they are pretty cute. I'm just a sucker for those puppy dog eyes and cute little ears and noses. (Although Dog Nose Heaven makes that part into a sick sort of fetish—see site number 21). If you want something to make your dog even cuter, you've come to the right place.

185

Whip Store
www.whipstore.com

Whip it! Whip it good! "Bullwhip, signal whip, snake or stock whip—it doesn't matter what you use. The first time you make one crack, you'll be grinning from ear to ear." Buying a whip just to hear it crack? Yeah, right.

PRODUCTS: Bull whips, stock whips, and snakes whips, for starters. Snake whips, are "especially suited to indoor whip crackers, who may be working in places where the extra length of a rigid handle makes life tricky." They're available in kangaroo hide and nylon, which make "ideal first whips for 'adult' whip crackers." Adult whip crackers? And just do what do juvenile crackers use?

VERDICT: You know what was a really good example of great whip use? Halle Berry in *Catwoman*, one of the obviously great cinematic masterpieces of our time. Didn't she use the whip for fighting crime? Yes, even though the original (and much better Julie Newmar) Catwoman was a villain. The Whip Store is an ideal place for wild animal lovers, collectors, and sick people looking to indulge their secret fetishes.

186

The War Store
www.thewarstore.net

This means war! The War Store is a place for fans of war games, acted out through action figures, board games, and/or card games. There are even hilarious "Celebrity Testimonials," a made-up joke section featuring "praise" from celebrities like Saddam Hussein, John Kerry, Donald Rumsfeld, big stars like Rosie O' Donnell, and even big (I mean really, really big) film makers like Michael Moore! Mr. Moore supposedly says "Neal of the War Store is providing today's youth with the pewter to destroy tomorrow."

PRODUCTS: Board games, Dice and Hobby supplies, Fantasy Miniatures, Futuristic Miniatures, and Collectible Card and Miniature Games. In Fantasy Miniatures, you can find the essential game for every self-respecting nerd: Female Fantasy Football, featuring miniatures from the Human Team, the Elf Team, the Sisters (Nuns) Team, and the Bunny Team. Female Elves playing football, oh goodness, I need my inhaler!

VERDICT: The War Store sells games guaranteed to please any anti-social band of geeky rejects. Hey, Michael Moore likes it, doesn't that say enough? Add to fact that such distinguished people as Justin T., Bill C., and Hillary R. heartily endorse the site. If they like it, it HAS to be good.

187 Beer Is Good for You
www.beerisgoodforyou.com

It is? This site touts the boundless benefits of beer. Sections include "Health Benefits," with "articles" like "Beer May Help Prevent Alzheimer's," "Beer May Prevent Dementia," and, the biggest surprise, "Beer May Help Control Obesity."

PRODUCTS: Shirts, hats, stickers, and other accessories with the Beer is Good for You logo: a rather attractive blonde woman in a, um, "nurse's outfit" holding a beer. Don't forget that if you "order twenty dollars worth of crap (you) get a FREE 'Got Beer' baseball hat!" Well, they're honest about their products, at least.

VERDICT: Who knew about the health benefits of beer? We can get drunk every night AND lose weight? Reality check, guys: lots of beer is NOT good for you. Stop trying to pretend. If you're somehow convinced that beer is really good for you, or, if you just love beer, you'll find it at this delusional, "healthy" web site.

188 Presidential Pet Museum Store
www.presidentialpetmuseum.com

What do the names Lucky, Nelson, Buddy, Socks, Barney, and Spot all have in common? They're names for pets, true, but they're also presidential pet names! This site is dedicated to the extensive history of the pets of the various first families of the United States. A list of the pets of recent presidents, along with a "best books about" link for each president, are also available. Strangely, books about George W. Bush include *Supreme Injustice: How the High Court Hijacked Election 2000* by Alan M. Dershowitz, and *The Betrayal of America: How the Supreme Court Undermined the Constitution and Chose Our President*, by Vincent Bugliosi. Those are the "best books" about George W. Bush? And I thought this was supposed to be about pets.

PRODUCTS: Keepsakes, books, clothing, and collectibles featuring the presidents and their pets. The real attraction, though, is the "Presidential Pet Statues" collection, with ceramic shepherds, poodles, terriers, cats, and...alligators? That's right! John Adams, our second president, had an alligator as a pet! A far cry from the miniature terriers and cats of our recent presidents!

VERDICT: According to this site's history section, the worst presidents have had no animals! "Only rarely did presidents choose to not own pets, and that decision evidently doomed them to obscurity, or worse. Chester A. Arthur, for example—do you know anything about him? No? Well, now you know why—HE HAD NO PETS. Ditto for the equally insignificant Franklin Pierce." Perhaps this site is trying to convince us that pets make the president, not policy. With the ambiguous morals and, at times, sheer incompetence of the government, perhaps that's true. The Presidential Pet Museum takes a rare, lighthearted look at the personal lives of our presidents.

189

Zoltron
www.zoltron.com

Welcome to the enigmatic world of Zoltron. Zoltron is "a design company, specializing in web design, CD design, poster art, and free pony rides." Free pony rides. Right. They've done web and poster designs for Primus, Arj Barker, women.com, and Club Bastardo. I've heard of all of those, haven't you?

PRODUCTS: Zoltron posters, with several Primus designs, including a Primus Halloween poster with a creepy, haunted mansion in the background. Other designs include the purple-skinned soldiers, with the phrase "Zoltron: Enlisting Abnormality." Most other designs have something to do with portraying George W. Bush as evil, including George W. Thug Life. Don't you love how the election year bought out the activist in everybody?

VERDICT: Zoltron sounds more like an alien villain from a bad science fiction movie than a design company. The mystery surrounding the origin of the ideas that make up Zoltron are as mysterious the origins of its name.

190

Cloud City
www.cloudcity.com

These *aren't* the products you're looking for, unless you're a *Star Wars* fan, that is! "Cloud City Collectibles is a site that deals in collectible toys from the '60s to present. We do however, specialize in vintage *Star Wars* toys with a primary focus on high grade production items, rarities, and prototypes." Prototypes as in, new toy designs, or prototypes of planetary weapons of mass destruction like the Death Star?

PRODUCTS: Choose from the rare vintage *Star Wars* toys, modern *Star Wars* toys, "other" *Star Wars* toys, and toy cases. Vintage *Star Wars* products include twelve-inch dolls like C-3PO, a Jawa, and the IG-88 robot assassin. Be warned, however—the cheapest of these dolls is two hundred fifty bucks. That's what you pay for when you get cheaply made toys from the 1970s. Modern *Star Wars* toys include cheaper original trilogy products, disappointing *Episode One* and *Episode Two* toys, and Lego toys, Micro Machines toys, the "Power of the Force" toys, and more.

VERDICT: These products may not be from a galaxy far, far, away (unless you define Atlanta, Georgia as another galaxy), but for young *Star Wars* enthusiasts and collectors alike, Cloud City is a must see. However, at thousands of dollars for some old toys, may the force (and a Platinum Mastercard) be with you.

191

Pushin Daisies
www.pushindaisies.com

"You'll love what we dig up for you!" Pushin Daisies is a "mortuary novelty shop." What a respectful way to approach death, huh? "Pushin Daisies offers everything relating to the mortuary business, from the funny to the bizarre. Items include cemetery art, five-foot-tall mummies, outrageous T-shirts, funeral videos, music CDs, and even dead roses for that very special someone!" Just what I'd like: a batch of black, limp, moldy smelling roses.

PRODUCTS: There's Cardboard Coffin Gift Boxes, Mini Milk Chocolate Hearses, and the Niocide Coffin Ashtray. Just what you're asking for if you need one! You can also buy the *Six Feet Under* First Season VHS set, a show on HBO about the funeral home business. VHS? Where are the DVDs? Get with the program, people! Finally, there's the Five-Foot-Tall Mummy, which "has a skull face and is very realistic looking." It looks more like a skull attached to a straitjacket.

VERDICT: We all die sometime, so why not have a carefree attitude towards it? It's as certain as the sun rising, increased taxes, an Oprah Winfrey diet, or another new reality TV show every month. So why not just take it with a smile? Pushin Daisies can help you discover the lighter side of death.

192

Celebrity Rants
www.celebrityrants.com

They could have called this "Celebrities: Uncut and Uncensored," but that's taken already, so instead, it's Celebrity Rants! What are these rants? "Celebrity Rants presents animated portraits based on actual uncensored recordings of your favorite stars." Be warned, though: sample rants are saturated with anger and profanity, but they can be quite funny at times if you've heard these celebrities talk before.

PRODUCTS: You can buy an entire collection of rants for only two dollars for an MP3 download. Forty-five short, uncensored recordings of various celebrities. "MICHAEL JACKSON admits to sleeping with children! MARIAH CAREY's mental break down caught on tape! ELVIS PRESLEY gets stoned and threatens the press with violence! BILL CLINTON's comment after 'Getting a Lewinsky!'" Getting a Lewinsky? I wonder if the press heard that one. Rants apparel is available, with shirts featuring the Celebrity Rants logo as well as different rant quotes from celebrities.

VERDICT: I will warn you again: some of these rants may be inappropriate for kids. But, if you're mature enough to see that you should never say nasty things when others are listening, you'll find Celebrity Rants to be highly hilarious.

193

Dressy Tresses
www.dressytresses.com

For odd hair accessories, Dressy Tresses is the place to be! "Combining hair accessories with…experience as a licensed cosmetologist lead to the creation of Dressy Tresses. In the creation of each jewelry piece may be found Karlie's interest in renaissance, gothic, celtic, and fantasy themes." "Licensed Cosmetologist"? You mean makeup lady?

PRODUCTS: Pony Tail Holders, Hair Sticks, Claw Clips, Hair Snaps and Magnets, and more are all available at Dressy Tresses. If you're a fanatic of Victorian style jewelry, consider the Victorian Girl Dangles in the "Earrings" section.

VERDICT: Renaissance, gothic, celtic, fantasy themes: what great ideas for hair products! Now you can look like the elves in *The Lord of the Rings*, or keep up with the styles popular hundreds of years ago! If you want something a little more contemporary or stylish, however, you might want to look elsewhere. But, frankly, I do not care to have any knowledge of what's "in style," so judge for yourself.

194

Vegas Weddings
www.vivalasvegasweddings.com

Viva Las Vegas, baby! For the ultimate in spur-of-the-moment, alcohol-induced holy matrimony, look no further than Viva Las Vegas Weddings! "I decided to open my own chapel and to give brides and grooms the respect and dignity they deserve on the most important day of their lives. Most of all, I wanted to make the day fun and exciting, and give the couples the flexibility to express their own tastes and wishes on their wedding day." If you want respect and dignity, don't marry someone after only thirty minutes and five drinks together! Or was that five minutes and thirty drinks?

PRODUCTS: Various wedding packages are available for your very special day. You could select a traditional wedding, but who wants that? If you're gonna get married in Vegas, you want something like…like…the James Bond wedding! "This Las Vegas wedding package includes…two dancing Bond girls!" The real James Bond part is after the wedding though; finding a way to escape from your quickie marriage. Don't forget the Friday the Thirteenth Weddings, Halloween Weddings, and the upcoming 05-05-05 weddings. I got married on May 5, 2005! Isn't that cool?

VERDICT: Every Vegas wedding I know about has lasted a lifetime. Look at Britney Spears. How long did her marriage to Jason Allen Alexander last? Oh yeah, two days. Well, how about Dennis Rodman and Carmen Electra? That was nine days, but they got back together—for six months. The point here is that if you're serious about getting married, don't do it in Vegas.

195   Helmet Store
www.helmetstore.net

With "over thirty-eight styles of airbrushed helmets," you can't go wrong with the Helmet Store! From German army helmets to helmets with flaming skulls, and even full face motorcycle helmets, the Helmet Store has helmets galore!

PRODUCTS: Helmets. Lots and lots of helmets. You can buy skull helmets, eagle helmets, American flag helmets, and skull and eagle helmets WITH American flags. Perhaps the most masculine helmet, though, is the Unicorn Airbrush Motorcycle Helmet. Nothing says "macho man" more than a biker with a cute little unicorn on his helmet. If you're not concerned with safety, check out the "Novelty Helmets" section, with the super-stylish German Chrome Novelty Helmet with Spike. It's World War One all over again!

VERDICT: Not all of the helmets on the Helmet Store are DOT certified, meaning if you get in a crash, some of these helmets won't prevent a broken skull. Sure I'm risking my life by riding a bike or motorcycle without proper cranial protection, but I still look cool! Some of these helmets are certified, but if you couldn't care less about your safety, you can wipeout and break bones in style with the novelty helmets from this radical retailer.

196

Old Computers
www.old-computers.com

"Welcome to old-computers.com, the most popular website for old computers. Have a trip down memory lane." And what a trip it is! Old Computers has several articles, timelines, and a museum with computers dating back to 1960, when sticking wires into sockets was how you "programmed" it. Now we use computers for dating, dieting, looking at stupid websites, and buying weird products!

PRODUCTS: Apparel, stickers, clocks, mugs, and of course, mousepads, with old computer names and old computer games. Designs include a red, alien-like, pixilated figure with the phrase, "Destroy All Humanoids!" More like destroy all old, crappy computers. You can also buy the Wimbledon 1975 products, with a scene from a game of *Pong* on the shirt. Finally, there's the "I (heart) my ORIC-1." What's with this "I (heart)" stuff?

VERDICT: While people like me may not remember the old days of the primitive, crappy, very expensive computer and computer entertainment systems (better known today as videogames), those who do remember the humble origins of the super-advanced supercomputers of today will remember those days with a smile at Old Computers.

197

Mojo Scooter
www.mojoscooters.com

Forget skateboards. Scooters are all the rage these days! "Motor Scooters…are fun, inexpensive ways of transportation. MoJo Scooters offers a wide selection of scooters and scooter accessories. Scooters are providing a safe, fun, reliable, cost-effective way of alternative transportation." Cost effective?

PRODUCTS: Not really. In the "Gas Scooters" section, there are motorized scooters like the Thunder 50cc. While it does get eighty-five to ninety-five miles per gallon, the scooter itself is going to set you back about $1,800. It gets worse. The Mainstreet 260cc is more like a small motorcycle than a scooter. It can go a top speed of eighty miles per hour, with similar gas mileage as the Thunder, but it's gonna cost you $3,700. I'd rather get a used car for that price! If you're short on cash but still want to get in on the fun, there's exciting Mojo Gear, apparel, mugs, bags, and other products with the Mojo Gear logo.

VERDICT: While this site does offer some less expensive scooters, the gas-powered ones cost more than a good used car. The Mojo Scooter gear seems to be targeted towards loyal customers of this site. Even the regular, manually powered scooters cost an arm and a leg. Unless you're willing to spend hundreds on a trendy new transportation method, you're better off riding a bike.

198 Area 51 Collectibles
www.area51collectibles.com

Area 51 Collectibles has nothing to do with the top-secret site in Nevada that's become the center for hundreds of ridiculous government conspiracy theories. "Unlike gift shops that have a few pieces of dozens of different lines we only carry a few lines but we carry virtually every item in that line. So if you are a collector of Emmett Kelly Jr., Hummels, Pocket Dragons [I'm not going to comment on that…no], Willow Hall, or one of our other lines, you have just found the ultimate source!" If I had ever heard of *any* of them, I might be interested.

PRODUCTS: Charming Tails animal sculptures, Disney Sculptures, Emmett Kelly Jr. products, M.I. Hummel Figurines, Pocket Dragon Collectibles, as well as movie posters, rock 'n' roll collectibles, and Miniature Cowboy Hats! A sample from this small hat section includes the Stetson Miniature Hat Oregon Trail which is "Popular with modern day cowboys." Also, "this hat genuinely reflects the hearty pioneer's ultimate western migration." And this is on a site named Area 51. Strange.

VERDICT: If you happen to be a fan of any of these collectibles, you'll love this site. But most of you never have heard of Pocket Dragons or Emmett Kelly Jr. There are some fairly normal collectibles here, however, so Area 51 Collectibles can help you discover some neat vintage products, although it can't help you discover if "the truth is out there."

199

Think Geek
www.thinkgeek.com

Well, at least they're honest. Think Geek "started as an idea. A simple idea to create and sell stuff that would appeal to the thousands of people out there who were on the front line and in the trenches as the Internet was forged." Front Line? In the trenches? You make it sound like World War I brought about the Internet! Load your slide rules, fix bayonets, and charge into the fray!

PRODUCTS: Buy a Swiss Army knife with a USB storage drive, or a wristwatch color TV. There's also the Frustration T-shirts, like, "No, I will not fix your computer." Also available are confusing Coder/Hacker T-shirts, like the SYN/ACK shirt, which states, "If TCP/IP handshaking was less formal, perhaps SYN/ACK would be YO!/SUP! instead." Ok, whatever that means. Finally, there's the some-what sad Ladies apparel, with the Chicks Dig Unix T-shirt. Scary.

VERDICT: It was geeks who founded the Internet, and for that, I thank you. Without you giving the people of the world the voice to express their sick, twisted thoughts, my books would not be possible. But, then again, I am a geek, so I'm thanking myself. Boy, am I good.

200

Mardi Gras Zone
www.mardigraszone.com

Need more beads for your Mardi Gras trip? How about "great masks for any occasion"? Mardi Gras Zone is your supply HQ for the spring holiday where everybody goes "crazy," for lack of a better term. Like "intoxicated." "Mardi Gras Zone is both an online and traditional brick-and-mortar busi-ness located in New Orleans." Once again, "brick and mortar" translates into "offline, real-type, non-high-tech store," except it sounds better.

PRODUCTS: Tons and tons of beads, as they're in high demand dur-ing Mardi Gras (I wonder why?). From deluxe beads to "jazzy beads" to "big beads," you can get any type of beads here. They must make millions off of beads when Mardi Gras rolls around. There are even special beads just for throwing, mostly to women up in balconies, where everybody can see them flashing their fabulous, um, faces. Hats, dolls, masks, and other traditional Mardi Gras party goods are all here at your fingertips, ready to help you have a swingin' time on Fat Tuesday.

VERDICT: If you're a regular down in New Orleans on this sinfully delightful holiday, a trip to the Mardi Gras Zone is a necessity. It may not be my cup of tea, but if you live to party, attending this outrageous occasion at least once, with proper party supplies from this website, is a must.

201   Ornithopter Zone
www.ornithopter.org

The Ornithopter Zone: "Fly with Flapping Wings!" Ornithopters are devices that fly by flapping their wings, similar to how a bird flies. "And yes, they really work!" They do work, but what can you use them for? "Although some researchers focus on manned flight, the main goal in our field is to mimic bird or insect flight at its own scale." In other words, they're essentially complicated mechanical kites.

PRODUCTS: The Freebird and Luna Ornithopters are two of the manually powered flying apparatuses. "This unique flapping wing model kit was designed for ease of construction. That makes it the perfect introduction to the exciting field of flapping flight." Pretty cheap, too—only $13. Let's just hope the quality of the construction is as good. Radio-controlled Ornithopters are also available for a slightly higher price—slightly meaning about $200. I'll take the rubber band motor, thank you very much.

VERDICT: What inspired these people to make these strange devices? Perhaps a little too much birding (see number 6)? Maybe one too many "accidents" trying to fly as a child? Some "birdman" falling off the roof and hitting his head is how I'd imagine this idea came up. Still, if you're looking for an interesting alternative to your standard kite, the Ornithopter Zone is the way to go.

202   Legendary Heroes
www.legendaryheroes.com

What do Arnold Schwarzenegger, a teen heartthrob, and a warrior princess jacked up on steroids have in common? They all are elements of the exotic adventures on Legendary Heroes! Legendary Heroes sells merchandise related to certain TV and movie fantasy series. Examples include *Highlander* and the hit movie series *Lord of the Rings*, starring teen idol Orlando Bloom. Other series on Legendary heroes include *Conan the Barbarian*, a series about a muscle-bound guy who became governor of California, and the cult-hit *Xena: Warrior Princess* starring the buff Lucy Lawless and her female, um, "friends."

PRODUCTS: DVDs with seasons from *Xena* and *Hercules*, as well as the *Highlander*, *Conan*, and *LOTR* movies. The *Highlander*, *Hercules*, and *Legendary Swords* stores sell collectible swords, like the Sword of the Witchking, a "sensational, fully authentic reproduction [that] is crafted from the original film prop that so effectively menaced The Fellowship." It also comes with a "Certificate of Authenticity," which justifies its ridiculous price tag of $350.

VERDICT: *Conan* had to be Arnold's best movie. Better than *Terminator*, better than *Total Recall*, and definitely better than *Jingle All the Way* (I'm very serious on that one). Legendary Heroes in actuality is only for faithful followers of these fantasy series.

. . . .

203   Cool Moose
www.thecoolmoose.com

Let loose the moose! The Cool Moose is "Maine's Original Moose Store." It's probably Maine's (and the world's) ONLY moose store. You can buy moose merchandise, but you can also view the very cool Moose Cam! "A resident outside of Anchorage has set up a monitoring camera in his yard…generally, your best viewing times will be dawn or dusk in Alaska, which is four hours behind Eastern Standard Time. Good luck!" While I'd imagine it's quite a sight during those periods, the rest of the day has you staring at nothing. Maybe it's not so "cool" after all.

PRODUCTS: Moose clothing, crafts, belts, and toys and other stuff for kids. A few memorables are Maynard and Harry, the Humanitarian Bear and Moose Trophies. "These Maine-made humanitarian trophies are popping up in bedrooms and boardrooms across the country. It's the fun, humane way to bag a moose or a bear!" Good thinking, since you'd be crazy to try to kill a moose or a bear without a machine gun or automatic rifle in hand.

VERDICT: If you do your homework, you'll discover moose aren't the nicest creatures out there. According to an article on Mooseworld.com, moose abandon their young shortly after they're born! Next time you think about buying some moose gear for your kids, ask yourself if you'd condone those repulsive parenting habits. Shame on you, moose!

204 International Dodgeball Federation
www.dodge-ball.com

While the movie flop *Dodgeball: A True Underdog Story* may seem like a stupid movie for a stupid sport, there is actually a real league for this child-ish sport. "The IDBF promotes the sport of dodgeball by standardizing rules, courts, equipment, and acts as the central agency responsible for sanctioning tournament play." I didn't play with equipment when I was in grade school; why should they have to now?

PRODUCTS: The official IDBF T-shirt features a player in green shorts and a purple shirt who seems to be jumping into the path of the incoming ball. He wants to get hit by a ball, and his clothes don't match? Like, what a loser! You can also buy the official tournament ball and the official dodgeball rulebook. Now football, or hockey, I can imagine elaborate rules, but, dodgeball?

VERDICT: While dodgeball may be somewhat popular among adults, the glory it once had was with grade school children has now been wiped out by "safety rules" and the threat of lawsuits. Oh, my kid got hit by a ball and now we have a bloody nose on our hands! Call my attorney, I'm suing the school for millions of dollars! Lawyers. Can't live without 'em, can't shoot 'em.

205

Weather Shop
www.weathershop.com

Next on the forecast, we have a strong gathering of unnecessary products, with a weak front of stupid sales pitches coming in from the Internet! The Weather Shop sells various tools for measuring elements of the weather like rain, temperature, radio waves, and even lightning! Ok, so what if I'm not a desperate, unemployed meteorologist?

PRODUCTS: Barometers, atomic clocks, hygrometers, and even lightning detection gear. One of the latter tools is the StrikeAlert Personal Lightning Detector, a pager-like device that "provides an early warning of approaching lightning strikes from as far away as forty miles. Perfect for all outdoor sporting events, work, and recreation, or for professionals needing early warning. Only $79.95!" Only?

VERDICT: Unless you want to broadcast a weather show from your garage over public access television, the Weather Store only offers a handful of useful products. Do you really need (or want) the Irrigard system that shuts off your lawn sprinklers if it looks like rain? Useless. Thermometers and clocks, maybe, but anything else is overpriced and overrated by this strictly stupid site.

206

Zombie Nation
www.zombie-nation.net

"When there is no more room in Hell, the Zombie Nation will rise." What is Zombie Nation? This site is basically about anything and everything zombies. They even have a plan for where to go if there's a zombie attack. The safe haven: the mall! Like, there's everything at the mall!

PRODUCTS: Clocks, stickers, shirts, hats, and other apparel and accessories with different Zombie Nation logos: red and green zombie hands, Zombie Attack, with a creepy blood-red zombie face, and the Zombie Skin Gear, discolored, spider-vein skin with the words Zombie Nation on it. And I thought eczema was a bad skin disorder. The heartbreak of psoriasis is nothing compared to Zombie skin.

VERDICT: Don't zombies need brains to survive? They're available at BrainsforZombies.com (another classic from my original book). Perhaps Zombie Nation needs to get a contract with them. Whatever the case, if you like horror movies, reanimated corpses, or undead fiends in general, Zombie Nation is for you.

207

Bundyology
www.bundyology.com

Bundyology is "a non-official site dedicated to the sitcom *Married...with Children*." Information on the series, the characters, the cast, quotes, and other interesting *Married* facts are here as well.

PRODUCTS: DVDs featuring season one and season two of *Married...with Children*. There's also a *Best of* DVD, as well as another offer that seems a bit suspicious. "TVonDisc.com offers the entire series on twenty-five region-free (play anywhere) DVDs." This dubious set costs about US$185. I don't know any details about this offer, especially if it's legal. Well, the Feds haven't shut it down yet, so hurry while it's legal! Also sold are books (*Pig Out With Peg*, an actual cookbook of bad recipes), comics, and sources for the Be Like a Bundy game.

VERDICT: Love and marriage. They're kind of like a horse and a carriage. This site is a good resource if you want to learn more about this quirky series, and fans will go nuts over it. Just look out for that TV On Disc offer. It's like bringing back Crystal Pepsi...too good to be true.

208 Bush and Zombie Reagan
www.bush-zombiereagan.com

"Difficult times call for great leaders—men of vision, strength, and courage. Men like George W. Bush and the shambling, reanimated corpse of Ronald Reagan." Sounds like a plan to me! Not convinced of Zombie Reagan's qualifications? Check out the FAQ, with questions like, "Will Zombie Reagan require the brains of the living to feast on?" "Yes. However, enough young Republicans have volunteered to donate the ones they aren't using that this will not be an issue." Young Republicans? What young Republicans? Don't look at me. What about the opposition? "Is Zombie Reagan really that much of an advantage? Doesn't John Kerry have the zombie vote locked up?" "No. John Kerry, in fact, isn't really a zombie. He is more akin to Frankenstein's Monster, built out of parts stolen from graveyards under cover of night. He simply claims to be a zombie for political advantage." Ah, it's so clear now.

PRODUCTS: Hats, shirts, mugs, and mousepads with the Bush/Zombie Reagan logo, as well as a sticker that says, "It's morning in America...again!" But, no tote bags? No clocks? NO THONGS? What's up with that?

VERDICT: While this site may be old news by the time this book is released, its extreme abnormality can't be ignored. In memory of the potentially unstoppable presidential ticket that could have been, Bush/Zombie Reagan keeps its place in this book and in our hearts.

209 The Nanny
www.thenanny.com

It's da Nanny! What was this crazy show about? "When the show premiered...the plot was...simple: Fran, fresh out of her job as a bridal consultant in her boyfriend's shop...appeared on the doorstep of Broadway producer Maxwell Sheffield (Charles Shaughnessy) peddling cosmetics, and quickly stumbled upon the opportunity to become the nanny for his three children." Not to mention the opportunity to peddle her really annoying voice to the rest of the world.

PRODUCTS: Books, movies, and CDs like *The Wit and Wisdom of the Nanny: Fran's Guide to Life, Love, and Shopping*. Gotta have the shopping! Don't forget the appropriately titled *Enter Whining*, by none other than Fran Drescher herself.

VERDICT: Unless you're a fan of Drescher's high-pitched whining, the Nanny website is just more of the same annoying excuse for a babysitter. Her equally annoying New York accent makes it all the worse. I'd prefer to see a non-stop marathon of Arby's Oven Mitt commercials than watch one episode of this sordid show.

210

Prince of Pets
www.princeofpets.com

The Prince of Pets sells art and posters featuring dozens of animals, including dogs, cats, elephants, birds, bears, monkeys, and even zebras. You can also participate in fun things like the "Feline/Human Relationship Quiz." "Is your human attendant well trained?" Human training? What, now I need papers to poop on?

PRODUCTS: There must be hundreds of different types of animals here! There are almost one hundred dog breeds alone, not to mention cow, moose, tiger, and hippo products. Perhaps the ugliest shirts are the Pekinese and Pomeranian shirts; dog breeds that look like monkeys and foxes respectively. The stupidest poster is the Ostrich poster, a black and white close-up of an ostrich's face that is meant to look artistic, but ends up being just plain weird. Finally, the strangest poster is the "Let the Little Things in Life Tickle You," a poster of an elephant foot hovering over a little mouse. It looked good when it was taken, but any later and it would've been a poster with mouse guts.

VERDICT: If you have a favorite animal, you'll definitely find something to like at Prince of Pets. I mean, where else could you find (or want to find) a poster of prairie dogs sniffing each other? Whether you're mad for monkeys, crazy for crocodiles, or bonkers for bison, you'll find at least one product that gives your favorite creature the artistic merit it deserves. No mosquitoes, though; I thought everybody liked those.

211

Friends of Hillary
www.friendsofhillary.com

Who would participate in such devil worship? Somebody, apparently. This site is for supporters of this evil woman seeking to get her re-elected to the Senate. If you're drawn in enough by the brainwashing of this site, you can join "Hill's Angels," which describes how "the right wing is waging a personal attack against her…You can help Hillary fight back against these untrue, unfair attacks by joining Hill's Angels—a very special group of friends who are working right now to be sure she has the support she needs." Hill's Angels? More like Hill's demons. There's even the "en espanol" version, to assist in multi-lingual propaganda.

PRODUCTS: T-shirts. Scary, repulsive, abominable, immoral, downright disturbing T-shirts. "With a Marc Jacobs 'Hillary' T-shirt, you can show you're proud of your politics. Support Hillary in style and get yours today!" Does the madness ever end?

VERDICT: Why do I despise HER so much? Look at it this way: she stays with Bill, after what he did and did and did and did. Any other woman would have dropped him like a one-hundred-pound sack of potatoes. It's obvious what I think, now ask yourself: do you want to support a woman who tolerates that kind of crap from her husband? Stand up for yourselves!

212

The Cellar Store
www.thecellarstore.com

"The Cellar Store is the result of our attempts to bring neat things to life for our customers." Neat being defined as "Cast Iron Pots, Fine Oak Wine Barrels…Classic Pedal Cars, [and] Portable Thermoelectric Coolers and Warmers." All those in one place? So much for specialization.

PRODUCTS: Some of the weirdest products include the Pot Belly Pot w/Stand, that stands 6.5 inches tall. Normal enough, until you consider the other products they sell. They not only sell pots, they sell GPS units, like the Meridian Color from Magellan, "The first Meridian GPS Receiver for serious navigators who want a vibrant outdoor viewable color display in a go anywhere handheld system." Quite a far cry from cooking pots, huh? There's also Classic Pedal Fire Trucks, like the Deluxe Sad Face Pedal Powered Fire Truck. Hey, fire trucks have feelings too!

VERDICT: The assortment of products on this site is so strange. One minute you're looking at cookware, the next you're looking at high tech satellite technology, and then you're on to collectible model cars. While all of these products have their uses, it's rare to see them all in one place, much like the celebrities on *The Surreal Life* (Gary Coleman AND Vanilla Ice? Tammy Faye Bakker and Ron Jeremy? Talk about a combination!). If, by some chance, you need nineteenth-century cookware, GPS equipment, and collectible cars, the Cellar Store is here for you.

213

E Bead
www.ebeadstore.com

Bonkers about beads? Check out this site. "Our mission is to provide you exceptional value for all your beading needs." More like beading "wants." Beads are no more of a "need" than one hundred channel satellite TV or cell phone text messaging.

PRODUCTS: So many beads, you won't know where to start! Animal Print Beads, Basic Glass Beads, Chevron Glass Beads, Fancy Gold Line Beads, and other obscure types of beads. The oddest selections include the Elephant Bone Beads, bone beads in the shape of elephants; Bug Beads, beads in the shape of little ladybugs; and Fancy Zebra Line Beads, pipe-like beads with zebra patterns.

VERDICT: Buying beads from a website is a sure sign of obsessive compulsive accessorizing. Do you really need to order ten individual elephant-shaped beads just so you can have little elephants around your neck? Do you really need to get red, white, and blue beads shipped to your house so you can show off your American pride in style? Buy some cheap beads from a craft store and make your own necklace. "Needs," these are not.

214

Sky Houndz
www.skyhoundz.com

Are you fond of flinging the Frisbee to Fido in the backyard on warm summer nights? (Oops, I used the "F" word—Frisbee—the official doggie disc is the Hyperflite, according to this website.) If you're a little too fond of this seemingly casual hobby, you can check out Sky Houndz, and compete for the "Top Dog" flying disc title. "Skyhoundz was founded in 1998 by Peter Bloeme, the only person to win the World Championship twice—once by himself and a second time with his dog Wizard." How can you win this crazy competition without a dog?

PRODUCTS: Discs, videos, books, accessories, and T-shirts all related to disc dog competition. Check out the *Skyhoundz Images* Coffee Table Photo Book, which has artistic photos of dogs catching discs. So poetic, those disc dogs are. T-shirt designs include the "Every Canine Deserves a K-10," and the classic "Best Toy for Dogs Since the Cat." I don't know, those cats are pretty good toys for our pooches.

VERDICT: All of the strange sports in this book can't have a big following. I mean, dodgeball, kickball, kiting, pole vaulting, and now this? Did enough people like throwing discs to their dogs so much that they decided to make a sport out of it? The obvious answer is "hard to believe, but yes."

215

Mr. Cranky
www.mrcranky.com

Sometimes it's good to find someone who finds the bad things in everything. Mr. Cranky is full of witty, zinging anti-reviews of movies, meaning they are rated not on how good they are, but how BAD they are. The rating scale ranges from one bomb, rated as "almost tolerable" to an atomic explosion that says, "proof that Jesus died in vain." An example includes a review of *Catwoman*, which got a dynamite; "So godawful that it ruptured the very fabric of space and time with the sheer overpowering force of its mediocrity."

PRODUCTS: You can buy Mr. Cranky's book, ShadowCulture's *Mr. Cranky Presents: The 100 Crankiest Movie Reviews EVER*, which features one hundred of Mr. Cranky's best (or worst) reviews. Mugs, T-shirts, hats, stickers, and other products are available featuring either the Mr. Cranky logo (a face sticking its tongue out), or the Mr. Cranky rating scale from one bomb to an atomic explosion.

VERDICT: I spent almost an hour looking at the reviews before I wrote this down. It's that good. While some of the reviews are a little too frank and over the top with the language (read: not for kids), most people will enjoy the insulting comparisons and dead-on descriptions that make the reviews so thoroughly enjoyable.

216

Giant Robot
www.giantrobot.com

"*Giant Robot* magazine covers cool aspects of Asian and Asian American pop culture. Paving the way for less knowledgeable media outlets, Giant Robot put the spotlight on Chow Yun Fat, Jackie Chan, and Jet Li years before they were in mainstream America's vocabulary." Good for Jet Li and Chow Yun Fat, but helping Jackie Chan achieve American stardom? Shame on you.

PRODUCTS: Strange products relating to Asian movies and cartoons, including the Jason films. Not the masked serial killer who appeared in the cinematic masterpiece *Freddy vs. Jason*, but rather Og Jason. *The Iron Wagon* by Jason is a detective story with questions like, "Who killed game warden Blinde? Why won't he stay dead? What dark secret causes landowner Gjaernes and his butler to act so suspiciously? And—most maddening of all—precisely what is the invisible 'Iron Wagon' whose clatter and tumult accompanies these sinister occurrences in the otherwise idyllic Norwegian countryside?" Your guess is as good as mine.

VERDICT: If this is how Asian culture is, I have no idea how they understand this stuff. Do we Americans just think differently than they do? Do we consider corny love stories and films about saving the universe normal, as compared to these perplexing plotlines? It just shows how incredibly diverse this small world is.

217

Stan the Caddy
www.stanthecaddy.com

Stan the Caddy is a character from the mega-popular TV series *Seinfeld*, which means that Stan's site is a *Seinfeld* site. Besides its impressive inventory, Stan the Caddy has *Seinfeld* scripts, sounds, character profiles, and a large collection of classic *Seinfeld* quotes. Some quotes include "I would drape myself in velvet if it were socially acceptable," "Nobody carries wallets anymore. I mean, they went out with powdered wigs," and "Hey, you know what I think it is? I think it's that East River. I think it might be polluted."

PRODUCTS: *Seinfeld* season DVDs, posters, books, caps, and stickers. In the description of one of Jerry Seinfeld's books, *Seinlanguage*, Simon Leake proposes that, "Eons hence, scholars may ponder the mysteries of this book in the same way that they now ponder the fragments of Heraclitus. Until then, *Seinlanguage* will continue to provide guaranteed chuckles in a neat and tidy package. Kind of like Jerry himself." Ah, the philosophical mysteries of Jerry Seinfeld.

VERDICT: Stan the Caddy matches the show in its, shall we say, "unique" humor. Some may like *Seinfeld*, others may loathe it. Nobody, however, can doubt the appeal the show held until the "epic" finale. Of course, the series ended with them in jail. How else could it end?

218

A Little Bit Hippy
www.alittlebithippy.com

Flower power! Save the world! Make love, not war! True to its name, this store sells almost anything hippy that you can imagine. In fact, the folks at Little Bit Hippy are "sure that you'll find something to satisfy the little bit of hippy in you." What if we don't have ANY hippy in us?

PRODUCTS: Start with an essential for every hippy: Tie Dye T-shirts! Stained Glass Tie-Dye shirts, Rainbow Tie-Dye shirts, and the absolutely necessary Peace Sign Tie-Dye shirts. Perfect for angry anti-war protests! T-shirts with hippy bands like the Grateful Dead and Phish, along with hemp hats (smoke 'em if your stash is gone), jewelry, and sandals are also in stock. A favorite for women is the "Bohemiem" dress. Guess it's hard to spell "Bohemian" when you're stoned. And, of course, how could a hippy exist without the essentials like blacklights, incense, door beads, and candles?

VERDICT: While I may not have any bit of "hippy" in me, teens and young adults who revel in defying authority and sixty-years-olds with ponytails do. So if you're looking for something to satisfy that little "peace and free love" part of you, visit A Little Bit Hippy.

219

Platinum Pen
www.platinumpen.com

"Platinum is forever, and we put it in writing." A very poetic slogan, but, "to Platinum Pen, this is not just a slogan, it has been their way of doing business since 1919." Putting platinum in writing doesn't sound like a "way of doing business." Nevertheless, this site is the Internet's premier purveyor of platinum pens, and perhaps the only platinum pen peddler on the planet. Sorry, the P key got stuck!

PRODUCTS: Pens, made of platinum (what did you expect?). The pens are well crafted and attractive, but extremely expensive. Pens like the Eightieth Anniversary pens, available in red and black, cost about $1,000. Who would pay that much for a writing utensil? It gets worse. The Plantain Makie fountain pen costs three times that amount. That's right, $3,000 for a pen. There are standard pens that only cost a few bucks, but its obvious they make the most off of the ridiculous prices of the fountain pens.

VERDICT: The prices for these pens are like Britney Spears tabloid stories: just when you think you've seen the worst, something else totally outrageous comes along and blows it away. Nobody, save for mega-business conglomerate CEOs, can afford these pricey pens. There are reasonable pens on this site, but the others can and will vacuum everything out your wallet if you are foolish enough to buy them

220

Harry Potter
Wizard Store
www.hpwizardstore.com

Milkius cashcowius! That's the spell the Harry Potter Wizard Store is cast-
ing. While there is a reason it's sold millions of copies, selling a billion
copies wouldn't warrant the milking of the cash cow that's going on here.

PRODUCTS: Harry Potter candies, games, books (strangely not the
title books), and unfortunately, ties, scarves, and clothing. How sad is
that? The strangest products, however, are the broomsticks, including
the Nexus 100 Flying Broomstick, which warns parents, "It is advis-
able that children be given flying lessons from a qualified instructor
before attempting to use any of our brooms." They're actually telling
you that you can fly with these? "Here, son, jump off the roof with this
and fly." Can you say "lawsuit"?

VERDICT: I like the *Harry Potter* books, but these products have
gone too far. Only fanatics of the series will even think of buying
these, and even the "fanatics" should think twice about wearing the
clothes regularly. The books may not be overrated, but these products certainly are.

221

Speed Racer
www.speedracer.com

Go, Speed Racer, Go! *Speed Racer* was a cartoon imported from Japan and
"Americanized" with different voices. The episodes were full of crazy car
stunts, predictable plot twists, and characters talking really fast (as a result
of the rough translation). This site has message boards, episode summaries,
and wallpaper downloads.

PRODUCTS: T-shirts, collectibles, gifts, hats, and more. Notables
include the Speed Racer neckties, with ties featuring the Mach 5 (Speed
Racer's car that may be able to exceed the speed of sound), the Racer X

tie (such an original name for a mysterious character), and the Go Speed Racer Go tie. Don't forget the Bumper Sticker Set, with stickers like "My Other Car is the Mach 5," or "Go Speed Racer Go."

VERDICT: *Speed Racer* was a strange show. Cars would spin out, go over the edge of a cliff and explode (how nice for a kid's show), but the Mach 5 and other cars could fly and drive over each other with elevated wheels. Plus the little boy had a monkey named Chim Chim that he traveled with who could foil evil plots by the other racers. If you're a fan of totally unrealistic, but still classic cartoons, though, you should race down to SpeedRacer.com.

222

Pairs on Ice
www.pairsonice.net

It's a boring, yet somehow popular sport: ice skating with partners. "These pages feature recent and historical elite pairs skating competition results, pair profiles, photos, and online resources." Historical? You mean like Nancy Kerrigan and Tonya Harding? More like hysterical!

PRODUCTS: Books, magazines, movies, and music all straight from the "intense" action of figure skating. New releases include *Artistry on Ice* by none other than Nancy Kerrigan, the woman unfortunate enough to get in the way of Tonya Harding's blackjack wielding cohorts. Also available are books for kids, like *Ice Dreams*, where "seven-year-old Randi Wong wants to give up her violin lessons for skating, and, with the help of her friends, Anna and Woody, she comes up with a creative scheme to persuade her parents." Today, "creative" skating lesson schemes, tomorrow, "creative accounting" fraud schemes. And, really, truly, do you seriously, personally, know anyone who admits to the nickname Woody?

VERDICT: Who wants to watch a man in tights and a woman with an ugly dress spin around each other? The Harding-Kerrigan scandal was the only good thing ice skating ever produced. It shows us that if you can't beat someone, you should convince your ex-husband and his shady friends to club her in the knee. Such valuable life lessons from good ol' Tonya Harding.

223

The Box Store
www.theboxstore.co.uk

Unlike the Unique Box Shop that sells intricate works of art, the UK-based Box Store makes no bones about it: they sell cheap, reliable, bland, and boring cardboard boxes. "The Box Store was set up to simplify the purchase of boxes. If you are about to move house, need to relocate the office, or simply want to tidy your garage or shed, the Box Store has the answer." The wacky Brits may be dismal at dental hygiene, but they are tops at corrugated cardboard.

PRODUCTS: Furniture protectors, adhesive tape, marker pens, and of course, boxes. Sure, some of them have fancy colored patterns on them, but in the end, they're all just boxes. However, the best product on this site is the cheap but magnificent Bubble Film, or as we Americans know it, BUBBLE WRAP! Six-hundred-millimeter wide sheets for only sixty pence (about $1.10 in US currency) a "metre," VAT included. A dollar ten for six hundred millimeters of bubble wrap? Let the popping party begin!

VERDICT: Not only is this site a great supplier of bubble wrap, the boxes they sell are cheap, and assumingly semi-reliable, too. If you need some boxes for that big move, or if you just want countless sheets of bubble wrap for hours of simple fun, you need to visit the Box Store.

224

Jaded Ape
www.jadedape.com

Jaded Ape is another site with humorous downloadable videos. *Can I Call You Tomorrow?* shows several guys being extremely insensitive to women who don't appear to be, well, present. Quotes like, "Dessert? For her? No," "I will have a burrito, and for the lady, something of equal or lesser value," and, "So, I basically started wearing bigger pants, and the rash cleared right up," saturate the video. I don't think they'll be getting that call. The best, however, is the *French Chef* video, where they make a "Surrender Sandwich." Although the actual making of the sandwich doesn't make much sense, we all know that the French reign in the realm of resignation.

PRODUCTS: Shirts, hats, clocks, mousepads, and teddy bears are available, but as the description of the store says, "If you're keeping track, you'll notice we offer a lot of chick stuff. Very observant Sherlock. That's because Jaded Ape is made up of lonely guys, who love the ladies. That is, the hot ladies. Send us your pictures, hot ladies!" At least they're honest about the lonely part. They might add "loser," too.

VERDICT: Jaded Ape's humor isn't laugh-out-loud funny, but it is funny. To the FAQ comment, "I watched your stuff, but I don't get your humor," they answer, "You're an idiot. Lame jokes, snappy one-liners, and cliché characters may pass for humor in your house, but your house probably has a Ford in the driveway."

225 Not without My Handbag
www.notwithoutmyhandbag.com

Take one part pop culture, add a little quirkiness, and throw in some crazy junk with no purpose whatsoever, and you've got Not Without My Handbag. In addition to a store, the site has links to other online sites with a female audience (but remember, men can use handbags, too!), along with "bad baby name" stories, a message board, and a letter of the day.

PRODUCTS: A wide array of unusual products, like the album cover purses and coasters. Want your favorite Beatles album on a stylish purse? You can have it. How about *Elvis In Hawaii?* It's yours. Another cool and undoubtedly unique product on NWMH is the selection of Keyboard Jewelry. Yes, you read right - you can have any key from your keyboard made into a stylish necklace. We all know there's nothing sexier on a woman than a Caps Lock hanging from her neck!

VERDICT: The keyboard jewelry is cool, but those album purses are, like, so totally cool! Wouldn't it be so totally fabulous if we could get some Backstreet Boys purses? Of course, they are, like, so four years ago. Yo, what about some shiznit Snoop Dog coasters. Ain't nothing but the d-o-double-g, dawg, fa shizzle. Regardless of your tastes in music and fashion, if you're a girl who's into music or computers, Not Without My Handbag is worth a look.

226

Atomic Tiki
www.atomic-tiki.com

Atomic Tiki carries the self-proclaimed title of "The Coolest Retro Shop on the Internet," and it has some right to say so. "We have put together some of the coolest Mid-Century, Tiki, Rockabilly, and Vintage items on the net. So, grab yourself a cocktail, settle in, and prepare to go for a wild ride back in time!" I guess I'll have to settle for a Kiddie Cocktail.

PRODUCTS: The "Atomic Pad" section sells bar furniture sets, books about the fabulous '50s, and '50s-style signs with phrases like Good Coffee, Double Dip Cones, Twinkle Beverages, and Nugrape Soda. I know I still drink Twinkle Beverages and Nugrape Soda! In the "Thug" section, there are tons of wild Tiki shirts with dancing Tiki idols, fiery Tiki idols, and Shag T-shirts like the Space Brain and Shag Pirate T-shirt. Shagadelic, baby!

VERDICT: Once again, this site caters to a wide variety of tastes, so you're bound to find something you like. What else appeals to so many different people? Perhaps *Trading Spouses*? Or *Extreme Makeover*? Or *Queer Eye for the Straight Guy*? When people like to watch others swap life partners, buy a new look through plastic surgery, and make ugly losers look better by turning them into "metrosexuals," you know society has gone far, far down the drain.

227

Caribbean Soul
www.caribbeansoul.com

Jamaica me crazy, mon! Caribbean Soul sells "vibrantly illustrated clothing and other products that feature parrots, lizards, iguanas, and the casual lifestyle found in paradise." Not to mention that casual lifestyle requires mountains of money to live! Or that "paradise" is often a dirty and dangerous place if you stray too far from the beachfront hotels and tourist-trap bars and restaurants.

PRODUCTS: Products like clothing, hats, shotglasses, and more, with Caribbean creatures and other Caribbean culture symbols. A few that stand out are the Party Gods Curtains, with threads strung together to create an image of Tiki idols. Then there are the Parrot Patriot products, with an American flag and red, blue, and black and white parrots on them. Beach towels, camisoles, T-shirts, and other apparel with Caribbean-style designs are also available for purchase.

VERDICT: Why does everybody love parrots so much? Because they can talk! A few voice lessons, and you've got a pranking parrot! That, or a companion to talk back to you when you're lonely and desperate. Whatever the case, Caribbean Soul loves parrots, as is shown in their plentiful selection of interesting products.

228

Chrome Cow
www.chromecow.com

Chrome Cow seems to have no mission or purpose. It's just another one of the millions of personal online journals. The difference is that Sean Hyde-Moyer, the owner of this site, makes money from his journal! Stories about developing Game Boy Advance games, information on "projects" with lasers, and programming tutorials are all here, and all have nothing to do with Chrome Cows.

PRODUCTS: Clocks, T-shirts, mugs, and Frisbees with three main designs: The Big Robot design, with a giant metallic man; Microcosm, with the planet Earth surrounded by a forest; and Panoptic Skull, a real skull shaped like a giant peanut. A nuclear mutation, perhaps?

VERDICTS: Why is this site called Chrome Cow? Does this guy own a giant metallic cow? I think this site should be called "Confessions of a Programming Geek," but that's just me.

229

Odd Hobby
www.oddhobby.com

Odd Hobby is self-explanatory: they sell supplies for odd hobbies. The Odd Hobby E-zine is "A strange publication for strange people and their odd hobbies. Places that exist in your head, in dreams, in other points in time, and just in case you're really lost, it's right here on the Internet!" Why not just say "it's on the Internet" instead of creating all those abnormal analogies?

PRODUCTS: Action figures, snow globes, gadgets, games, dolls, plushies, and more. The best product, however, is the *Hole in the Head* documentary. It explains itself with a rather disturbing warning: "This video contains graphic scenes of trepanation (drilling a hole in one's head to facilitate a higher level of consciousness), including a scene in which a 'witch doctor' scrapes a hole through the skull of his patient with a tool made from a tin can. It's gruesome!"

VERDICT: This is indeed an odd store. Any store that sells Eminem Action Figures, *Addams Family* Snow Globes, the *Eat a Bug Cookbook*, and *Buffy the Vampire Slayer* Candy Bars can't be considered as anything remotely resembling normal.

230

Big Hat Store
www.bighatstore.com

Big Hats is not a store full of sombreros, huge foam cowboy hats, and other novelty headgear, but rather a store for people with big heads. "We decided to open our store in 1998 when we found few extra-large baseball hats available for my brothers and father who, like me, have large heads!" Perhaps because 99 percent of the population have regular sized heads.

PRODUCTS: Cotton baseball caps, mesh baseball hats, wool baseball hats (who wears those hot, itchy things?), and cotton bucket hats in nearly all the colors of the rainbow including Blaze Orange with

Nutmeg Visor, Blueberry, and Citrus hats. Sounds more like something you'd eat than wear! You can also get custom made hats if you want a hat with your name on it.

VERDICTS: While most people do have regular-sized heads, there are a few celebrities who come to mind as oversized fatheads. Whoopi Goldberg, Rosie O' Donnell, Michael Moore, Howard Stern…oh, wait, those are oversized egos. Perhaps large hats can fit large egos. If so, the Big Hats Store is probably for everyone.

231 Ready Teddy Death
www.readyteddydeath.com

I used to think that everybody loved teddy bears. So cute, cuddly, gentle. They don't ask for anything, they aren't mean to you, they just listen and watch with those cute little plastic eyes. Who wouldn't love that? Apparently, not the folks at Ready Teddy Death. RTD invites you to "watch in horror as pathetic, sentimental, and utterly defenseless bags of fluff are shot, burned, beheaded, electrocuted, drowned, roasted, torn apart by machines, and more." Think that's creepy? Then try playing the RTD game, where you can use scissors, rubber gloves, clothespins, nails, mousetraps, matches, and more to torture a defenseless teddy bear. Sick!

PRODUCTS: Of all the disgusting DVDs in this book, the RTD DVD is the most disgusting. For 9.99 British pounds (about nineteen dollars American), you can own fifty full minutes of sadistic teddy bear violence. "No plot, no dialogue, no computer graphics, and no subtitles. Just endless cheesy music as whole boxes of brand new bears get wasted." Well, isn't that nice? There are also RTD T-shirts and mugs.

VERDICT: These guys need some serious psychological help. And it won't stop here, either. First it's teddy bears, tomorrow it's dogs and cats (although the latter is more of a service than a problem), then before you know it, we've got an insane group of axe murderers on our hands. All because of a little grudge against teddy bears. There's still hope, guys. Get help.

232

Robert E. Ham Store Fixtures
www.robertham.com

While you may not need a shopping basket or a mannequin, retail store owners will be in paradise here. "We stock a large inventory of store fixtures, retail packaging, gift wrapping, slatwall, gridwall, garment racks, showcases, mannequins, hangers, bags, display fixtures, and much, much more." Anything for the average Joe WITHOUT a store?

PRODUCTS: If you see it in a store, it's here. Mannequins, racks, display cases, and even pricing and tagging devices. A few of my favorites are the Wet Dry Carpet Sweeper QPU, the Visitor Chime security device (I would think of that as more of a friendly welcome than a security device), and the Folding Board Flip 1 (the working version of that funky Styrofoam gadget that folds clothes—as seen on TV). Plus, you can chose from fifteen types of pegboard hooks!

VERDICT: If you're a retailing entrepreneur or a store manager, you could find something to use here. But, unless you have a use for a huge shoe rack at your home (then again, if you're Imelda Marcos or a *Sex in the City* afficianado…), you'll only find a select few items at Robert E. Ham useful.

233

Cowboy Outfitters
www.cowboyoutfitters.com

Cowboy Outfitters, "The World's Premier Cowboy Store," sells a wide assortment of apparel right out of an old West movie. It even draws in rich business moguls with a quote from Will Rogers: "Why play Wall Street and die young when you can play cowboy and never die?" Such a deep analogy! And I thought cowboys could only herd cows and spit snuff.

PRODUCTS: Hats, boots, saddles, décor, music, gift selections, and other cool products. Apparel is sorted by "Cowboys," "Cowgirls," and "Cowbabies." I thought they were called calves? The "Rodeo" selection is quite interesting, with products like the SB2000 Protective Vest, which has "an impact resistant, shatterproof shell with high density foam for added protection." Sounds like a fun time, getting trampled by angry bulls while your vest takes all the abuse. Remind me to try it sometime.

VERDICT: It's always so hard to get a good picture of the old West. Is it more like *Dances with Wolves*, with Civil War officers dancing with vicious animals, or is it more like the classic Will Smith movie flop *Wild Wild West*, with giant, fire-breathing mechanical spiders? No matter what kind of old West film you're into, Cowboy Outfitters appeals to the little bit of cowboy in everybody.

234

Bumper Power
www.bumperpower.com

Want to make a statement with your car? Bumper Power is the place to do it. "We've got everything from political bumper stickers, slogan T-shirts and sportswear, funny ballcaps, custom coffee mugs and steins, and other sorted products customized with thought-provoking statements." So, "Don't Mess with Texas" is considered "thought-provoking"?

PRODUCTS: Bumper stickers, with phrases like "Love is Grand...Divorce is a Hundred Grand," "Democrats are Wimps, and Whiners, too," and "Money Makes it Right." The stickers are sorted by category, with environmental, political, redneck, and other classic categories. Shirts, mugs, hats, and more are also available with similar phrases.

VERDICT: Bumper Power might as well be called "Attitude Power." All the products on this site are full of outrageous opinions and even more outrageous attitudes. If you're looking to express yourself, look no further than Bumper Power.

235

Blue Honey
www.bluehoney.org

Blue Honey also calls itself "The Infinite Mushroom." What exactly is the infinite mushroom? "This website is dedicated to anyone interested in "inner-space exploration. A deeper understanding of self and reality via sacred plants is not a new concept, it is a surprisingly archaic concept." In other words, "organic" drug-induced "exploration."

PRODUCTS: Books and videos on philosophy, alternative religions, and other strange stuff. Read *The Psilocybin Solution*, which will tell you how these "magic" (i.e., they will get you higher than a kite) mushrooms "can save the planet." You can also buy the usual apparel and accessories with phrases like "Question Reality," "I do ~~Drugs~~ Plants," (aren't they the same thing in this case?), and of course, shrooms, cacti, do-it-yourself kits for growing "sacred plants," and more stuff that pushes the drug laws to the limits.

VERDICT: Is this site even legal? Last I checked, hallucinogenic mushrooms and cacti were illegal, except for certain Native American religious purposes, which this site certainly doesn't seems to be about. My advice: Don't do drugs. It's something parents tell kids, and it's true. Besides, why do shrooms when you can do crazy websites?

236

Rattius Maximus
www.rattiusmaximus.com

You've heard of dog breeders and horse breeders, but rat breeders? "We hope to bring, to the rat community, a more perfect pet. The betterment of the rat species as a whole is our #1 goal and is always what guides us to breed only the best." "Best" and "Betterment" should never, I mean, not ever, never be used in reference to rats.

PRODUCTS: Shirts, mugs, hats, etc. (To get to the store, you have to click on "Links" on the home page.) Phrases include "Once you go rat you'll never go back" (I'll never go rat to begin with), "My rats are smarter than your honor student" (even former MTV VJ Carson Daly is smarter than any rat), and "My rats are scary, want to come play with them?" (One word: NO.) You can also adopt rats from the rattery. When does this vermin factory stop?

VERDICT: Breeding rats is more disgusting than a watching Ben Affleck in a *Gigli* and *Jersey Girl* all-day movie marathon. Rats are called vermin for a reason: they're dirty, disgusting, and revolting. To say that they're smart, cute, or even worth existing is an insult to the human race. Rattius Maximus is a futile exercise in trying to make repulsive, repugnant, ratty creatures almost tolerable.

237 Stick Figure Death Theatre
www.sfdt.com

Stick Figure Death Theatre is "breaking the rules of entertainment" by depicting stick figures in gruesome, often disturbing deaths. One video called Stick Thief shows a stick sneaking through a castle of some sort, cleverly hiding on sides of tables and desks to evade other stick figures. After he is discovered, he impales stick figures with swords, shoots them with crossbows, and blows them up using gasoline tanks. Not exactly lighthearted stuff.

PRODUCTS: Clothing, mugs, mousepads, etc. with the SFDT logo: a stick figure laying against a red circle, most likely implying a pool of stick figure blood, but looking more like a stop sign. There's also Stickman Jones for President, featuring a stick figure against an American flag. Can a stick figure hold an elective office? Based on political history, the answer must be yes, and they'd probably do a better job.

VERDICT: While SFDT is a bit violent, watching stick figures bleed isn't really a traumatizing sight. Just tell yourself it looks like ketchup and you'll be fine (or is it catsup?). SFDT is a creative, albeit unsettling site that's worth a look for fans of dark humor.

238

Tarantulas
www.tarantulas.com

Do you have an unusual attraction to those creepy crawlers known as tarantulas? Tarantulas.com is your hookup. "Our goal at Tarantulas.com is to become the #1 resource on the internet for those interested in invertebrates."

PRODUCTS: As gross as I find it, you can actually order tarantulas! The Brazilian Black tarantula, the Goliath Birdeater (let's hope that's not a literal name), the King Baboon, and more are all available to be shipped to your house. What a nice present for mom! There is a $200 minimum order, though, so you have to pay for the shock value of a live tarantula. Tarantula food is also available in the form of lesser insects like crickets.

VERDICT: Any site that has advice on "How to Sex a Tarantula" (no, not what you think, it's an article about how to determine gender) is just plain sick. Who cares if it's male or female? It's ugly and scary and should be squashed. End of story. But for all you sickos who need a furry arachnid to freak out your friends, this is the site for you.

239

Creatures in My Head
www.creaturesinmyhead.com

Something really weird must be going on in this guy's head. "'Creatures started as a daily illustration exercise that I felt the need to undertake for reasons that are now entirely beyond me…I don't go out much any more or see sunlight very often…I'm so very hungry and pale. Send help." I'd like to get away from you now, thank you. The drawings are as scary as his rhetoric, and are obviously inspired by a traumatic childhood experience.

PRODUCTS: Toys, clothing, books, accessories, and artwork featuring these disturbing drawings. T-shirts include the Monkey design, which encourages you to "Stay true to your roots with the albino mutant monkey shirt!" It gets scarier with the Scribble series of T-shirts, which truly do look like something produced after five minutes of pure scribbling. Finally, there's the *You've Gone too Far* book, with sixty-four drawings of "Creatures in My Head." Yes, you HAVE gone too far.

VERDICT: Besides Jewel's *A Night without Armor*, this is the most disturbing thing I have ever seen. However, if you want people to get as far away as possible from you, this will certainly succeed in doing that.

240   Bobble Head Store
www.bobbleheadstore.net

Introducing the most overrated "toy" of the new millennium: the bobble head! Popular as Beanie Babies but significantly less annoying, bobble heads are plastic dolls that you shake to see their heads "bobble" up and down. Right now, "Some of our best selling bobble head dolls are Jesus Christ bobble head, Hula Girl bobble head, and Scooby Doo bobble head dolls." The Jesus Christ bobblehead? Is nothing sacred anymore?

PRODUCTS: You can select from about a dozen bobble heads, including the aforementioned Jesus, Goth girl, monkey, and Lucha Libre Mexican wrestler bobbleheads. The best advertising pitch can be found in the mischievous Devil Bobblehead. "This cute little plastic devil girl nodder has a naughty gleam in her eyes. She's not really evil, just a little bad." Riiiight.

VERDICT: Even though I'm not much for popular fads or popular anything (I had a Furby phase that lasted about a day, though), these bobble heads are a deviously delightful distraction. Then again, I'm fascinated by bubble wrap, Bin Punched (361 from the original *505*), and flashing neon lights. But like you aren't.

241

Cherry Pit Store
www.cherrypitstore.com

Cherry pits may be useless from a cherry eater's standpoint, but they are actually quite versatile from this site's standpoint. Arts and crafts, beanbags, and heating and cooling pads are just some of the uses for cherry pits.

PRODUCTS: The incredible, non-edible cherry pits come in Pit Pads. "Down through the ages, people have used hot and cold compresses to relieve aches, pain, and discomfort. Cherry pits have the unique ability to retain and slowly release moist heat or stay cold for a long period after being heated in a microwave or chilled in the freezer. That's what makes our Pit Pads so soothing and comforting." Ok, but I can get an electric heating pad for seven dollars less. But it's environmentally friendly! Isn't that worth it? You can also buy pits by the bag for things like beanbags. "Delight your child with a beanbag toy. They'll love the sound they make while tossing them around." So do some grown adults!

VERDICT: The Pit Pads may be a bit expensive compared to other heating and cooling pads, but with a four pound bag of pits and a little extra work, they're incredibly useful for a number of things. Maybe we'll find new uses for orange and banana peels, or watermelon and grape seeds. Well, no. Nope. Never.

242

E-Bug
www.e-bug.net

Have some heavy-hitting pest problems? E-Bug can help you fight back. "We are a do-it-yourself pest control store that sells professional strength products to the general public. Whether you have a flea problem or an infestation of powder post beetles, we have effective solutions for you." Was that supposed to be serious?

PRODUCTS: E-bug is now encouraging you to defend against the cicada invasion that Miss Jolene Sugarbaker so smartly capitalized on (number 71). "Every thirteen or seventeen years, cicadas emerge from the ground…For treatment to kill cicadas and to prevent them from entering the home we recommend using Talstar." At $195 for 3/4 of a gallon, though, you better have a pretty catastrophic cicada problem. Products to eliminate roaches, fleas, ants, etc. are available, all on the same expensive price level of the aforementioned Talstar.

VERDICT: If I had bugs, I'd want them gone today. Unfortunately, orders from E-bug are shipped UPS ground and will probably take a week to get to you, and cannot be shipped to New York or Connecticut. (Why? Because!) While these products are expensive, you get what you pay for. If you have a bad bug problem and don't want to pay for an exterminator, E-bug is a great resource. After all, somebody has to stop the cicada invasion!

. . . .

243   Cool Gifts Store
www.coolgiftstore.com

How do you define "cool" gifts? Lighters and incense and clocks, of course. "Here at Cool Gift Store.com, you will find a huge selection of Zippo lighters and Zippo accessories, imported incense products featuring Nag Champa, Spiritual Sky, and other quality incense products and accessories with many more cool gifts to come!"

PRODUCTS: A gigantic selection of Zippo Lighters, including Special Edition lighters, Urban Style lighters, Pure lighters, Work and Play lighters, and many other categories. A few particularly "cool" lighters are the NHL lighters, with teams like the Detroit Red Wings, the Boston Bruins, and my personal favorite, the New Jersey Devils. Another cool series is the Elvis lighter series, with the Elvis Silhouette lighter and the Elvis Heart Emblem lighter. "Cool Collectibles" featuring the Robert E. Lee wall clock and Incense and Oils are also available in numerous varieties.

VERDICT: While I do like the large selection of lighters and collectibles, I don't get why incense and oils are so "cool." Does Cool Gifts want a piece of Bath and Body Works' customer base, or are they a crazy combination of aromatherapy and pyrotechnic fanatics?

244

RKDM
www.rkdm.com

Whatever RKDM stands for, it's "the source for all of your 'As Seen on TV' products!" Then it's probably safe to assume half of them don't work. However, this site is THE place to get those products you nocturnal TV watchers need and want. Where else can you pick up the Nyce Legs spray-on instant nylons?

PRODUCTS: Classic 'As Seen on TV' products like the Eggstractor, Deli Pro Knife, and the Talking Toilet Paper Roll. The latter is described as a "this year's hottest gag gift!" There are also sound clips and products featuring the politically ambiguous Taco Bell Dog (Communist conspirator or innocent Taco Revolution spokesdog?), as well as Giant Underwear, underwear so big three people can fit into it. Useful? No. Hilarious? Without a doubt!

VERDICT: Those 'As Seen on TV' products are big on talk but slim on delivering. The Perfect Pancake leaks batter and the Quick Chop is prone to jamming (I know from experience). The other products on this site are memorable memorabilia that are ten times as fun as the TV products are reliable (commercials excluded). Yes, that's even true of the giant underwear.

245

Greaseman
www.greasemanstore.com

Grease is not the time, the place, nor the motion here. "The Greaseman Show is a program of the highest order with a professional acumen and improvisational brilliance matched by no one else in the business...The Grease has done two NBC movies of the week with Brian Dennehy." And this is improvisational brilliance?

PRODUCTS: Greaseman CDs, including *A Very Greasy Christmas*, *Blasterpiece Theatre*, *Estelle Ya Pig Ya!!*, *Sing Like a Man*, and more. The covers of the CDs are quite, um, creative, with the Greaseman smiling, dancing, flashing, and reading. Yes, you heard me right.

VERDICT: While I may not have heard the Greaseman's radio show, it's important to remember that "he first came into prominence replacing Howard Stern at DC 101 in our nation's capital, and consistently out polled his rival in the local market when they were broadcasting opposite each other." He beat out Howard Stern? He MUST be good!

- -

246

Bob Barker
Prison Supplies
www.bobbarker.com

Bob Barker Prison Supplies has no association with *The Price is Right*, Plinko, or spaying or neutering your pets (although the last thing we need is more cats). Rather, Bob Barker is "America's Leading Detention Supplier." "Every product in the Bob Barker family has been tested to ensure it is appropriate for institutional use. We smash radios on the floor and grind toothbrushes on cinderblock walls to see how easily they can be made into shanks." Good to know broken radios and used toothbrushes won't result in bloody prison riots.

PRODUCTS: Clothing and accessories, bedding and linens, shoes and boots, and even "drug and alcohol screens." A few interesting products are the Specimen Cups with Lids, Adult Disposable Bibs, and the High Security Velcro-Closure Jumpsuit, Orange. Sounds like a daycare center, except with violent psychopathic murderers.

VERDICT: Prison supplies are good for keeping criminals safe and happy (they shouldn't be happy), but where are the Barker Bimbo action figures, or the *Price is Right* Stage Playset? I don't want prison supplies, I want a life-size Plinko board! Thanks for tainting the name of a radical animal activist/game show host, Bob Barker Prison Supplies!

247

T-Shirt Countdown
www.t-shirtcountdown.com

T-Shirt Countdown is a list of the top one hundred most popular T-shirts on the Internet. Topics for designs range from work, political, and electronics to "offensive" T-shirts, which cannot be mentioned here lest I have liberal activists banging down my door.

PRODUCTS: Today's Top Ten features T-shirts with phrases like "My job makes my life possible, but my job is not my life," "Speed Dater: Got a Minute?" and "My Inner Child Can Beat Up Your Inner Child." Maybe so, but my inner child is smarter. A very clever T-shirt has a father and son pair of monkeys saying "Now listen up—if you want to live a long life, don't go near New York." Smart monkeys. My favorite is a T-shirt with cats, dogs, rabbits, and other animals reading, "Animals Taste Great!" So true.

VERDICT: Let's face it: everybody has to make a statement sometime. Whether it's Fiona Apple describing the world with an expletive at the MTV Video Music Awards, anything by Michael Moore, or a three-hundred-page statement in this book, you have to stand up for your opinions, no matter how stupid or senseless they might be. The T-Shirt Countdown has hundreds of shirts with statements to fit any opinionated jerk. Where's my shirt?

248

Scrub Store
www.scrubstore.com

The Scrub Store sells the uniforms that nurses and surgeons wear in hospitals and clinics. The Scrub Store, however, sees them not as practical medical wear, but as a fashion statement! "Check out Crest for exclusive new prints every season, with coordinating colors from pastels to brights and everything in between." Hey, like, medical people have to, like, be fashionable too!

PRODUCTS: Tops and jackets, pants, lab coats, prints, and keepers. There's the very stylish Nighttime Sky print available on vests and shirts. With smiling moons and clouds, these scrubs look more like glorified pajamas than medical uniforms. The Geo Floral print looks like these scrubby people bought out an overrun of Hawaiian luau shirt fabric. The Keeper prints have dates on them to indicate when they won't be available. This way, an entire medical staff can be efficient, professional, AND fashion-coordinated!

VERDICT: While every member of a medical staff needs scrubs, the Scrub Store caters to crazy, obsessive-compulsive control freaks! "Today's flower day, everybody! I expect to see smiles and flowers, people! Smiles and flowers!" Control Freaks: one in every workplace, none that anybody wants.

249   Fun with Words
www.fun-with-words.com

Fun With Words.com is "dedicated to amusing quirks, peculiarities, and oddities of the English language: wordplay. Playing with words and language is both entertaining and educational." I love it! More people who can read, more people who can buy books...my books! Ha ha ha!

PRODUCTS: A book store and a game store with "edutainment" games like Scrabble, meant to help children learn and have fun at the same time. General wordplay books include *The Game of Words: The Remarkable Exhuberance of the English Language* by Willard R. Espy. "Explore ABC language, acrostic verses, alliteration, anagrams, Anguish Languish, Parody, Chain Verse, Clerihews, Chronograms, Cryptograms, Epigrams..." This long list goes on for another paragraph. Anybody can do alliteration! I've been excessively including it throughout this entire book!

VERDICT: Believe it or not, "fun learning" is not necessarily an oxymoron. Look at the *Magic School Bus* or *Captain Planet*. While they were fun shows, they taught us useful lessons, like that psychopathic teachers always have magic buses, and that superheroes can save the world AND help the environment! Another trend in children's shows is using "magic" to summon friendly mythical or extinct creatures. Are the children's "friends" evil spirits? Perhaps. But, are they good teachers? Absolutely!

250 Villisca Axe Murderers
www.villiscaiowa.com

Ever heard of the Villisca Axe Murderers? Not many people have, until now. "On June 10, 1912, the tranquility of this 'Pretty Place' was shattered by the discovery of the Villisca Axe murders. The Moore Family, well-known and well-liked Villisca residents, and two overnight guests were found murdered in their beds." This site has an extensive treasure trove of information on the murders, including suspects, evidence, and, surprise, surprise, reports of supernatural beings in the house.

PRODUCTS: You an buy a "complete reprint of the *Villisca Review* published the day after the Villisca Axe Murders," books, a CD featuring the "Paranormal Boogie," along with VAM clothing, lunchboxes, Frisbees, mugs, and stickers with an ominous house and the words "I survived the Villisca Axe Murder House." There's also the "organic tee," so you can show off your pride in axe murderers in an environmentally friendly way.

VERDICT: It's almost automatic that any tragic death involves ghosts later on. This site even has blatantly faked photographs "proving" this. Ghosts and mass murders seem to be like peanut butter and jelly, or Bill and Hillary: you can't have one without the other. Come on, you know they were meant for each other.

- -

251 Dead Quail
www.deadquail.com

"Another quail dies every time someone visits this web site. Over 18,544 quails have died needlessly since June, 2001. Do not contact P.E.T.A. for further information." Don't worry, I won't. This site is actually about "The misdirected adventures of the Mexican wrestler." Six videos (with a seventh to come soon) show the Mexican wrestler running around senselessly in a forest, a beach, Central Park, Afghanistan, and other strange locations.

PRODUCTS: Clothing, mugs, mousepads, stickers, etc. with Mexican Wrestler designs and other Dead Quail designs, including "Lead Paint: So Deadly Yet So Delicious," and "It's decision time," featuring the blue and red pills from the overly-spoofed and popular *Matrix* series, and "Blame the Parents." Sounds good to me!

VERDICT: While the videos on Dead Quail featuring the senseless, silly, and stupid Mexican Wrestler are only mildly amusing, the wide assortment of products is amazingly awesome. After all, nobody can resist the Skip Taylor's Disco Frenzy line of products. Get Down Tonight, baby!

252

Stuff-O-Rama
www.stuff-o-rama.com

Unlike other sites, Stuff-O-Rama has little explanation as to where they came from, how they got here, or what their special mission to make the world a better place is. Rather, they get straight to the point and let you browse their vast selection of retro-age products in their decidedly low tech website. No flash animation, just clunky, wordy explanations with a few picture perfect depictions of the things you can buy.

PRODUCTS: Stuff-O-Rama sells various '50s products, like books, magazines, party lights, retro postcards, clocks, pin-up girls, animal-fur-covered light switch plates and so much else it'll make your head spin. A few products stand apart from this extensive inventory, however. One is the Yeti Yule Cocktail Napkins, with a yeti resting in a lounge chair with a broken leg. Another is the Pin-Up Girl light switch cover, a checkered light switch color with an attractive, '50s style pin-up girl on it. Finally, there's the Smoking Bunny iron-on patch. No varsity or military patches for me; give me a rabbit smoking a fine Cuban!

VERDICT: Even though the presentation of Stuff-O-Rama is bare bones, the selection of retro products they offer couldn't be better. With Tiki products galore, leopard-skinned anything, and merchandise with icons like the Pink Panther and Elvis, you can't go wrong with Stuff-O-Rama.

253

Freedom to Groove
www.freedomtogroove.com

Despite its name, the artists and songs on Freedom to Groove are anything but "groovy." "Freedom to Groove is an online music marketing and promotions company offering Internet services specifically for those in the music industry…today's independent artist can look forward to the potential of a viable career without the need for the major label machine to make or break them." Freedom to Groove sounds more like an alternative market for failing artists and bad boy bands than anything to do with "grooving."

PRODUCTS: CDs from artists like Andrea Klas, Anomalous Disturbances, Costar, Cripple Creek Fairies, Jack Tripper (do they "come and knock" on your door?), and the Hermit.

VERDICT: Unless you're a fan of the alternative markets, you'll never have heard of any of these people. If you like something a little different in your music, feel free to give Freedom to Groove a look. Just don't come expecting any disco or dance music that you can "groove" to.

254

Mr. Piercing
www.mrpiercing.com

If you have a desire to endure pain by jamming a ring of metal through some part of your body, check out MrPiercing.com. They offer rings for nose, navel, lip, eyebrow, and tongue piercing, as well as "male" and "female" piercing. Nice way of naming such, um, "sensitive" body parts.

PRODUCTS: Body Jewelry like Captive Bead Rings, Curved Barbells, Horseshoe rings, and Straight Barbells. Some selections from the latter include the Black Barbell with Cones, UFO balls barbell, and even Straight Barbell with glow-in-the-dark balls. (Let's just refrain from comment here, ok?) Glow in the Dark products are more in demand than a new Stephen King book, or poorly written celebrity autobiographies, if this book is any indication. Also, check out the silver nose screw. Gee, I'll have to put *that* on my Christmas list!

VERDICT: A pierced ear I can see as sorta normal, but somebody with more than ear piercings just creeps me out. Same with tattoos. But then again, it's called body art for a reason: one person sees a piece of art as crappy, another sees it as a work of genius. Even defending celebrity criminals in court is considered an "art" these days. Johnny Cochrane, artist. What a concept. That's America for you.

255   Turtle Expeditions
www.turtleexpedition.com

"If you had stopped Gary Wescott on his way to journalism class…in 1967 and told him he would spend his life traveling around the world; or if you could have caught Monika Mühlebach Wescott as she peddled her bicycle home from school…and tried to explain that she would join Gary in Mexico ten years later—well, you might have encountered some disbelief." Well, I never imagined I'd be writing part of this book about them and their crazy adventures. "For the past thirty years these two intrepid adventurers and photojournalists have globetrotted from the arid deserts of Afghanistan to the deepest jungles of the Amazon with sometimes no more than a camera and a backpack."

PRODUCTS: Their store has clothing, mugs, and caps that "clearly identify you as part of the Turtle Expedition Field Support Team." "Field Support Team" translates into "I gave you money and all I got was this lousy T-shirt." There's also a VHS video tape chronicling select portions of Gary and Monika's amazing adventures.

VERDICT: While their story is interesting, I wouldn't want to explain to my friends exactly how I "support" the Turtle Expedition team. I guess I'd have to say: "I don't know these people, I have no idea exactly what they do, but I do support them just by wearing this T-shirt. Aren't I cool?" I'll pass on buying your T-shirts; I'd prefer not to be a member of your incredibly impersonal "support team."

256

Hong Kong's
Born to Party
www.borntoparty.com.hk

It's party time, Far Eastern style! "Every Born to Party party is personalized, age-appropriate, and one-of-a-kind. Our number one priority is for the kids to have fun. Between the three of us (BTP, you, and your child), we accomplish just that. Your child gives us the vision, you give us the practicals, and we supply the rest."

PRODUCTS: Select one of about four dozen selectable themes. The selection ranges from classic themes like Barney, Barbie, and Sesame Street: P is for Party, to more modern selections like Powerpuff Girls, Lizzie McGuire, and Buzz Lightyear. Supplies like plates and cups, napkins, thank you notes, party hats, and loot bags are available for each theme. Be warned, though: the full selection of products for just one theme will cost you dearly. An eight pack of themed party hats is $40, an eight pack of cups is $30, and other supplies have similar costs. Even for reusable cups, that's a ripoff!

VERDICT: Are these prices in yuan (Chinese currency), or are they just outrageous? I mean, forty dollars for an eight pack of party hats? What are they made out of, titanium? And that's not including shipping. Unless you want to spend hundreds on a children's party for eight guests, forget about Born to Party.

257

The Honey Store
www.thehoneystore.net

Real bees, real honey, real expensive! "In a world of artificial this and manufactured that, The Honey Store is a wonderful demonstration of the things that come from nature."

PRODUCTS: Nobody ever said nature's bounty was cheap, though. Twelve ounces of this stuff costs $3.25. Sounds reasonable, until you factor in that you need to pay shipping and handling when you could get it at the grocery store for the same price. If you buy a larger package, you can save a bit of money: a five pound jug is $11.25. If you REAL-LY want the savings, though, aim for bulk. You can buy a fifty-five gallon barrel or three thousand POUND plastic tote of honey. They don't show the prices, presumably because it's so darn outrageous.

VERDICT: Who would want three thousand pounds of honey? Maybe if you work for a grocery store or large restaurant chain it would be reasonable, but why would the average Joe (or average Jane) want that much honey? Perhaps they're toting the Honey Diet. Drink honey all day and lose weight. Most people prefer the "see-food" diet, though (see food and eat it), which results in a lot of overweight Americans. Starve yourself and get thin, or eat everything and get fat? You just can't win.

258 The Original 1966 Batmobile Site
www.1966batmobile.com

Holy retro superhero vehicles, Batman! This site is the unofficial home of the original Batmobile used in the classic *Batman* TV series. Along with some amusing personal stories, this site has a full history on the origins of this ultra-cool superhero ride. Originally a car designed by Bill Schmidt for Lincoln Mercury in 1955, the Lincoln Futura enjoyed limited success on the auto-show circuit until it ended up in the hands of George Barris. Barris was commissioned last minute to design a car for the new *Batman* series. He made a few modifications to the Futura, and the Batmobile was born.

PRODUCTS: Photos, shirts, hats, postcards, and patches featuring the 1966 Batmobile. The shirt, hat, and sew-on patch have a logo with a picture of the vehicle and the words "Batmobile Barris." The postcard has an old concept drawing on the front, with a short history of the Batmobile on the back side. Finally, in addition to regular Batmobile photos, there are rare eight-by-ten collectable photos of the Batmobile, and for the size and prestigious value, the prices ain't too shabby either.

VERDICT: While fans of the original series will eat this site up, it has a lot of value for anybody eager to learn a little about classic Americana history. The shirts have a stylish retro look, and the photos are a must-have for collectors. A very interesting site for just about anybody.

259

Chick Saddlery
www.chicksaddlery.com

You can't ride a horse without a comfortable saddle, can you? "Chick's Discount Saddlery is your home for English saddles, western saddles, horse tack, equestrian equipment, and horse and pony products."

PRODUCTS: Click "Chicks Online" to get into their store. I was pretty interested until I found out there were no scantily-clad ladies here, just horse and pony products. Products like the Baron Plaid Show Sheet. "Classic plaid styling! A superbly crafted sheet from the world's leading manufacturer of horse clothing." Like Chanel, but for the equine set? What an honor! Then there's the nutritious and delicious five pound Apple Crunchers Horse Treats. Even horses have to splurge once in a while! Dozens of other product categories, like medication, boots, and western and English style horse products.

VERDICT: I don't know one kid, girls especially, who has never wanted a horse sometime. How can you say no to a horse? They're such sophisticated animals, too. You won't see a horse chasing some silly ball, unlike those dirty, stupid dogs. They just stand there, eat, run, and unleash incredibly huge piles of waste. "Sophisticated" also means "boring." Unless you're already a horse fanatic, Chick's Saddlery won't do anything to alleviate the non-fascinating "sophistication" of horses.

260

American Racing Pigeon Union
www.pigeon.org

"We find that this hobby has a great appeal to those who enjoy working with animals, to those who appreciate athleticism, to those who like friendly, wholesome competition." After seeing mountains of pigeon poop on cars, how can anybody see the "athleticism" of these flying rats? The ARPU has information on pigeon training and becoming a member of this union of perturbed pigeon lovers.

PRODUCTS: ARPU sweatshirts, polo shirts, hats, posters, and stickers are here to buy, including a sticker reading "Join the Excitement: Pigeon Racing: Race Horses of the Sky." I'll take a horse any day over these putrid birds. This crazy club of pigeon lovers even sells videos, like *Marathon in the Sky*, which is a "thrilling documentary on our fascinating international sport." Can this get any stupider?

VERDICT: There's a great song about pigeons by '60s satirist Tom Lehrer called "Poisoning Pigeons in the Park." It's very cathartic listening to it after spending way too much time staring at this extremely stupid site. If you're as disturbed and disgusted by this site as I was, I suggest finding the song. Trust me, it's worth it.

261

Taken by Aliens
www.takenbyaliens.com

Are we alone? Not on your afterlife, according to this site. "Here you will find UFO and alien abduction stories, sent in by people…who have either been taken by aliens or experienced a UFO sighting…and several stories that were just too good to not post." One of these "too good" stories is about a man emailing his father's long-lost friend, who was dead. The email was "delayed" until five days after he sent it. It "arrived" in his widow's mailbox on what would have been their wedding anniversary. "A true 'Happy Anniversary Darling!' from across the great divide!" Simple coincidence, or supernatural email tampering? You decide.

PRODUCTS: Clothing, mugs, stickers, etc. with numerous alien logos. One includes an alien head and the word "Believe." I'll believe when they land on the White House lawn. Another is the "Got Taken?" T-shirt, the one billionth parody of the "Got Milk" slogan.

VERDICT: I do believe that it's possible there could be other life forms in the universe. What I DON'T believe is that they have the technology to travel trillions of miles to examine the human race. And even if they did, why don't they land and introduce themselves? Maybe they know we're too busy tracking which guy J.Lo is dating this week to care about some boring new galactic neighbors.

262

Regis Jack
www.regisjack.com

Regis Jack likes to put humor in everything they do. You may ask how much of this site is serious and how much is just joking around. They'll tell you that "we are very serious about our business at RegisJack.com and the RegisJack.com: Original Designs on T-Shirts and More store. But, we put humor in absolutely everything we do...We make jokes even though we are serious." Serious humor. Sounds like honest politician. This site also touts "The Ministry of Life," which is a real religion. If you don't want to see that kind of thing, don't go here.

PRODUCTS: Products like the Regis Jack Soccer Fan shirts for the Regisjack.com indoor soccer league. If you're looking for something a bit more risqué, try one of the Perception is Reality products. Another line of products have the State of Mind logo, with the words "Arrogant," "Impulsive," "Emotional," "Unstable," and "Obscene." "Want people to know what you might be thinking? Want to warn others that you may be a tad unstable? Want to make the people around you nervous? Well, this stuff can help!" Sounds like it can help, and so can the phrase "stay away from me."

VERDICT: Regis Jack is a pretty controversial site. If you value sheltering yourself from the inevitable exposure to the outrageously stupid opinions of others, stay away. If you're set in your ways, however, you'll find this site a refreshing reminder of how weird and wacky people can be.

263

Red vs. Blue
www.redvsblue.com

"What the hell?" That's probably what you're thinking about this site. Their answer? "Yeah, we know." In the next question, they answer the question seriously by saying that they "just write scripts and then use videogames to act them out." The videos are made of footage from the videogame *Halo* and usually consist of people talking about shooting things and nodding.

PRODUCTS: Hats, mousepads, messenger bags, shirts, and even bean-ies with the Red vs. Blue logo: a rooster and a wind-up set of teeth with the words "Red vs. Blue." If you think that's weird, try figuring out how they can sell two DVDs full of this stuff. "Relive the season over and over again with this surprise-filled DVD, chock full of more than two hours of content!"

VERDICT: I'm a big videogame player, and even I found this stuff to be incredibly boring. Guys in armor suits nod and talk about shooting things and how to not be shot. I would rather see Britney Spears make a sequel to *Crossroads* co-starring Mariah Carey than be forced to watch two whole DVDs of this. It's that bad.

264 Dolphin World
www.dolphinworld.org

Ever wanted a chance to get up close and personal with a dolphin? (No, no like THAT, you naughty people!) Now's your chance. Dolphin World offers trips that allow you to swim with dolphins. "Swimming with dolphins is a very natural and rewarding experience in their dolphin cove or lagoon. Beside the excitement of the swim with dolphin program, you will have memories that will last a lifetime."

PRODUCTS: And you can relive those memories with dolphin products. Dolphin jewelry, dolphin clothing, household items, sculptures, and more are all here for *Flipper* fans young and old alike. Dolphin World also caters to the foot jewelry phenomena with the Gold Dolphin Toe Ring and the Dolphin Anklet. Are people supposed to be looking at your feet? You can even buy a full Dolphin Vacation package where you can swim with these graceful mammals (they're not fish, people!).

VERDICT: As we've seen in *Flipper* and at Sea World, dolphins are very intelligent creatures. Perhaps a little too intelligent. We've got so many smart animal species—dogs, dolphins, mice—sometimes you wonder how long they're going to tolerate our waste, our expansion-ism, and Yanni's music. How long will it be before the animals take back the Earth? As long as we have Regis Philbin, the human race will always be the greatest. But after he's gone, I don't know what we'll do.

265

Rant.com
www.rant.com

Rant is yet another monthly satire magazine. It's more of the same here, with a few clever features, like the Martha Stewart Lying graphic, with text reading, "Martha looks at the bright side of losing her legal battle: at least Michael Moore won't be making a documentary about me." Was that really necessary? No, but it was funny.

PRODUCTS: The usual selection with "Rant" in graphic word art, and the phrase, "Beyond the perhipheral vision." Of course, what store would be complete without political products? T-shirts, mugs, etc. have a sheep on a couch with the phrase, "How the Republicans stay in power." Boy, do I hate politics.

VERDICT: Why did I have to write this book during an election year? It's amazing how many of these comedy sites have to open their big mouths about politics. Hopefully, you'll visit Rant at a time where the world has moved on with life, and we only have Ben Stiller movies to worry about.

266

Uncle Bubba's
www.unclebubbas.biz

Uncle Bubba's is another store selling a little bit of country, with a confusing front page. "We love Bubba for the sheer fun of it! Learned a long time ago that everyone knows a Bubba, has a Bubba, or is a Bubba." It may be true, but exactly what IS a "Bubba"?

PRODUCTS: Country classic Bubba Wear. One shirt says "Bubba's Roadkill Café" on the front, and "You kill it, we grill it" on the back. If you actually know what on Earth a "Bubba" is, you can buy Bubba and Bubbette T-shirts. Finally, there are the Bear Whiz shirts, shirts with a bear urinating in various settings. How classy! How quaint! Collectibles, furniture, Christmas products, and other country collectibles are here too.

VERDICT: I'd still like to know what a "Bubba" is. Is it a hick? Is it an outdoorsman? Is it missing teeth? Is it all three? Whatever kind of person this mysterious slang word describes, they'll be at home shopping at Uncle Bubba's. Stuff for Bubbas, by Bubbas.

267

Bad Movies
www.badmovies.org

Is your favorite guilty pleasure watching horrible special effects, even more horrible acting, and senseless destruction by creatures from other worlds? Don't feel guilty. "Here is a safe place to indulge in your more unsavory cinematic tastes." Finally, something in this book I can enjoy! There's a rating system to find the worst movies, with criteria like the words in the title (the more words, the worse it is), the director (ten points for being directed by Ed Wood), and the main actors (if George Kennedy is in it, "Put the film down and RUN LIKE HELL!").

PRODUCTS: The Bad Movies lessons learned T-shirts. On the back, there are five classic lessons that you learn from Bad Movies: "The lessons are: If it looks like a man-eating plant, then it probably is a man-eating plant," "Fruit bats are, strangely enough, carnivorous," "Special effects need not be so special," "Sweat-soaked shirts burn easily and make excellent torches," and finally, "Dinosaur is Latin for 'stuff glued on lizard.'"

VERDICT: B-Movies are so bad, they're good. I have spent more time viewing this site than any other site in this book. They even review my personal favorite, the classic *Leprechaun*, where a psychotic midget Irishman goes on killing sprees to recover his gold coins, while rhyming like an insane rap star. Most people will hate these movies, and for good reason. But some people (myself included) have the innate ability to find humor in horrible works of art. Besides, everybody's got to love a movie about a killer elf bred by the Nazis (*Elves*, 1989, Rated PG-13)! Admit it, you can't resist.

268

Sea Shell World
www.seashellworld.com

Sea Shells make great, all-natural souvenirs from a visit to the beach. Now you can have the shells with out the shoreline sojourn! Seashells aren't just pretty rocks, though. In fact, they're not rocks at all. "A shell is the most universally identifiable part of a creature known as a mollusk. Mollusks are invertebrate animals (think of a snail) with an unsegmented, basically symmetrical body, generally consisting of head, foot, visceral hump, and mantle." I didn't need the detailed description, thank you.

PRODUCTS: The two kinds of seashells you can buy include univalves and bivalves. Univalves come in a spiral shape and are commonly known by the fact that you can "hear the ocean" by putting your ear up to it (the sound is actually sonic vibrations bouncing back into your ear, not the ocean). The bivalves are shaped like a flat cone. You can also buy other static marine life forms like starfish, sand dollars, coral, and others.

VERDICT: It's hard to believe these were once parts of living animals. The question then arises, "If these things look dead but are really alive, could it work the other way around?" Look at Ted Koppel, Al Gore, and Colin Powell. There's your answer right there.

269

Solar Power Store
www.solarpowerstore.com

The Solar Power store is a merchandiser on a mission: "To successfully promote with passion and integrity the effective use of solar energy and other sensible alternatives to address electrical challenges to improve living standards everywhere while respecting the environment." From the photos provided, this "higher living standard" includes a set of five-yard-long, ten-foot-tall solar panels on your front lawn. Talk about luxury! Of course, you must remember, this site is created by Canadians, the "wannabe" Americans.

PRODUCTS: This site contains links to providers of modules, batteries, inverters, and controllers; your essentials for a solar-powered lifestyle. For those who are actually interested in buying this stuff, you're gonna have a tough time navigating this maze of solar power products. You must go to a different site, decipher complicated electricity terms, and deal with a host of other purchasing problems.

VERDICT: What kind of person would go through all this to get a gaggle of giant metal gadgets on their property? Even if the financial benefits were considerable, I wouldn't take the chance that some big storm system would come along and leave me without power for days on end. Call me pampered, but if I don't have a TV, microwave, computer, telephone, and the true essential: a George Foreman grill, I don't think I can survive. Especially without those juicy cheeseburgers.

270

McDonald's Store
www.groupii.com/mcdonalds

Ba ba ba ba ba, I'm lovin' it! This is the official website for McDonald's merchandise. Looking for a McDonald's T-shirt that doesn't make you look like a burger flipper? How about the best kids stuff with Ronald McDonald and the gang? You've come to the right place.

PRODUCTS: Youth and adult T-shirts, McDonald's sports apparel, collectibles, and other gear featuring the highly catchy (and highly annoying) "I'm Lovin' It" slogan. Two interesting products are the Crystal Restaurant and the Retro Crystal Restaurant, two small crystal replicas of the modern and retro McDonald's restaurants. The most expensive product is the McDonald's Golf Bag, a bag that is "heavy on features," but still weighing "a mere 5¾ pounds."

VERDICT: McDonald's advertisement tactics sure have changed over the years. First they were using the Big Mac jingle ("two all beef patties, special sauce…) that appealed to just about everybody, and now they're using pop and hip-hop music that only appeals to their primary customer base: college students strapped for cash and looking for a convenient, good-tasting, extremely unhealthy meal. So little time, so many fat-packed choices.

271   **Generations**
www.generationstore.com

Can't get enough of that retro merchandise, can you? "If you are in the market for high-quality items with that classic, vintage, or retro flair, you have come to the right place. The variety of merchandise you will find here will astound you."

PRODUCTS: And indeed it does astound me. Beaded curtains, tapestries, nostalgic tin signs, "cool clocks," and a whole host of other retro products are here, ready for the picking. Other products are just strange, like the "Warning: Fishing Pox" sign. "Never heard of fishing pox? Note the symptoms of this disease...Hangs out in sporting goods stores longer than usual. Secret night phone calls to fishing pals. Mumbles to self. Lies to everyone. NO KNOWN CURE." If he wants to fish forever, fine, but lying to everybody is more serious than spending pox (the disease that compels people to buy hugely overpriced Gucci bags and Manolo shoes).

VERDICT: Retro merchandise is like water, or love, or Geico commercials (you're bankrupt, but there is good news...): you can't get enough of it. There's something about novelty light fixtures, neon signs, and old drink labels that appeals to everybody. The Generation Store is another generous helping of these groovy gifts.

* *

272   **Llamas and More**
www.llamasandmore.com

Llamas and More: "The catalog store where the discriminating llama shops!" How can llamas discriminate? They just make noises and spit! Whatever they may be discriminating against, it's not the products in this snazzy store.

PRODUCTS: Llama gifts, like the Llama Welcome Sign, a sign with "welcome" and a silhouette of a llama. Another "great" gift set is the

Llama Cookie Cutters, allowing you to make llama shaped cookies for your guests. For those who actually own llamas, you'll find llama grooming products, halters, hay bags, and leads. Finally, there are children's books like *Hummingbirds to Elephants and Other Tales* by Murray E. Fowler. Gee, that's what I'd want to read if I was a kid.

VERDICT: With all these llama products and a little creative decorating, you could throw a llama-themed party for you and your friends! Llama cookies, llama T-shirts for everybody, llama decals. You could even rent a live llama! That does it, I'm planning my llama party now.

273   Jerry King
www.jerryking.com

Jerry King is "one of the most published, prolific, and versatile cartoonists in the world today." He has an impressive list of credentials, including being mentioned by Bill Clinton in a *USA Today* article! Well, it depends on what the meaning of "mentioned" is. His "cartoons features" section has cartoons on subjects like sports, relationships, office life, and technology. One cartoon in the health section reads, "My son here is failing out of medical school. So, to earn extra credit, he'll be operating on you." Sounds like a good idea to me!

PRODUCTS: Jerry King cartoon prints can be bought, along with a book by King called *You Know You're a Golf Addict When...* Finally, a very disturbing stuffed animal. "Jerry King's cat cartoon has been made into a stuffed animal! Now you can own this adorable kitten." With a star coming out of his head, and a bandaged hand and foot, this seriously injured cat looks more like a demented Teletubby. I was offended, and I hate cats!

VERDICT: While the stuffed cat looks like it has a swollen nose and a bad ear-hair problem, the cartoons on Jerry King are pretty funny. And he's got a fantastic credit on his resume: he's worked for the *National Enquirer!* After working for what is, without a doubt, the highest quality news magazine in the world, you can't doubt his talent.

274

Short Fat Guy
www.shortfatguy.com

It's another personal blog from—you guessed it—a short fat guy. What's the story behind this rather embarrassing name? "I used to work with a lovely girl who was tall and slim. I began to tease myself that she was not interested in me because she had something against 'short, fat guys.' I liked the rhythm of the term and soon adopted it as a description for myself." Good to know he can accept such a demeaning description of himself.

PRODUCTS: This store offers something new: you can get fleeced! These soft, comfy fleece sweatshirts, shirts, and pullovers can be bought with the SFG logo: a smiley face with a large nose and curly black hair. Mousepads, mugs, regular shirts, and the usual assortment of products can also be brought with a similar logo.

VERDICT: It's good to know that some people can accept themselves for who they are. So what if he's short and fat? He'd probably be just as happy if he were Fabio. It's the personality that counts, not the looks. Unless you're a shallow pretentious idiot who doesn't want any conversation with a shred of intelligence and who needs to look in the mirror every ten seconds…Then, yes, looks do count.

275

Mars News Store
www.marsnews.com/store

For all your Martian desires, it's the Mars Store! The main site provides information on the latest efforts to explore the red planet. The store offers a bevy of Martian books, games, videos, and more.

PRODUCTS: Books like *The Martian Race*, a fictional novel about a different kind of space race. There's also the Mars 2020 board game, where "You'll repair malfunctions by answering questions on space related science and technology. If all systems are 'go,' you'll then need to be the first to land on Mars to win!" And if you can't answer the question, your ship will blow up and you'll die a horrible death in the frigidly, forebodingly vicious vacuum of space!

VERDICT: In the world of science fiction, Mars has always been associated with hostile extraterrestrials on a quest to destroy the human race. I'm almost hoping we'll find a superior race bent on the destruction of mankind. We could use an invasion to unite our planet. No time for partisan politics and flip-flopping: we've got aliens to destroy! But, no invasion yet, so it's back to arguing and name calling.

276   Bad Bones
www.badbones.com

While this site offers rock and roll apparel, the actual company has different roots. The founders saw "a void in Personal Watercraft Vehicles and the existing after-market performance industry was not filling it." The story goes on to say how a T-shirt promotion campaign for parts for jet skis turned into the apparel line you see on this site. Yes, of course.

PRODUCTS: Bad Bones T-shirt designs with phrases like, "Believe in the Bones," "Bar Fights, Whiskey, and Women," "Bad Bones Illegal," "Bad Bones Forever," and "Generation Hawg." You can also buy Bad Girl designs, featuring clothing with a crossbones heart design, including the seemingly obligatory Bad Girl thong undies. All the Bad Bones designs have skulls or bones. It's bad, but it's supposed to feel good. But, it's just bad.

VERDICT: Any site that prominently features Vince Neil, Motley Crue singer and amateur porn actor, is definitely bad. I still want to know where the stupid personal watercraft equipment is! I don't need some crazy hard rock biker design, I want jet skis and speed boats! The apparel here will suit some tastes, but others will be left wanting more; namely insanely fast recreational water vehicles.

277 Colour Therapy Healing
www.colourtherapyhealing.com

Now your favorite COLOR (notice I used the correct spelling) can help cleanse you of stress! What is Color Therapy Healing? "Using the seven colours of the spectrum, Colour Therapy aims to balance and enhance our body's energy centres/Chakras and also to help stimulate our body's own healing process."

PRODUCTS: This site advises you to find the right color for you through a certified color therapist." But who has time for that and, more importantly, who has the money to waste? My advice is to select your own favorite color and start shopping! There are Colored Silks, which are placed "directly onto the body of the patient." The "light box" therapy sounds a little more believable. A light box uses a color filter over a light to provide another way to "apply color to the body." I can see colors, but I can't feel them.

VERDICT: While there has been reliable scientific research on the benefits of meditation, yoga, light therapy, etc., I can't fathom the notion that putting a colored cloth on a specific body parts can help "heal" you. Mostly, however, I disagree with the spelling of "colour." So there, all you "colour" weirdos. Take your excess "u" and get out!

278 Life Sentence Records
www.lifesentencerecords.com

While Life Sentence Records doesn't have a "how we got here" story or a "we're the best because…" r0Eech, they do have a number of interesting records.

PRODUCTS: CDs by bands like Deadlock, Bloody Sunday, With Dead Hands Rising, and Wings of Scarlet. They also carry clothing products: a hooded sweatshirt and a T-shirt saying, "Go Ahead Keep Smoking: I!Want You to Die." Brutal honesty can be a good thing sometimes.

VERDICT: I have no idea what this record label is all about and frankly, I don't want to know. All of the bands have the word "metal" in their description, which translates into "loud screaming about how horrible life is."

279

GPS Store
www.thegpsstore.com

Thanks to the GPS Store, "Getting lost is a thing of the past!" Obviously, real men don't need this store. We never get lost. "You are welcome to give us a call and speak to a staff member who actually uses GPS and is qualified to answer your questions." So, we call you for customer support when we're lost and can't figure out how to use your products? So much for "getting lost is a thing of the past!"

PRODUCTS: GPS units, accessories, software, and even "marine products." The award for the most exorbitant, overpriced, and totally unnecessarily product goes to the Furuno FCV-582L Color Echosounder. Described as "High power for serious fisherman," the echosounder uses sonar to detect the positions of fish underwater. How much will this indulgence cost the avid fisherman? $1,240. I am not kidding. Twelve hundred bucks to help find a creature that you can lure to bite a hook and then toss back in the water. Catch and release, no. Catch and sauté. Yes!

VERDICT: The idea of not getting lost on a hike or road trip is extremely attractive, but it's also extremely expensive. A handheld unit can run well over $400 at this site if you want reliable GPS equipment. It may be the wave of the future, but the future is extremely expensive for now. My handheld navigation system? A map.

Lucy Lawless Store
www.lucylawless.info

It's Xena the Warrior Princess, also known as Lucy Lawless. We all know she's Xena, but this site cherishes her for being (gasp) an actress! "Lucy Lawless is better known to many as Xena the Warrior Princess but Lucy is a multi-talented actress and singer. This site brings together and showcases the talents of this amazing actress." She has appeared on the movies *Eurotrip* and *Boogeyman*, and as Aunty Kate on *Tarzan*. I never heard of any of those failures...but she IS Xena!

PRODUCTS: At the bottom of the page, you can buy Xena, er, Lucy books and DVDs. There's the book *Lucy Lawless & Renee O'Connor: Warrior Stars Of Xena* by Nikki Stafford, along with the *Xena: Warrior Princess* soundtrack, the *Xena* season one, two, three, and four DVDs, and the *Xena* series finale video. Where are the afore-mentioned *Tarzan* and *Boogeyman* in that list?

VERDICT: Lucy Lawless, Xena, what's the difference? Like she can actually do anything else! Listen to the mp3 files of her "singing" and you'll be certain of one thing: Lucy will only be remembered as Xena. She can't change that, and neither can anybody else.

The Kilt Store
www.kiltstore.net

Sometimes, dress pants just don't cut it. Sometimes a man just needs a stiff breeze up his shorts to cool him down. Sometimes a man just needs, well, a skirt. The Kilt Store hasn't always been the place to shop for tra-ditional Scottish clothing. "Until 2004 we specialised in promoting other companies who we felt offered the best of [Scottish clothing]. But now we can supply you directly ourselves, putting into practice everything we've learned about easy-to-use and secure online trading." You spent nine years peddling other people's products? What is wrong with you? Where is your pride?

PRODUCTS: Traditional kilts, modern kilts, "kilt jackets," and other traditional Scottish and Irish clothing. There's the Budget Casual Kilt, also known as the Sports Kilt, which is "A five-yard, medium-weight kilt worn in the traditional way, in the full range of tartans." Be warned, though: even the "budget" kilts are extremely expensive: 160 pounds, or $292 U.S. Ouch. That's one expensive skirt. The "Modern Kilts" section features camouflage kilts. Who said army tactics and Scottish tradition couldn't mix? And, of course, the Kilt Store stocks a wide variety of sporrans. What is a sporran, you ask? In logic terms, kilt is to skirt as sporran is to purse. Yes, a purse.

VERDICT: Some people may find it weird, but a lot of Irish and Scottish people are looking to get back to their roots with this traditional clothing. The unfortunate reality, though, is that these kilts are expensive. If you're looking forward to a traditional Scottish/Irish themed wedding, family reunion, or party, though, you just might want to indulge yourself here.

282

Karate-Mart
www.karate-mart.com

Everybody was kung fu fighting! Okay, karate and kung fu are different, but it's close enough. "Karate-Mart.com [is] the largest online retailer of martial arts supplies, karate equipment, karate supplies, martial arts weapons, ninja gear, and martial arts equipment." Did you say ninja gear? Sweet.

PRODUCTS: Uniforms, belts, boxing equipment, sparring gear, and of course, weapons. Here, you'll find swords, nunchakus, kamas (miniature handheld scythes), and tonfa (a wooden nightstick with a handle). You'll also find fans ("using fans as weapons is very common." FANS?) and pathetic training weapons, like a rubber pistol and a rubber knife. Screw that, I want ninja weapons with razor sharp edges!

VERDICT: Even though it's probably wise to train for years on end until you use the real weapons, very few people have the time or patience for that. Unless you're a trained martial arts master, you'll probably end up hurting yourself with these weapons. They're still exceptionally useful as decorations for the avid collector and strangely enticing to ninja crazed teenagers.

283

The Rebel Store
www.rebelstore.com

The folks at the Rebel Store proudly proclaim that "We ain't jest a-whistlin' 'Dixie'!" By that, they mean that they have an excellent selection of historical Confederate products. Don't bother shopping elsewhere; if you "Compare our prices to what them Yankee stores charge…we're sure you'll agree…We got them Yankees Beat!" Last I checked, the war was long over, guys.

PRODUCTS: Confederate flags, clothing, collectibles, bumper stickers, and art. The bumper stickers have designs with Confederate flags and phrases like, "We fought the first war on terrorism," "We may be politically incorrect, but we vote too," "Death before dishonor," and "Why apologize for being right?" Right about what? Splitting our country in half? Supporting slavery? I'm not a big fan of the Confederate movement. However, I do support one product on this site: Confederate bikinis.

VERDICT: As long as there are humans, there will be arguments. Arguments about who's better, arguments about who's right, arguments about what's better. The Rebel Store is an example of how some of us would rather get our teeth pulled or move to Siberia than give up our right to argue and disagree. Even if the disagreement is about a war that ended well over a century ago.

284

I Dig Pig
www.idigpig.com

Yet another misleading website, I Dig Pig isn't about plump pork products, nor is it about salivating over swine. It's about cleaning supplies! "I DIG PIG has it all to keep your home clean inside and out!" If you're about clean homes, why did you choose a filthy pig as your mascot?

PRODUCTS: Cleaning products for the garage, kitchen, basement, and boat, as well as cleaning supplies for hunters and their guns. If you find yourself wiping out on icy steps in the winter, try the Ice Breaker Mat. If you're fortunate enough to live on a lake or ocean, try the Pig Bilge Sock. "When you're out cruisin' in your buoyant beauty, the last thing you want on your mind is the bilge. The awful smell and all that gross-looking oil floating around in there…"

VERDICT: How do "clean" and "pig" fit together? Pigs are dirty, and muddy, and disgusting. Not to mention delicious. Irony aside, I Dig Pig does have some cleaning products that could make your house less of a pigsty.

285 Pig Pals Sanctuary
www.pigpalssanctuary.com

Another porcine product place! Pig Pals Sanctuary is a home for a most unfortunate creature: the orphaned pig. "Pig Pals Sanctuary was founded seventeen years ago, in 1987, when the plight of the unwanted pet pig first came to our attention…As with any animal, the more popular they became, the more people there were [who] got them as babies and then couldn't handle the grown animal." Handling a grown pig is simple: season nicely and put it in the oven.

PRODUCTS: The PPS store sells T-shirts, tote bags, and decals. Most have the PPS logo with different pigs from the sanctuary including Toonie, Arnie, and Chops. Chops sounds like a good name, if you add "pork" to it! Mmm…pork chops… There's also the Fence T-shirt, with a mosaic of pig pictures around the sanctuary's sign.

VERDICT: Despite my opinion that pigs are at their best on our plates, I do think that if pigs are destined to live, they should be treated as well as a dogs, or at least better than cats. Either let them feed a family, or let them live with a family so they can be loved, and maybe eaten later.

286

Bowie Wonder World
www.bowiewonderworld.com

Bowie Wonder World is a fan site dedicated to David Bowie, the singer behind the famous *Ziggy Stardust* album. This site contains an extensive one-hundred-plus question FAQ, answering virtually every question you could have about Bowie, including how tall he is, where he proposed to his current wife, right down to the name of this site and even the meaning behind a prop in one of his movies!

PRODUCTS: David Bowie books, albums, tour posters, and even an A&E biography. Even David Bowie postage stamps from the island of St. Vincent. Bowie's biggest film, *The Man Who Fell to Earth*, is a film where "David Bowie plays the alien of the title, who arrives on Earth with hopes of finding a way to save his own planet from turning into an arid wasteland. He funds this effort by capitalizing on several highly lucrative inventions, and in so doing becomes the powerful leader of an international corporate conglomerate." Sounds deep, deranged, and depressing.

VERDICT: I'm not Mr. Bowie's biggest fan, but anybody who has even a slight liking for the singer/actor will find something to like here. If you have a question about him, it's practically guaranteed to be answered by the amazingly thorough FAQ. What other site has a complete list of the famous people mentioned in Bowie's songs?

287

Trepanning
www.trepanning.tv

"Welcome to Trepanning, the world's first twelve dimensional settlement." If you're already confused, don't expect fathoming anything more. "Trepanning is a village in Cornwall so isolated that it is located a short way from the outskirts of itself…It is an independent village-state with a population of less than fifteen hundred and borders built from elliptical quantum formulae so twisted that they make immigration not only difficult but also perplexing and unaccountable." Um…what?

PRODUCTS: Shirts with the You are Here design, with a map of Trepanning pinpointing village locations like the Stone Circle, the Waiting Room, the Chakra Field, and the Off Centre Centre. Okay... There's also the Nan Uren's Quantum Bakery mug, with the said phrase and a map of Trepanning. Finally, you can buy the Trepanning postcards, postcards divided into four images: a flower in a pseudo-divine light, the Eiffel Tower in an open field, an image of a seashore, and a picture of a forest with the phrase "A village so isolated it lies on its own outskirts," and a UFO in the middle of the forest. Right...

VERDICT: Trepanning is more confusing than *Xanadu* (a movie about glowing, roller skating Greek muses), *Zardoz* (a futuristic saga starring Sean Connery and a giant flying stone head), and *Barbarella* (a movie where Jane Fonda battles an evil scientist while constantly losing her clothes) COMBINED. If you go to Trepanning, don't expect to understand anything. It's that weird.

288 Canadian Favourites
www.canadianfavourites.com

"What do you miss most about Canada?" I don't miss the metric system. "The Moose? The Mounties? The Mountains? Chances are it's a favourite Canadian food you're craving." Just what is Canadian food? Proper spelling aside, this site has a ton of Canadian foods that are really rare in America.

PRODUCTS: "Shop safely online from the widest available selection of Canadian food products including Tim Horton's Coffee, Nestlé Chocolate, E. D. Smith Jams, Red Rose Tea, Humpty Dumpty Chips, Body Smarts, and so many more we know you'll be happy to see." The Nestle Chocolate bars aren't the Butterfinger and Crunch bars we're so accustomed to here, but rather the After Eight, Big Turk, and Mirage bars. And what Canadian wouldn't sell his soul for a pound of Maple Leaf Tenderflake Pure Lard or a box of Post Shreddies?

VERDICT: Canadians will find all their "favourites" here, but Americans might find some new "favorites" here as well. Whether you're a Canadian looking for old "favourites" or an American looking for new "favorites," there's something to like for everybody at this Canadian food site.

289

Perfect Clock
www.perfectclock.com

The Perfect Clock Store sells radio-controlled atomic clocks, which are, true to the name, perfect. How do theses marvelous timepieces work? A radio station in Fort Collins, Colorado transmits a low frequency signal to the clock, telling it the correct time. The radio station keeps the correct time, so you don't have to! Radio waves sending atomic signals into my home? Sounds like a commie plot to me!

PRODUCTS: Atomic watches and clocks, including projection clocks and wall clocks. Watches like the Casio MTG900DA-9V have tons of funky features, like world time from thirty cities (Gee, I really need to know the time in Buenos Aires! Right now!). Even more feature-packed are the atomic clocks, with an AM/FM Radio with Thermometer and ExactSet Clock and six user-selectable sound soother modes: bird, wind, river raindrop, waterfall, and ocean waves. Now even time can be relaxing.

VERDICT: Let me clear up the confusion behind the word "atomic." "Atomic" does not automatically mean weapons of mass destruction (or, as they used to be called, "nukes"). "Atomic" is a physics concept, not a word for nuclear weapons, (or, as George W. Bush would say, "nuke-yuh-lur"). Definitions of doomsday weapons aside, the Perfect Clock is a boon to punctual perfectionists everywhere.

290

Back to the Future
www.bttf.com

You may not have Doctor Emmett Brown's DeLorean time machine, but you can still follow news and buy products from this popular time travel movie series. BTTF has a news page that gathers any news that has the slimmest link to the BTTF series, like the article "Actor Tom Wilson of the *Back to the Future* Trilogy Releases 'Big Pop Fun,' a Series of Paintings, Prints, and Posters of Nostalgic Toys." Biff is making toys instead of screwing up the space/time continuum? What a letdown!

PRODUCTS: Autographed items, home video, music, novelty items and more from BTTF. Marty McFly colorshifter hats made of "lenticular material" from the year 2015! The music section sells several iterations of the *Back to the Future* soundtrack, some of which are so out of date and out of style that they're on cassette tapes! For you young ones, cassettes were what music was played on BEFORE CDs and mp3 players. Amazing, isn't it?

VERDICT: The mechanics of time travel have always fascinated me. If I went back in time and was stupid enough to kill my grandfather, what would happen? Would I be stuck in that time period? Would I cease to exist? Or would that stupid stunt cause the collapse of the entire universe? The bottom line is that, much like movie classics like *Casablanca*, *The Wizard of Oz*, and *E.T.*, time isn't something that should be tampered with.

291 Pasha Oksana Grishuk
www.pasha-grishuk.de

She's one of ice skating's most well-recognized stars. And you've probably never heard of her! Pasha Oksana Grishuk (POG) is "the only ice dancer in sport history who has won Olympic Gold two times!" Along with a wealth of information on this artist of the ice, she also has her own equally elegant store!

PRODUCTS: Autographed photos of POG, which are "real photograph[s], not printed paper!" Yeah, but is the signature real? Don't forget the POG T-shirts, hats, ties (what self respecting man would wear a tie with an ice dancer on it?), scarves, and tote bags. But the best item by far has to be the "water filled glass ball with dolphins swimming around Pasha!!!!" Four exclamation points? They seem overly excited about this glorified water globe. And don't forget the red trucker hat with Pasha's smiling face beaming from the chic polyester fabric.

VERDICT: Pasha looks like she's touting her looks more than her ice-skating skills. How many Olympic ice dancers sell T-shirts and hats with their faces on them? If you're a fan of Pasha's, you'll be delighted with this store, but if the last time you cared about ice skating was the Kerrigan/Harding scandal, you'll find this site less than stellar.

292

World of Celebrities Stores
www.world-of-celebrities.com

The World of Celebrities has hundreds of profiles of celebrities, all of them with their own stores where you can buy their movies and books. Almost everybody you could possibly imagine is here: Britney Spears, Angelina Jolie, and Johnny Depp.

PRODUCTS: One memorable store out of the hundreds here is the Steve Irwin store. Steve Irwin is better known as The Crocodile Hunter, perhaps even better known for his stunt where he placed his infant son only a few feet away from a live crocodile. At least we'll know who to blame when the dingos eat HIS baby. You can buy his feature film debut, *Crocodile Hunter: The Collision Course*, in which "The Crocodile Hunter mistakes some CIA agents for poachers and sets out to stop them from capturing a wily croc which, unbeknownst to him, has swallowed a tracking drone." Sounds like a sure Oscar winner!

VERDICT: If you're the slightest bit interested in the celebrity scene (as disgusting as it is, it's incredibly fascinating), The World of Celebrities site is your one-stop shop for CDs, DVDs, and books about your favorite celebrities. Whether you're looking for classics by Bing Crosby or Nat King Cole, or you MUST have former Playmate of the Year Jenny McCarthy's diary, the World of Celebrities has a store for you.

293

Buffy Collector
www.buffycollector.com

Battling evil monsters, juggling boyfriends (some even being undead), and kicking butt with great hair: all in a day's work for Buffy the Vampire Slayer! "The Buffy Store focuses on *Buffy the Vampire Slayer* collectibles by providing links to online collectibles, information about finding collectibles online and offline, and news about *Buffy the Vampire Slayer* advance orders." If you're looking for a vintage Slayer action figures or a set of Buffy trading cards, you'll find something good at the Buffy Collector.

PRODUCTS: Buy Buffy busts, like the Fyarl Demon Giles bust, which is "Based on the demon form of Giles from the season four episode where Giles was transformed into a Fyarl Demon." First he was a bookish undead hunting expert, now he's a demon with goat horns! But how did he change back? Did he change back? And what's up with the goat thing? All that transforming back and forth from being alive to being dead is too confusing for me. You can even buy a real wooden stake! Be warned, though: "This is the real thing. This is not a toy. This is not for children."

VERDICT: Sarah Michelle Gellar never struck me as an effective vampire hunter. It seemed like she'd be too concerned about breaking a nail or messing up her hair to effectively fight hordes of undead demons. For the avid Slayer fan, Buffy Collectibles is a must.

294

Moto-ya
www.moto-ya.com

Moto-ya is quite different from the other "Moto" in this book, Motopets (number 45). Instead of using bad English to advertise ridiculous, fake motor-powered pets, Moto-ya sells kimonos and "fine kimonos obis." What are obis, you ask? "The Japanese obi is the sash worn around the kimono wearer's waist. It is an extremely important part of the kimono ensemble." I can at least see the importance of a kimono not falling off, and imagine what would happen if it did

PRODUCTS: Antique obis, contemporary obis, and bargain obis! One interesting bargain obi is the Fukuro Obi, which has "Dark orange and silver circles surround[ing] colorful carts on this fukuro obi. Simplicity prevails allowing you to see every charming detail." If there are carts on kimonos, maybe I should wear a tuxedo cummerbund with cars on it! To complete your kimono ensemble, you can buy the actual kimonos, with men's, women's, children's, and wedding kimonos.

VERDICT: This site, like the Kilt Store (number 281) is ideal for people looking for a traditional, ethnic-themed party or wedding. But, what other uses could these high priced bathrobes have? How about none.

295

The Warhol Store
www.warholstore.com

Here's a brief lesson in art history: Andy Warhol was one of the pioneers of modern art. His works include the famous Campbell's Soup Cans and the four-multicolored frame pictures of cultural icons like Elvis Presley and Marilyn Monroe. He also created the phrase "fifteen minutes of fame" with his quote, "In the future everybody will be world-famous for fifteen minutes." Now you can buy art inspired by Warhol at his official store.

PRODUCTS: Andy Warhol accessories, books, calendars, clothing, posters, photographs, and more. His books have three worded titles like *Shoes, Shoes, Shoes*; *Love, Love, Love*; and even *Cats, Cats, Cats*. Three too many cats for me. There are also photographs of the artist himself in various poses, like Kissing John Lennon, Kissing Liza (seeing Warhol kissing Liza Minnelli is extremely disturbing, though not as disturbing as seeing David Gest kissing her), and even Working Out. The price for each eight by ten picture is even more confusing than the photos: $500. Seriously. I am not joking.

VERDICT: While some modern art appears to be a creation of a three-year-old, Warhol's art is unquestionably unique. While some of it may be a little too "avant garde" for me, for better or worse, Warhol was one of the most influential artists of the twentieth century. Now that influence has led to the creation of T-shirts, calendars, and even refrigerator magnets with his art. Strange times we live in.

296

The Gavel Store
www.gavelstore.com

Order in the court! The Gavel Store sells tons of different varieties of gavels, including traditional, checkered, hand-carved, and even crystal gavels. Crystal gavels? Sounds like a product liability lawsuit waiting to happen.

PRODUCTS: One memorable miniature gavel features an apple for a head! You can also buy New Gavel Styles, with designs like diamond, spiral, rope, and eight sided. And what would a gavel be without an appropriate sound block? Sound blocks in walnut, oak, and rosewood are here so you can have that satisfying smack when using your gavel. Finally, there are the gavel watches, which are designer watches with an image of a gavel in the time display.

VERDICT: I can see no practical use for a gavel in my home. Maybe toddlers can put these gavels to good use. Instead of shaking a rattle, they can slam a gavel on the floor! If you're a judge, and you need a good gavel to control your court, the Gavel Store is a good place to start looking. Anybody else will find these glorified mallets utterly useless.

297   Exploding Dog
www.explodingdog.com

Exploding Dog is another abnormal art site. This site creator, whose name is Sam, draws pictures from titles people suggest. People send him phrases, and he draws cartoons that reflect what he thinks of when he hears the phrase. An example is the phrase, "and even you can find love," which has a drawing of a poorly drawn, shall we say, "person," giving another "person" a brochure with hearts on it. The only recognizable features on these "people" are the misshapen arms, legs, body, and head. Weird stuff.

PRODUCTS: The Exploding Dog book, *Wish for Something Better*, which has "all new pictures and stories about moon monsters, love, flying, and other fun Exploding Dog stuff." Moon monsters? Flying? I don't want to know what "other fun stuff" is in this sick storybook. There are also T-shirts with similarly cryptic drawings, and another with the phrase, "I am a moon monster." Aren't we all?

VERDICT: Drawing whatever comes to mind when hearing a certain phrase doesn't make for great art. It doesn't even make for good art. It doesn't help that "Sam's" drawing skills are horrible at best. The only redeeming product is the Moon Monster shirt, as people like Boy George (the star of Rosie O'Donnell's flop play *Taboo*) may very well be moon monsters and should wear such a shirt to warn us all.

298

Court TV
www.courttv.com

As if we didn't get enough courtroom drama from *Law and Order* and *Boston Legal*, we forgot about the twenty-four-hour cable courtroom channel, aptly named Court TV. Along with information on programs, there's also an entire section devoted to famous trials. The list is comprised of shameful scandals with celebrities like O. J. Simpson, Kobe Bryant, Martha Stewart, and any other legal issue that appears frequently in the *National Enquirer*.

PRODUCTS: Visors, golf balls, tote bags, and other apparel, along with select Court TV videos. You can buy the *Florida vs. Wuornos: Female Serial Killer* video, which details the case that was the basis for the 2004 movie *Monster*, starring Charlize Theron. This movie is known for the fact that Theron ate two boxes of Krispy Kremes a day to gain the weight required for the movie. Why can't I get paid to eat Krispy Kremes?

VERDICT: If you're a fan of TV shows with courtroom drama, or an avid reader of John Grisham books, Court TV is a good channel to tune into to get your daily dose of riveting law enforcement and litigation shows. The main strength of the channel is probably the endless reruns of *Cops*. Watching police officers arresting and interrogating drunks, druggies, and prostitutes has an appeal all of its own.

299

Samadhi Cushions
www.samadhicushions.com

The Samadhi Cushions Store is "the internet's premier source for quality meditation cushions and supplies." Achieve inner peace while keeping your tushie comfy. What a concept! Along with cushions and benches for meditation, you can also buy gongs, incense, and books on transcendental subjects.

PRODUCTS: Take a look at the Half-Moon Zafu cushions. This meditation cushion is "sewn short at the front and taller at the back for a wedge effect in your meditation posture." We all know how important a proper wedge posture is! In the "Gongs and Bells" section, you can listen to the sounds that the gongs make. As I strain to hear a purpose for these gongs, I can only observe silence. Be one with the sound…of nothing.

VERDICT: There's a confusing picture on this site that I just have to mention. On one page, there is a meditation cushion with a person on it. You'd think it would be a man or woman in deep meditation, but instead, it's a smiling *baby*. How many babies meditate? Their attention span is limited to a few seconds, so don't count on your bundle of joy achieving inner peace anytime soon. Then again, happiness is a dry diaper. Oooooooooooom.

300

Ahh Products
www.ahhprods.com

Ahhhhh…this site's beanbag chairs are soooo comfortable. Ahh Products is assumingly named after the sound you make when you settle into a quality beanbag chair. If you want proof that Ahh Products knows what comfort is, check out their client list, which includes the Smithsonian Institute and the Jim Henson Co., as well as A-list celebrities like John Travolta, Pink, Metallica, and even former *Dark Angel* beauty Jessica Alba! If it's good enough for her, it's good enough for me!

PRODUCTS: Several categories of beanbags, each with their own distinct style. The "Featured Spots" has the cream-colored Uptown design and the traditional Autumn Leaves design. By contrast, the "City Panache" section contains more modern designs like the "shapely" Geometric design, and the marvelously modern Martini design. The really cool section is the "Exotic Flair" section, with cow spot, Moroccan, and Persian designs. Cow spots are exotic? Right. While the beanbags do look cool, they are also costly: the average price is around $100.

VERDICT: While these beanbags may be expensive, I know from experience that most beanbags aren't very durable. The constant plopping down on the chair can often break the bag within days. With the numerous customer testimonials here, however, it's obvious that you get what you pay for. If you want a comfortable beanbag chair that's durable and reliable at the same time, your money may be well spent at Ahh Products.

301

Funeral Depot
www.funeraldepot.com

It's like the Home Depot. If you're dead! The Funeral Depot not only "guarantees free next-day casket delivery," they also "eliminate the anxiety of the traditional funeral purchasing experience" by providing "the opportunity to save time, money, and most of all have freedom of choice, all from the comfort of their own home." At last, the chance to plan the funeral of a loved one in total solitude and isolation.

PRODUCTS: A wide selection of caskets, cremation urns, vaults (to protect the casket from decomposition), and custom markers for the gravesite. The upright monument markers are available in traditional, contemporary, alternative, and even designer markers, like the Rose Bud Red marker, a funeral marker in the shape of a red and pink heart. Hey, my gravestone has to look good too! The cremation urns are equally unique, with urns shaped into nature scenes and even a golf bag! Now, when my loved ones look at the ashes, they'll think of golf instead of me!

VERDICT: The Funeral Depot's advertising policy for their products is disturbingly lighthearted. Instead of having sentimental messages throughout this site, they have phrases like "Absolute Lowest Price Guaranteed!" and "Savings up to 70 percent" on gravestone markers! Rather than comforting you in your time of need, Funeral Depot gets right to the important part: death at a reasonable price.

302

The Magickal Cat
www.themagickalcat.com

The Magickal Cat: "All your metaphysical needs in one magickal place." If you find yourself "Want[ing] to try magick but have no idea where to start," rest assured, "you aren't alone." Well, you have plenty of options to waste your money on good luck charms, spells, and other superstitious trinkets here!

PRODUCTS: "Start out simple" with the selection of amulets and talismans. "We carry over one hundred amulets and talismans for love, luck, prosperity, and everything in between." How about gullibility and insanity? Move on to the Divination devices, which tells how "a simple pendulum can be a fabulously effective tool." How can you use a pendulum in magick? "Get to know your pendulum with basic yes/no questions then move on to use with prepared charts." I'm sure the pendulum knows the answers to all of my burning questions? How about, "Is this site for weirded-out whackos"? All signs point towards yes.

VERDICT: Perhaps they think the extra "k" makes "magick" more effective. Perhaps the "k" appeases the divine spirits that govern magick. Perhaps this site should be called the "Stupid Superstitions Store."

303   Eastern Bison
www.easternbison.com

Eastern Bison sells "America's First Red Meat," a.k.a. bison, a.k.a. buffalo. That's right! Now that bison are off the endangered species list, companies like Eastern Bison are wasting no time in slaughtering them to provide high quality meat! Now the only place they're endangered is on your plate. Not only does this site claim that bison has a "hearty, sweet, and richer flavor than beef," it's also healthier! For those that care about weight watching, 3.5 ounces of bison only has 2.42 grams of fat compared to the 9.28 grams for beef, and 143 calories compared to beef's 211 calories. Calorie counters win here!

PRODUCTS: Tons of delicious bison products. There are several varieties of steaks, including flank steak, T-bone steak, porterhouse steak, and tenderloin steak, which is described as "maybe the best of the best." Maybe? What kind of advertisement is that? More like "without a doubt" or "definitely!" If you're into "tube steaks," you can try the bison hot dogs or ground bison to "cook up a super burger." Finally, be sure not to overlook the bison stew meat, chipped steak ("for a delicious steak sub"), kabob meat, and many more tasty treats.

VERDICT: If the claims that bison is healthier and tastier than beef are true, we might just have a new favorite meat. However, compared to beef, it's a bit pricier. Ground bison costs twice as much as its beef counterpart. If you're looking for the best quality meat, though, you need look no further than Eastern Bison.

304

When Pigs Fly
www.whenpigsfly.bz

"Special shaped hot-air balloons come in many different shapes, sizes, and colors. Ours just happens to be a pink pig standing over one-hundred-feet tall, sixty-feet wide and eighty-feet long!" That's one big pig! This site is where you can learn more about Ham-Let, "The World's Largest Flying Pig." You can see Ham-Let's tour schedule to see when you can see the big pig lift off, or take a gander at the "Pig Puns." One pig pun says that "When Pigs Fly, they…Go through mud-al detectors for sow-cureity." If you think THAT'S bad, check out the other pig jokes.

PRODUCTS: Embroidered apparel, T-shirts, Pig Pins, yield signs, and the Flying Pigs category, which contains such products as Pig Noses, Pig Hats, and the Battery-Operated Flying Pig! And if you're "looking for a great way to get your foot in the door or go for that order, thank a customer, or push a boss for that raise, our Flying Pig Cookie Clusters are an excellent way to toast your success now that your pig flies." I'm sure a flying pig cookie cluster will get me a raise.

VERDICT: Ham-Let is not a flying pig. It's a balloon that flies and looks like a pig. I could recommend this site as a cool store with cool products. Yeah, when pigs fly! Until then, I'll pass on the pig products here.

305

Black Jungle
www.blackjungle.com

Who said plants don't eat meat? On Black Jungle, you will find one of the healthiest selection of carnivorous plants on the Internet, along with a host of other exotic flora and fauna. If you can find in the rainforest, you can find it on this site.

PRODUCTS: Venus Fly Traps, Pitcher Plants, Sundews, and other carnivorous plant supplies and accessories. One prime pitcher plant is the "Nepenthes diatas," an "exciting species" from the "montane meadows of Gunung Bandahara" in Indonesia. Maybe they should stay in the montane meadows of Gunung Bandahara. Black Jungle also offers poison dart frogs and answers the burning question we all ask when thinking about poison dart frogs: "What are your chances of getting a sexed pair of frogs from unsexable froglets?" According to this site, your chances of getting your frogs to make some lovin' increase with the number of froglets you purchase. Get eight, and frog babies are practically guaranteed.

VERDICT: The only thing I'd worry about with a carnivorous plant is that it might try and eat my finger when I'm handling it. If it loves live flies, who says my finger isn't next on the menu? But more importantly, is there anything more exciting in life than getting a pair of sexable poison dart frogs to mate successfully? I think not.

306
Jose Silva Ultra Mind ESP System
www.silvaultramindsystem.com

I feel a strange premonition…that this site is NONSENSE! "Imagine having a guide who actually knows what lies ahead, who can point you to success, happiness, and fulfillment you deserve." The story goes on to say how Jose Silva taught children meditation and, as a result, they earned special mind-reading powers. Riiiiight.

PRODUCTS: The Silva UltraMind ESP System Home Study Course, which allows you to "gain insights in your dreams," "create 'good vibes' with anyone you meet," and—this one is scary—"influence people from a distance for good causes." Nobody's gonna use their maniacal "mind control" to "influence" me! Silva has also anticipated the obvious: "Skeptical? Many people were…until they proved it to themselves." At the very bottom of the page is the price for this crazy instructional course: $130 for the CD set, and $110 for the cassettes.

VERDICT: Unless you're an incredibly gullible fool, you can see right through this psychic nonsense. If this course is so successful, why don't I see anybody accurately predicting the future or using mind control to further their own personal agendas? Then again, I have felt a strange compulsion to buy Suzanne Sommers products on the Home Shopping Channel now and then.

307

Museum of Modern Art Store
www.momastore.org

The Museum of Modern Art Store should be called "The Museum of Subjective Art Store." What is the mission of this "artistic" store? "Now more than ever consumers appreciate that everything we live with—from tape dispensers to dish racks—can, and should be, well designed." I want a tape dispenser to be practical, reliable, and affordable. If the "superior design" sacrifices any of those, it's useless.

PRODUCTS: Products for men, women, children, and the house, as well as posters and accessories. Some extremely stupid products include paperweights, including 1040 Tax Form, Architect's Blueprint, and the Stock Market paperweights. All of them are designed to look like crumbled-up paper. It gets worse with the children's book *When Pigasso Met Mootisse* where "the two artists become fierce rivals, calling each other names and ultimately building a fence between them. But when the two painters paint opposite sides of the fence that divides them, they unknowingly create a modern art masterpiece, and learn it is their friendship that is the true work of art." Finally, a children's story to encourage becoming a stuck-up, reclusive, starving artist!

VERDICT: Earlier, I said the "Subjective Art Store" would be more appropriate, because the true "beauty" of all of this "art" is in the eye of the beholder. I think that scribbles and shapes don't qualify as "art." But, others see a deep meaning in modernistic paintings. I'll take the Mona Lisa and American Gothic anytime over this crap.

308

Trumpet Geek
www.trumpetgeek.com

For all you band camp geeks, you've found a home at Trumpet Geek! How do you know who a trumpet geek is? Check out the very easy and very detailed diagram, showing all the key features of a trumpet geek, including the "Reamer for opening up mouthpieces," the "Pocket trumpet for practicing in the car," and the "Horn [that] has been Cryo-treated at the freezer at the local Baskin Robbins." Other features include articles on trumpets, the "Trumpet Geek Anthem," and the "Trumpet Geek of the Week."

PRODUCTS: Instead of just selling T-shirts, hats, or other products with Trumpet Geek logos and sayings (Geekus Trumpetus), they get straight to what true Trumpet geeks seek: Trumpet supplies! Valve guides, cleaning supplies, mouthpieces, metronomes, and tuners. For trumpet geeks, it's like being a kid in a candy store! The only other non-trumpet supply products are the Christmas cards, with trumpet geek themed cards.

VERDICT: For the true trumpet geek this site is sheer nirvana. There's even a trumpet geek chat room so you can talk with others of your kind and actually (gasp) make friends! But, talking with other trumpet geeks wastes valuable trumpet-tooting time! Decisions, decisions.

309 Dr. Thessalonia De Prince, Master Voodoo Priest
www.voodoodeprince.com

This site is home to "Dr. Thessalonia De Prince Master Voodoo Priest." "This modern magical master can help teach you how to overcome any special problem that you may have. Magic that is so powerful, it will change your life forever!" Making a buck off of supernatural phenomena? Seems like déjà vu after seeing the Silva Ultra Mind ESP System (number 306).

PRODUCTS: "Powerful Spell Kits from the Master himself," featuring the Boss Fix Kit. "Control your boss and make them give you a raise." Or, the Gay Lover's Kit to "find that special him or her," only $24.95. But wait, is the Dr. discriminating against gays? I mean, the heterosexual She She Lover Queen Kit and Man Man Voodoo Drops Kit each cost only $14.95. Maybe it's time for a "Queer Eye for the Voodoo Guy" makeover. Remember when using these kits to "Use with Care! If in doubt consult with a voodoo master or email me." I can imagine that email: "I have summoned an evil demon that's tickle torturing me! Please help ASAP!"

VERDICT: I doubt this "magical" merchandise actually does anything other than cast a spell of gullibility on you. These crazy products have the power to "change your life forever" only in your own insane imagination.

310

Top Secret Recipes
www.topsecretrecipes.com

Top Secret Recipes: "Creating Kitchen Clones of America's Favorite Brand-Name Foods!" "With over two million Top Secret Recipes books in print, Todd can often spend days at a time and dozens of attempts creating the perfect clone of a famous brand-name product." Dozens of attempts! That's a lot of wasted ingredients. And do you really need to whip up a batch of cloned Arby's Horsey Sauce when you can just grab a handful of those little foil packets?

PRODUCTS: You can buy the Top Secret Recipes Steak Rubs, which contains "A secret blend of spices that will make your homemade steaks taste like they came from a famous steakhouse chain." Aside from these salivatory spices, the rest of the store contains the Top Secret Recipe books, including *Top Secret Recipes*, *More Top Secret Recipes*, *Even More Top Secret Recipes*, *Low-Fat Top Secret Recipes*, and a few more Top Secret cookbooks. I slave away on a computer seeking the worst of the web, he slaves away in a kitchen. The things we do to bring you good books.

VERDICT: If done right, these recipes may be quite tasty. This site has several sample recipes, so you may want to give them a shot. From making your own Twinkies to unraveling Colonel Sanders's secret blend of herbs and spices, there's a lot of potential at Top Secret Recipes. However, you can save a lot of time by simply buying the actual products instead of trying to recreate them.

311

Grand Illusions
www.grand-illusions.com

Grand Illusions is "this site for the enquiring mind." This site contains tons of optical illusions, scientific puzzles, and interesting riddles. Examples include a piece of paper folded into a dragon that always appears to look at you, no matter where you stand in the room. Another is a variation of the classic "car speed" riddle.

PRODUCTS: The products are equally puzzling. One neat product is the Snail Ball, "A small, metallic gold ball just over two centimeters in diameter. Place it on a sloping surface, and you would expect it to roll down in the normal way. Well, this ball does roll, but it does so incredibly slowly." How does this puzzling product work? You'll have to visit this site to find out.

VERDICT: If you like products and experiments that make for incredibly challenging brain-teasers, you'll be drawn in by the mystery of this site. For the inquisitive person with a knack for figuring things out, this site is a must see. For the lazy person who has no interest in taxing their brain, it has no purpose whatsoever.

312

Butt Ugly Decor
www.legitimate.org/ugly

"Home decor in bad taste…is our specialty and what we pride ourselves on." If you're looking for "absolutely the last things you would want to have in YOUR home," you've come to the right place. These gifts truly are butt ugly. Sickening statues, perturbing paperweights, uniquely ugly unicorns, and abnormal animals; they're all here.

PRODUCTS: "Wildlife," "Humanoid," and "Unknown" products. The "Wildlife" section includes products like the Mutant Wolf, a three-headed wolf statue. "The detail and craftsmanship is stunning. You'll find your cats running from the room when you bring this beast home." Another is the Bulbous Bison, a large, light-bulb shaped bison head. Another from the "Humanoid" section is The Brain, a set of three statues. Two of them are semi-normal, but one looks like "that lab rat known as BRAIN from the *Pinky & The Brain* cartoon. Beware, he will take over the world if you let him." Sure.

VERDICT: These decorations are so incredibly ugly, they're more hideous than Gene Simmons *without* makeup. From toothless gargoyles to a skeleton figure called "Anorexia Deathosa," if you're looking for a particularly insulting gift for that annoying coworker or evil in-law, Butt Ugly Decor will truly make for an incredibly offensive present.

313   Nifty Threads
www.niftythreads.com

NiftyThreads.com: "We scour the nation for the coolest thrift store clothes so you don't have to." All the products on this web either have stupid phrases, haven't been in style for ten years, or are from bad movies or TV shows (*Teenage Mutant Ninja Turtles*, *Power Rangers*, etc.). And, they all are the COOLEST clothes you'll ever see.

PRODUCTS: While the selection changes rapidly (most are bought from thrift shops and sold for a profit here), you'll always find something so bad it's good. My visit to the sight saw the Teenage Mutant Ninja Turtleneck and the ALF Stuffed Animal. I loved ALF when I was little, and I still love him now (he eats cats, after all). Another product I saw was the All Your Base Are Belong to Us T-shirt. This phrase came from an incredibly bad video game translation. Other examples include the That's Chicago! hat, and the My Lucky Sweater, a hideous green sweater with white wool stripes and four-leaf clovers.

VERDICT: I have mixed feelings about this site. While many of the T-shirts are so bad they're amazingly awesome, they're really simply overpriced thrift store clothes. Your thrift store may carry remarkably similar items. Still, if you're a fan of super-lame, yet super-cool T-shirts, you might find your new favorite shirt here.

314   Buffalo Wing World Domination
www.bwwd.org

"Warning: Eating Buffalo Wings is HIGHLY addictive." BWWD is on a mission: "to peacefully take over the world through the use of nanite laced buffalo wings...Once in control of the world we will continue in the pursuit of the perfect Avian Bison. Their wisdom cannot be questioned." Their four-phase plan is to use the buffalo wing sauce to "infect" people, then activate a radio signal to make the world population "receptive to our commands."

PRODUCTS: "No soldier should be caught out of uniform behind enemy lines. Make sure to order your uniform right away." The "uniform" is a shirt with a winged bison standing on top of a globe, and the words "Buffalo Wing World Domination" on the back.

VERDICT: Even if this pathetic plan were actually real, only a fraction of the world's population have actually tasted buffalo wings! We'll see a Spice Girls comeback before we'll see Buffalo Wing World Domination. And, maybe I'm being a little Jessica Simpson-like here, but do buffalo really have wings?

315   Captain Quack
www.captainquack.com

Rubber Duckies, they're the ones, they make bath time lots of fun! Captain Quack sells rubber duckies, with a selection that would be the envy of Ernie from Sesame Street. Captain Quack is also "the name under which goodtastic! operates…Our mission is to provide novelty gift items of the highest quality, at a competitive price." "Goodtastic," what an original name!

PRODUCTS: Classic rubber duckies, Devil Duckies, Duckcetera, and Celebriducks. The Celebriduck selection is full of celebrity duckies with beaks, including Santa Claus, Uncle Sam, Elwood and Jake from *The Blues Brothers*, and Beethoven. Beethoven's "hair is done back in a fluffed sort of way, and his eyes are wide open and ready to create." A master music composer, except now he has a beak! The devil duckies are equally comical, available in black, pink, violet, polka-dot, and camouflage. A camouflage devil duckie? Now I've seen everything!

VERDICT: If you have kids, Captain Quack is a good place to get rubber duckies to make bath time a little more bearable. For adults, only gag gift lovers and demented duckie collectors need apply.

316   Cthulhu for President
www.cthulhu.org

Cthulhu for President: "Why vote for a lesser evil?" Cthulhu (pronounced kuh-THOOL-hoo) is some kind of octopus creature taken out of H. P. Lovecraft's books, an early twentieth-century horror/science fiction author. According to this site, Cthulhu "should return from his slumber to take over the U.S. government and make this country a whole hell of a lot better as the leader of our executive branch." Should, but won't.

PRODUCTS: H. P. Lovecraft shirts, statuary, miniatures, and "map and play aids." On the "Cthulhu page" link, scroll down under the heading, "What propaganda should I read about the illustrious one?" In answer to that creepy question is a link to Amazon.com with a large selection of H. P. Lovecraft books, and *Encyclopedia Cthulhiana*, by Daniel Harms.

VERDICT: First Mike the Headless Chicken (number 105), now this thing? From what they're promising, Cthulhu won't get my vote. Unless, that is, it's running against she-who-must-not-be-named, as she might in 2008 (see number 211 for her extremely evil site). If that were the case, Cthulhu could say he'd make us watch *Baywatch Nights* reruns and I'd still vote for him.

317   Bugs Bunny Burrow
www.bugsbunnyburrow.com

For all you Looney Tunes fans out there, "this is the place to be to find information about Bugs Bunny, Marvin the Martian, Tweety, Taz, Daffy Duck, Foghorn Leghorn, Miss Prissy, Chickenhawk, Dawg, Wile E Coyote, Road Runner, Speedy Gonzalez, Pepe Le Pew, Penelope, Porky Pig, Elmer Fudd, Lola Bunny, Honey Bunny, Sylvester, Michigan J Frog, Duck Dodgers, Hippity Hopper, Gossamer, Mac n Tosh, K9, and all the other classic Cartoon characters!" Information on Disney, Pixar, and anime (Japanese animation) movies is also here.

PRODUCTS: Looney Tunes figurines, collectibles, T-shirts, magnets, watches, DVDs, and a whole lot more. One particularly odd product is the Ashton-Drake Galleries Tweety Touchdown Doll. "Catch the team spirit with Tweety's favorite cheerleader by Cindy McClure." Tweety never used pompoms!

VERDICT: While most of the classic characters on this site were very nostalgic, I still regret being reminded of Lola Bunny from the movie mockery *Space Jam*. We seem to notice a trend with basketball stars who try to act: disaster. Look at Shaquille O'Neal's films: *Kazaam* (Shaq is a rapping genie), and *Steel* (Shaq wears a bulletproof steel suit and uses a hammer to shoot lasers). Aside from the *Space Jam* references, BBB is a super site for animation information and products.

318 Demetri for President
www.demitrionline.com/president

"I know what you're thinking: This is another website for another presidential candidate." Yeah, only number 1,358,657. "But Demitri is not just any candidate. He is the World's Cutest Candidate, and he wants to be your president."

PRODUCTS: Five varieties of buttons, including the plain "Demetri for President: Big Enough for the Job," and "Vote Cute: Demetri for Prez 2004." There are also "special interest" group buttons. The picture shows Doctors for Demetri for America, but "doctors" can be replaced with a group of your choice, like "Cannibals," "Door-to-Door Salesmen," "Fat Americans," "Harlots," "Hicks," "Nudists," and "*Xanadu* Americans." Harlots? Hicks? Fat Americans? Demetri may be cute, but he isn't polite. I wanted a "Carrot Top Haters for Demetri" button.

VERDICT: What in the world are *Xanadu* Americans? Are they glowing Americans? Do they dance and sing while glowing? Are they on drugs (as the makers of *Xanadu* clearly were)? Thankfully, the products page looks to be a joke, so we needn't worry about seeing Demetri buttons everywhere. Besides, with the support of NIN (Nine Inch Nails) Fans and Cat People, he won't be getting my vote.

319 Flamethrowers
www.flamethrowers.com.au

Shooting flames from your car exhaust pipe may not be safe, but it sure is cool. "We have heaps of cool cars, hot rods, imports, trucks, and motorcycles with tailpipes blazing...Our flamethrower kits are guaranteed to give you optimal flames." "Optimal" sounds a bit lame. Why not "wicked," or "awesome," or "monstrous"?

PRODUCTS: The Flamethrower kits are $165 each. "Will this work on my car?" you may ask. "Our Flamethrower kits will work on any vehicle, car, motor bike, truck, [Japanese] import, hot rod, classic, or even just your standard family/get-around car." Now even soccer-mom minivans can be radical rides! But, the burning question (no pun intended) is, "Are they legal?" "There is no law against installing our flamethrower kit…(but) cops just don't like these things for some reason." Gee, I wonder why?

VERDICT: It says in the FAQ, "To be safe just don't go shooting big flames while you're driving around on public roads." So, I'm supposed to save this for a lonely, deserted, dry grassy field? Right. As Dr. Nick from the *Simpsons* said "Inflammable means flammable? What a country!"

320 Greek Gear
www.greekgear.com

This site is not a site celebrating Hellenic heritage. It is a site selling sorority and fraternity gear! "Our mission is and has always been to provide the easiest way for fraternity and sorority students to buy Greek merchandise on the web…We think the Internet ought to be fun and that shopping should be as fast and convenient as shopping for anything else on the Internet." The Internet is fun, not to mention weird and stupid. Why do you think you're reading this book?

PRODUCTS: If you're looking to expand your sorority or fraternity, try the "Recruitment Ideas" page, with megaphones, mini footballs, flip flop sandals, and glassware. For drinking soda pop, of course. There's also Christian Biker Gear, with a very, um, believable shirt: "Jesus would have been a biker." Right.

VERDICT: This site is very confusing. Their name is Greek Gear, where the Greek alphabet is the only thing Greek about fraternities and sororities; the site also sells Christian gear, which has little to do with these party-hearty organizations, and in the "non-Greek" section, they say they make products for other organizations! Puzzling purposes aside, Greek Gear is the perfect place to shop for customized fraternity and sorority gear.

- -

321 The National Smokejumpers Association
www.smokejumpers.com

This is the official site of the NSA. They don't specialize in fighting terrorism, nor do they keep us safe via a worldwide spy network. They do specialize in aerial firefighting. The National Smokejumper Association is the "keeper of the flame for smokejumpers and others associated with or interested in woodland firefighting." Keeper of the flame...I wonder if that pyrotechnic pun was intended?

PRODUCTS: NSA artwork, books, apparel, mugs, and belt buckles! The Antique Brass Belt Buckle sports "superior design quality with amazing detail from the feathers of the eagle to the rip stop of the parachute." Lots of people stare at belt buckles, so it's important to have a good one! Finally, for around $200, you can buy a ten-year NSA membership, which gives you access to employment information for those in search of a smokejumper position.

VERDICT: I wonder if anybody has confused the National Smokejumpers Association with the mysterious National Security Agency. There's a lot of other NSAs on the Internet, too: the National Speaker's Association, the National Society of Accountants, the Neptune Shopping Agency, the National Stuttering Association (really, that's a real site), all with the NSA abbreviation. Coincidence? I think not. Recruiting tools? Very well could be.

322 The Lifeguard Store
www.thelifeguardstore.com

Think a lifeguard's workplace is all supermodel women and guys with chiseled abs? *Baywatch*, this is not. "We can customize your staff, swim team, or school's uniforms with your own logo. Minimum orders apply. All artwork must be clean." So, no "Barb Wire: Best. Movie. Ever" swimsuits?

PRODUCTS: Swimwear, apparel, rescue equipment, and "miscellaneous" gear, which includes megaphones, swim diapers to "improve overall pool sanitation" (the very thought sends chills up my spine), and sandals and thongs! Thongs, as in, thong sandals. There won't be any C. J. Parker look-a-likes in skimpy swimsuits rescuing you anytime soon, guys. Also available from the "Fun and Games" section are pool basketball nets and volleyball nets! I'll take a break from providing vital pool safety supervision to play some aquatic volleyball!

VERDICT: Just as every female lifeguard wants to be C. J. (for her looks, anyway), I'd imagine every male lifeguard wants to be Mitch Buchannon. He's David Hasselhoff, for crying out loud! Master actor (*Knight Rider* was the best, admit it), producer, writer (he was the head for *Baywatch Nights*), and of course, a master singer. Who wants to be David Hasselhoff? Everybody. For the money, at least.

323 The Restless Mouse
www.therestlessmouse.zoovy.com

The Restless Mouse is another of the countless gag gifts stores, but that doesn't mean it's not chock full of cool products! From the Big Excuse Eightball to the annoying, yet entertaining laser pointer, there's tons of gag gifts here, ranging from nifty to downright bizarre.

PRODUCTS: While you can find the standard fake vomit and fart machines here, those are nothing compared to products like the eerily authentic Amazing Fake Hand. As the description says, the hands "are alarmingly real looking!" What uses do they have, though?

"Some of my dog trainer customers use these as dog training aids, that's how real they look." (I guess dogs don't care that they don't smell human?) All they need to care about is getting smacked when they eat your garbage or drink from the toilet. Another "delightful" product from the "Desktop Delights" is the St. Clare, Glowing Patron Saint of Television statue.

VERDICT: Once again, a staggering selection of stuff is the main strength of this site. From the Big Bathtub Battleship to the Amazing Fortune Telling Fish, you can find all your essential needs here. When you can have a backwards clock and '50s-style signs with phrases like "Let's party 'till we puke" on the same site, you know you can find something good.

324

Purina Deerchow
www.deerchow.com

"It's gotta be the deer chow!" Besides their standard varieties of Purina Dog Chow, Puppy Chow, and Cat Chow, Purina now offers the more, um, "exotic" deer chow! Why the sudden need for this unique feed formula? "Supplemental feeding can be the difference between an average deer or elk and the world's biggest deer." Feed them Deer Chow now so we can fatten them up to kill them and eat them later! What a concept!

PRODUCTS: Deerchow with Antlermax Technology! Antlermax is "a power-packed nutritional package with ideal amounts and ratios of vitamins and minerals for superior antler density and strength, optimum reproductive performance, and healthy young." Purina offers regular Deer Chow, Elk Chow, and Exotic Deer Chow, which is "An 18 percent-protein pelleted ration uniquely tailored to the needs of exotic and non-native deer such as Red, Fallow, Sika, and Axis deer." Red and Axis deer: the favorite deer of totalitarian dictators!

VERDICT: Why settle for za puny, girly deer when we can "pump them up" with Deer Chow? Once they have massive muscles and loads of fat, then we can terminate zhem with our heavy-duty weaponry (just like Ahnuld terminated Gray Davis), and now, we have delicious venison to eat, so we can pump ourselves up! Hasta la vista, deery!

325

1-800-Porcelain
www.1-800-porcelain.com

Two hundred sixty years of quality porcelain production for this St. Petersburg business! "The Lomonosov Porcelain factory, founded in 1744 by Emperor Peter the Great, is one of the oldest and most famous manufacturers in Russia." Peter the Great was also known for taxing Russian beards, horse collars, and bee hives.

PRODUCTS: 1-800-Porcelain is "known world-wide for marvelous, high quality, and unique products." Like any other company, that "world-wide" recognition means some major money is needed to shop here. This site offers over a dozen different porcelain styles, Including Golden Garden, Lotus, Cherries, Snow Flakes, and Winding Twig. A three-piece Winding Twig tea set is $34, whereas a full twenty-two piece tea set is $319. Who knew precious porcelain was so expensive? If you think that's bad, try the company's most well-recognized set, the Cobalt Net Full Set: $1,592! You could get a used car for that!

VERDICT: You'd think that the Lomonsov Porcelain company would find a better domain name than 1-800-Porcelain. Phone service aside, 1-800-Porcelain does have quality (although expensive) porcelain.

326

Rejection Line
www.rejectionline.com

"Someone won't leave you alone? Give them your number: (212) 479-7990: The official New York rejection line!" That's right! If that annoying guy won't stop hitting on you, just give him that number and he'll be dumped by a rejection line "specialist."

PRODUCTS: The Rejection Line's current featured product is the limited edition Rejection Specialist mug. It's insulting, offensive, AND dishwasher safe! There are also products with the words, "ask me 4 my #," and the "Rejectionline.com," with a smiling, elderly lady wearing a headset. I'd picture an official New York rejection specialist as a woman with an annoying, Fran-Drescher-like New York accent, not a sweet grandma (see number 209 for *The Nanny* star's official website).

VERDICT: If you want to tell off that annoying guy, girl, or businessman without getting nasty, the Rejection Line provides a convenient, impersonal slap in the face for those losers. Don't forget also that "The Rejection Line is hiring! We are seeking creative, ambitious, motivated individuals to join our team." If your "ambitions" involve insulting desperate losers, the Rejection Line may be your dream job!

327   Youth of Britain
www.youthofbritain.com/yobsite.swf

This is not a British youth group, as the name suggests. Rather, the YOB "make music and visuals for a generation force fed a diet of bull****." Yeah, like this site. I never wanted this, but it's what I get for writing about weird sites. When you click on sections like "'oo are we?" and "'ooky videos," you get a strange audio rendition of the section's name. Isn't our language called "English" for a reason? This site explains that "If you have heard the music and had at least one of the resulting emotions: [one] A cheeky head nod, [two] smiled in agreement to lyrical content, [three] thought to yourself, yeah man, wicked…then chances are you have been infected already with…YOB attitude." I'm not infected! Thank goodness!

PRODUCTS: The YOB shirt, with "YOB" and a monarchial crown. The cost of this bloody weird shirt is 10 pounds, but "remember, it will be twenty-eight days to delivery." That long? You can also buy the YOB EP (extended play), which is described by Amato Direct.co.uk as a "satirical musical rollercoaster ride through the Britain we know, love, and hate." I don't like roller coasters, and I don't like this site either.

VERDICT: If this is a British website, why the .com abbreviation? It's not a true British site if it's not ".co.uk." And where is the bad dental hygiene and the tea and crumpets? Despite the American domain name, YOB is a weird site for a weird band.

328

Off Road.com
www.off-road.com

At Off-Road.com, "The Off-Road Lifestyle Awaits You!" While I'm not going out of my way for the "off-road lifestyle," this site paves the way for those who'd rather pave their own road. How big is Off-Road.com? "NASCAR.com is the single biggest motorsports site on the Net, and they're about three times bigger than we are. We're Number Two, and no one else is even close." We're Number Two! We're second best! We're the first in a long line of losers!

PRODUCTS: In the store, you can find ORC decals, professional photograph prints, off-road posters, T-shirts, and the *Monkey Butt* book, by Rick Sieman. Where the heck did they get the amazingly crude name? This book is smartly advertised as "a book you will be proud to display on the back of any toilet tank…(Because, let's face it, the wife is NOT going to let you leave it on the coffee table)." I wonder why?

VERDICT: It's odd that SUVs are touted as "off-road" vehicles, while most people use them for "navigating" large cities, or "adventuring" on quiet, suburban roads. Sure, they're horribly inefficient with fuel, and you'll probably never go off of a paved road with one, but they're such "rugged," cool-looking vehicles! The Off Road store is for true ATV and dirt bike fanatics, not those wannabe suburban SUV sissies.

329

Mean Kitty
www.meankitty.com

"Are you tired of sappy websites where owners post sweet kitty antics?" Yes! "While cutiepie sites have their place, do you know in your heart of hearts that kitties are not at all sweet?" Yes, yes! "Well, this is the place for kitty antics that are *not* so cute, the place where the real face of kitty is revealed. This is…Meankitty.com." Yes, yes, yes! This site has tons of pictures of cats looking mean, angry, or just plain evil! Finally, these nasty, ferocious feline furballs can be seen for what they really are!

PRODUCTS: Coasters, shirts, mousepads, mugs, hats, stickers, and postcards with the phrase "I love my mean kitty." I don't love "mean" anything! Especially not cats! The plain "Meankitty" logo comes with a suspiciously sinister cat picture.

VERDICT: As somebody who doesn't like cats a lot (one too many have given me that fearsome hiss), this site agreed with me on one level; that cats are angry a lot of times. But the folks at Mean Kitty seem content in putting up with the amazing anger of their cats. The things we put with from our animal friends.

330

Blythe
www.thisisblythe.com

Blythe is a doll created by Kenner toys back in 1972. Unfortunately "children found the large eyes that changed from green to pink to blue to orange with the pull of the drawstring at the back of Blythe's head a bit on the scary side." So Blythe was only made for one year. In 1997, a photographer named Gina Garan got hold of a Blythe doll, and while circling the world, took pictures of Blythe in all sorts of exotic locales. These pictures were made into a book that took the world by storm.

PRODUCTS: Everyone needs an eleven by fourteen print of this mutant headed doll. Only $325, plus shipping and handling, of course. Or accessorize your Blythe with a new hat for only "$11 (from $14.99)—pink, orange and white patterned visor." What a value. With Blythe's huge head, the hat has tons more fabric than your typical Barbie doll hat. What I found most troubling was the thong-like "original orange Blythe undies! In used condition." Used underwear? The site also has a forum where you can buy and sell "parts" like the "eye discs" that make Blythe's eyes change color. Trading in doll organs? What has this world come to?

VERDICT: Ahhh, the Japanese. The folks who gave us the Walkman, Pokemon, and Nintendo now give us a revival of an ugly, scary malformed moppet of a doll. If that's what eating with chopsticks does to your brain, I'll take my knife and fork anyday.

331 **Andean Gun Accessories**
www.andean-inc.com

I'm trigger happy, baby! Andean, Inc. is a company in the business of providing accessories for lethal firearms. They have a superb selection for dozens of different firearm types, including Glock, Colt, AR-15, Beretta, Remington, Winchester, Mossberg, and even the AK-47! Doesn't everybody need an automatic rifle to defend themselves from sadistic serial killers?

PRODUCTS: Bipods, tripods, flashlights, knives, magazines, lasers (to be sure that when you pull the trigger, your target dies!), and everything else to provide you with maximum firepower. For shooting in style, you can also buy gun jewelry, with sterling silver and gold pins in the shape of your favorite deadly weaponry. And what gun site would be complete without targets to shoot at? Not only standard paper targets, but also targets in the shape of turkeys and woodchucks. How much wood can this woodchuck chuck? None, because he's dead!

VERDICT: Finally, a site supporting the much-neglected Second Amendment. Our forefathers gave us the right to freedom of speech, freedom of religion, and the freedom to own lethal weapons! Celebrate your right to own a firearm by indulging yourself at Andean Firearms.

- -

332 **Cat and Girl**
www.catandgirl.com

Cat and Girl is a collection of extremely alternative comics. The *Cat and Girl* comics have appeared in the magazines *Flashbang*, *Sex* (a Swedish magazine, of course), *Grasslimb*, and *B**ch*. They sound very conventional, don't they? One comic has a cat person who "reduces himself to two dimensions" in famous paintings to "question Capitalism's two-dimensional linear view of progress" while uniting the paintings under the common theme of himself. Okay…

PRODUCTS: Very strange, ultra-alternative hats, stickers, and T-shirts, like the Iceland Tee, with the phrase "Kotter og Stulka" which is

Icelandic for (what else?) Cat and Girl. The shirt has a cat person and a girl in a Viking helmet sailing in a boat. The shirt is "Packed with blatantly stereotypical Viking action for extra super value." Think that's weird? Try the Mice in Space Tee, which has mice in a UFO "Fleeing environmental destruction and nuclear proliferation," while "seek[ing] asylum on a planet made of cheese."

VERDICT: Does alternative have to mean weird? Look at magazines like *Pretty Ugly* (number 174) and now the *Cat and Girl* comic and you'll get your answer. These comics prove that if you see a publication that makes you question the sanity of its makers, it's always classified under "alternative."

333   Shrunken Heads
www.shrunkenheads.com

Shrunken Heads get its name from a South American tribal practice of cutting off the heads of slain enemy warriors, mutilating them, and sticking them through the head of a spear. Such a nice tradition, isn't it? Rubber shrunken heads were popular in the '50s, '60s, and '70s among bikers of the time period. Now, they're back, and you can own your own shrunken head without going through the hassle of killing a rival tribal warrior!

PRODUCTS: Car accessories, T-shirts, novelties, videos, and music. One nifty novelty on this site is the Hula Gumby wobbler, featuring the famous claymation star wearing a hilarious hula skirt and playing a Hawaiian guitar. What about the other Gumby stars, Pokey the pony, Prickle the dinosaur, Goo the, um, flying gooey thing? The car accessories section has a wide selection of products. One irresistible item is the Rat Fink antenna ball, a "hot rod icon." The "icon" looks more like the green slime monster from *Ghostbusters* than anything resembling a rat. Or a fink.

VERDICT: While the selection of retro car accessories is extensive, I didn't need the unpleasant images derived from the "Shrunken Head" story section. Anything involving decapitated heads is not pleasant food for thought. However if you want an authentic shrunken head for your hog or ride, this is the place to be.

334

Stockings HQ
www.stockingshq.com

There's nothing better than a high quality stocking! Stocking HQ provides not only a stocking store, but stocking chat and discussion as well! I love putting on a sock over my foot, let's chat about it! Here, you can find discussion forums on everything from the "outfits/sightings forum" (I've spotted an unidentified flying stocking!), to the disgustingly disturbing "male stocking issues."

PRODUCTS: "Sheer Temptation" is the name of this stocking shop (I'm tempted to stop writing this and get as far away as possible). One featured section on my unfortunate visit was the Levee Ultra-Large Stockings and Hold ups. "At last! Someone who takes very large sizes seriously!" Yeah, seriously disgusting! The "Girdles and Shape Wear" section has products like the Rago 1361 six-strap zip contour open bottom girdle. "It's available in white or black in sizes up to 5XL!" 5XL? Is that even conceivable?

VERDICT: Even with sometimes somewhat attractive pictures of women wearing undergarments, shopping at this store is not a pleasant experience for men. I've already gone through this terrorizing torture, but that doesn't mean you have to. If you somehow stumble across this sick site, turn off your computer and run.

335

Shaddow Domain
www.shaddowdomain.com

The Shaddow Domain is "a store where dark and silly can scamper together in freakish harmony. If you like us, please pass the word along. We freaks have to stick together. If you don't like us, please let us know why. We want to be your supplier for the best dark merchandise." The only thing you'll be "supplying" me with is a desire to do whatever is necessary to purge this site from my memory. Believe it or not, this is a family-run site! "We're not exactly what you'd call the 'Average American Family,' obviously, but we have the love and perseverance to make this work. The family that scares together, stays together!"

PRODUCTS: Buy the Pile of Skulls night light. Need I say more? Or the Hypodermic Pen, which is "so realistic looking, strangers will be asking you for medical advice. It even writes in red!" For your Goth cosmetic needs, see the Manic Panic Semi Permanent Hair Color Raven Black, guaranteed to help you wallow in dark-haired abject misery and enjoy every minute of it. But wait, if black is the "obvious color," why do they have the Manic Panic Goth White face cream and powder? How terribly confusing.

VERDICT: This site is horrible, dark, disgusting, miserable, and disturbing. And you'll love every minute of it. The "Kids Stuff" section is perfect for raising your child to be that dark, pessimistic, black-clothes-loving, sun-fearing adult you'll be proud to call your own. If you're looking for a family-friendly Goth site, you've found it in the Shaddow Domain.

336   Roo Poo Company

www.roopooco.com

What better gift than kangaroo crap? "The world's most unique and unusual...gifts...from down under. Lovingly crafted from raw materials harvested in the outback from contented kangaroos." There's also a "word of warning" saying nothing on this site is "weird" or "freaky." The "word of warning" also contains very liberal use of the "s" word. Why the gratuitous profanity? "Believe us, we'd much rather use the word poo (like Disney does?), but it just doesn't work as well."

PRODUCTS: Kangaroo poo, koala feces, and even Tasmanian devil dung products. Their flagship product is a jar of pure, unaltered roo poo. "Kangaroo poo comes straight from the producer to you...250 ml presentation jars of genuine dried kangaroo poo nuggets direct from the outback. They're attractively labeled with a description of contents." Using the word "attractive" in describing excrement is just plain sick. There are also poo paperweights, and even poo earrings. Ugh...I'm gonna be sick.

VERDICT: This site is so repulsive, it makes dealing with telemarketers a pleasant experience. Giving a gift from Roo Doo to a friend or relative is without a doubt the ultimate in offensive gift giving. This online trip down under is revolting, repulsive, and should be avoided at all costs.

337

Luna Click
www.lunaclick.com

Luna Click is home to "Grandma's Revenge" and the "Muppet Liberation Front." Grandma's Revenge harkens that "The days that grandmothers played bingo and baked apple pie are over!" Okay, whatever. If you click on "Yo Momma," you'll discover the Muppet Liberation Front. "Every day thousands of hand puppets get killed to satisfy man's need for fashionable and retard[ed] looking gear. The slaughter of our childhood heros must end! NOW!" The MLF page shows celebrities wearing fuzzy clothing reminiscent of the fabric used to make Jim Henson's famous puppet troupe. Very frightening, and not just for the "slaughter" of Kermit and his friends.

PRODUCTS: "Scare your grandma (but watch out! They never get mad, they get even.), pet mouse, and postman with these Lunaclick goodies!" This store offers apparel, housewares, and bags with the Lunaclick logo: a cartoon face with a bad haircut and a Jay-Leno-sized chin. There's also a jersey with the phrase, "Don't look now, but you're being followed!" Hopefully, not by these lunatics.

VERDICT: Lunaclick sounds like Lunatic for a reason: whoever created this twisted site must be a raving maniac. As if Che Hamstera and his comrades at the Hamster Liberation Front (number 120) weren't weird enough, we've got another radical liberation front aimed at stopping Muppets from being made into fur coats. The lunacy never ends at Lunaclick.com.

338

The Straight Dope
www.straightdope.com

The Straight Dope: "Fighting Ignorance since 1973 (It's Taking Longer Than We Thought)." It certainly is. TSD provides answers to unusual questions, like, "Why do you seldom see sugar cubes in restaurants anymore?" The simple answer is that sugar packets are less expensive to make, but some restaurants still offer cubes because "they're considered more elegant." Also, some people prefer cubes because "sucking on them is an indescribable rush." Who needs illegal drugs when you've got packets raw sugar?

PRODUCTS: The Official Straight Dope T-shirt, bearing "Slug Signorino's favorite likeness of Cecil—he calls it 'Stupidity, I Smack Thy Face.'" Referring to the thin, pasty legs in the picture, the description says, "Actually, Cecil's legs are not quite this bad, and he threw out those polka-dot boxer shorts many years ago." Good thing. Also available is the Teeming Millions coffee mug, which contains TSD's motto of "Fighting Ignorance…" Unfortunately, if you live in Illinois, there is an 8.75 percent sales tax. That's what you get for living in "Bears Country"!

VERDICT: If the Straight Dope's mission is to fight ignorance, they're either going to go on forever or give up on changing the irreversible trend of growing ignorance in this country. I'm betting on the latter. Nevertheless, if you're looking for interesting stories and products to raise your level of competence in the field of trivial knowledge, TSD is the place to go.

339

Fork You
fork-you.com

"There is no spoon." People who have seen the hit movie *The Matrix* will remember this quote. In this case, "There is no fork." Fork You contains step by step instructions on how to "soften up" forks with your mind, then easily bend them using your hands. Despite the fact that this is sheer nonsense, the creator of this site is quite adamant about the fact that it's possible. "I admit it is weirdness of the highest order, but it's weirdness that is very real. Everyday people can do it, which is why I'm so amazed it's still controversial." Sounds confident, no?

PRODUCTS: This store sells Fork You clothing and housewares, with the phrase "Get Bent!" and a picture of the individual prongs of a fork bent and twisted into weird shapes.

VERDICT: I'm not crazy enough to try and see if this works. If, by some incredibly remote chance, there is a shred of truth to this site, then good for the people who have the power to deform perfectly good forks. True or not, this site is useless and weird. And thus, it's a perfect addition to this book.

340

Car Busters
www.carbusters.ecn.cz

Who ya gonna call? When you hate cars, that is. The Car Busters, of course! Car Busters is a resource center for "the grassroots global car-free movement." You've got a long way to go before people ditch their BMWs and Escalades for bikes and walking, guys. You can learn about World Car-Free Day, and you can even get information on a program called Autoholics Anonymous, which "admittedly…seems amusing at first, but…is intended to be totally serious." What is "intended" and what is reality are two very different things.

PRODUCTS: Buy subscriptions to the *Car Busters* magazine, a resource for alternatives to cars. There are also books like *Asphalt Nation: How the Automobile Took Over America and How We Can Take It Back*. This book is a "powerful examination" of how cars have "ravaged" America over the past one hundred years, along with the usual blah-blah-blah about how we don't need cars, there are better alternatives, etc. Car-Free bike stickers can be bought instead of the usual bumper stickers.

VERDICT: Let's face it: the world is just too big to get by on bicycles and walking. How are people supposed to commute to their jobs or Wal-Mart or the grocery store? Not all communities have everything within walking distance. Car Busters is an example of zealots with unrealistic expectations trying to force us to change an integral part of our daily lives.

341

Air Sickness Bags
www.airsicknessbags.com

Air sickness bags: convenient barf depositories, or works of art? " Some barf bags are no more than a baggie with a twist tie, while other sickbags could win international design competitions. Are they art? I think so. You decide." From the common Delta Airlines barf bags to the rarer Newt Gingrich Barf Bag (the former speaker of the house does have a tendency to induce nausea), there are tons of barf bag designs from all around the world. But it's not just air sickness bags you'll find here; you can find bus sickness bags, train sickness bags, and even computer barf bags.

PRODUCTS: The ASB poster, with over two dozen varieties of barf bags on the poster, along with their origin and year of inception. The bag designs include a McDonald's bag (I'm not loving that), a vomiting reindeer, a drawing of a dog, and the appropriate frowning face. I'd be just as sick when using these bags as I'm getting right now from looking at them.

VERDICT: Not only is the sheer notion of collecting these nauseating souvenirs absurd, but the sight of them is enough to make you want to puke. Unless you like feeling sick enough to vomit, you'd best stay away from this barf bag museum.

342

Dull Men
www.dullmen.com

The Dull Men Club is "A place—in cyberspace—where Dull Men can share thoughts and experiences, free from pressures to be 'in and trendy,' free instead to enjoy the simple, ordinary things of everyday life." Sounds like a plan to me! A "Monthly Events" calendar provides recommended activities, like "Napping Month." Occasionally, the "monthly itinerary" will have events to avoid, such as the World Cow Chip Throwing Contest, or the Snake Hunt.

PRODUCTS: The DMC T-shirt, mug, and hats, available for men and women. The "prototype" DMC mug is shown for the heck of it, but it was decided that the finished product wouldn't be in red (way too exciting, of course), but rather a "stunning gray." Gray is plain, simple, and boring; it's perfect! The ladies' caps section includes the Californian. The demand was high to make this hat hot pink, but of course, "Hot pink is not a color for dull men...We took a hot pink cap and gave it a washed-out look. The result is very attractive (we are tickled pink with it)."

VERDICT: As somebody who prefers plain vanilla ice cream over Rocky Road and long quiet walks over noisy parties, this site almost got me excited. Sure, you may think we're more boring than a Yanni concert, but we Dull Men like it that way.

343

Reality Shifters
realityshifters.com

Reality Shifters is home to the book *Aura Advantage*, by Cynthia Sue Larson, who is a "Bioenergy field researcher." This glowing appellation makes her sound more like a physics professor than a certified New Age nutcase.

PRODUCTS: "Play the eighty-minute *Aura Healing Meditation* CD any time you wish to reduce stress, enhance your energy field, improve your health, and increase your effectiveness." None out of four ain't bad. There's also the novel *Karen Kimball & the Dream Weaver's Web*. "It combines the mystery of a Nancy Drew with the metaphysical daring-do of a Harry Potter book—all into one. And it succeeds." If it's so great, how come it's not a bestseller? Perhaps Larson's negative aura is influencing her book sales.

VERDICT: Until I see a scientific study proving the existence of this "aura," I'm not jumping any hurdles to improve mine. While I do believe that some "guided relaxation" is helpful in reducing stress, I'd rather confront the issues in my life head-on than retreat into this wacky world of "positive auras" and "enhanced energy fields." However, Reality Shifters does generate some "positive vibes" for those seeking an easy escape from reality.

344

The Museum of Unnatural Mystery
www.unmuseum.org

The Museum of Unnatural Mystery is a site founded by Lee Krystek, whose mission is to "explore the fringe edges of science and at the same time use those subjects to get people interested in the more mundane aspects of scientific work... The world wide web provided a medium that was affordable enough for him to realize his dream." That's the beauty and bane of the Internet: anybody can have a website about anything.

PRODUCTS: The MUM store has "assembled what we consider the best books, videos, games, gadgets, and magazine subscriptions on unnatural and scientific subjects." How good are the "best"? Consider the *Usborne World of the Unknown: UFO's* by Ted Wilding White. Intended for children ages six to ten, the book "Includes articles on famous UFO incidents, hoaxes, disc-shaped aircraft, and making your own fake flying saucer photos." Making your own fake flying saucer photo? Such valuable and ethical lessons that books are teaching children these days.

VERDICT: So Mr. Krystek's mission has now been realized, thanks once again to our new friend, the Internet. The Internet, for better or worse, provides a voice for everybody, and the MUM provides a voice for a more logical approach to the paranormal. The real wonder of the Internet, though? It's tax-free! Take that, Infernal Revenue Service!

345 The Museum of Hoaxes
www.museumofhoaxes.com

Naturally, you'll find a ton of information on UFOs, the Loch Ness Monster, Bigfoot, ghosts, and psychic psychos here. That's because they all have one thing in common, the answer to most "unexplainable" phenomena: IT'S FAKE! They have a "gullibility test," a series of challenges for you to make the call as to their authenticity. One photo test contains photos of a deer going through a windshield (real), George W. Bush reading a children's book upside-down (obviously a hoax by a liberal Bush-hater), and a disgusting photo that shows "Michael Jackson's nose disintegrating." You guessed it: real.

PRODUCTS: Shirts, mugs, and stickers with phrases like, "Buy Striped Paint: Sold Exclusively at the Museum of Hoaxes." You can also buy products relating to the famous Jackalope hoax. The I Brake for Jackalopes sticker and Save the Jackalope T-shirt are the available testaments to this famous joke.

VERDICT: The Museum of Hoaxes reminds us how deceptive our world can be, especially in today's age of the "super-information highway," aka the Internet. The moral here is that more often than not (Jacko and California are an exception), if it seems too outrageous to be true, it probably belongs on this site.

346 Contortion Homepage
www.contortionhomepage.com

This page isn't just weird, it's downright gross. "Welcome to a special place on the net. Here, we shall celebrate those who take their physical abilities to the highest levels." "The highest level" apparently means the ability to become a human rubberband. The pictures you'll see here are downright scary; seeing somebody putting their head between their legs is truly a chilling and disgusting experience. Training information is available should you want to become one of these flexible freaks, as well as a photo section guaranteed to make you shudder.

PRODUCTS: DVDs and videos featuring exercises to increase your flexibility. The DVDs are "edited to contain the best footage of active flexibility training." Best? You mean grossest? Sickest? Most disturbing? You can also buy the *Classic Films* DVD, which "contains over one hour of historic performances and still photos from the dawn of the home-movie era." One hour of home movies featuring human Stretch Armstrongs. Wonderful.

VERDICT: Do you like seeing people twist their bodies into positions that make them look like true freaks? If you are a fan of the "art" known as contortionism, then you're free to wallow in the freakish glory that you'll find here. Any normal person will be scarred for life by visiting this sadistically strange site.

347 Happy Balls
www.happyballs.com

They're balls, and they're happy! Antenna balls, that is! Happy Balls is "the premier source for your antenna ball needs!" "Premier" translates into "we think we're the best," if this book is any indication. Every kind of ball is here, from the very popular Smiley Face balls to skulls, aliens, helmets from famous racers like Dale Earnhardt Jr. and Jeff Gordon, and the unsettling clown balls.

PRODUCTS: Some of the most interesting balls aren't even ball-shaped! The Star Flag ball, the Gary the Snail ball (the pet snail from the mega-popular cartoon *Spongebob Squarepants*), and the Lil Homie ball bear no resemblance to balls. The Lil Homie ball is a regular face with a goatee and a beanie pulled down over his eyes. He's supposed to be a "phat gangsta," or something similarly confusing, but he just looks stupid. The best balls are, naturally, the *Simpsons* balls, featuring Homer, Bart, Blinky the three-eyed fish, and the extremely dimwitted and extremely hilarious Ralph Wiggum.

VERDICT: If you like your car to be an attention grabber on the world, a visit to Happy Balls may be in order. I hope your visit to this site makes you as happy as the balls here are.

348 City Morgue Gift Shop
www.citymorguegiftshop.com

This is another site selling gifts having to do with death, the undead, skeletons, and the like. With a lighthearted and caviler attitude, of course. An example of this attitude is in the "Celebrity Cemetery," with a long list of any dead celebrity you can think of. Click on their name and you can see a picture of their gravestone! Elvis, JFK, John Wayne, even Sonny Bono! His former partner Cher isn't dead yet. However, considering her bizarre behavior, I wouldn't be surprised if she is really a zombie and starts looking for brains to feast on.

PRODUCTS: Apparel, toys and games, bobbleheads, and collectibles with a death theme. The featured product on my visit was the Munster Family Wacky Wobbler set. Another product that's "to die for" is the Tophat Lighter, a chrome lighter with a skull, wearing a top hat and smoking a cigar. The cost is five bucks, without the fuel, of course, so we don't have to worry about our mail being burnt to a crisp.

VERDICT: It seems society is becoming more accepting of death as a natural part of life. Now, we've got stores like the Funeral Depot (number 301) advertising low prices instead of "we're sorry for your loss," and now the CMGS with its death-themed gifts and its "celebrity cemetery." Our once morbid obsession with death has now become a mere sales pitch.

349

The Toilet Museum
www.toiletmuseum.com

If you're seeking descriptions and pictures of old, historic, antique toilets, you've come to the wrong place. If you're looking for meaningless pictures of plain, ordinary toilets, then this is definitely the right place! How did this museum of sanitation apparatuses come into being? "In 1982, my old roommate, Ed, suggested that we collect pictures of toilets and hang them in our bathroom. Now, Ed has left for a bathroom in the suburbs, but I'm still here, keeping the dream alive." Sounds like Ed made a smarter choice by moving on, away from this ridiculous "dream."

PRODUCTS: Books for adults and kids, as well as videos, CDs, toiletware, and posters. Some of the incredibly inappropriate books include *I Have to Go*, *The Scoop on Poop*, *The Gas we Pass*, and *Everyone Poops*. Of *Everyone Poops*, an Amazon editorial review says, "poop by any name seems an unsuitable picture book subject." Gee, you think?

VERDICT: Using the term "museum" in describing this site is a gross overstatement of its quality. It's more like a "disgusting toilet-picture gallery." The products are also, appropriately, a load of crap. This site is so bad, you can almost smell the shame.

350

The Toaster Museum Foundation
www.toaster.org

This site "pops" you straight into the history of those wonderful toasters! The TMF states that toasters reflect "the history of twentieth century cultural trends and industrial design." The less ridiculous answer is that toasters are "are fascinating, funky, and fun, demonstrate the better side of human ingenuity, and simply uplift one's spirits!" A machine that browns bread is the "better side of human ingenuity"? What about nuclear medicine, or computers? The museum features "exhibits" on toaster art, toaster toys, and toaster ads.

PRODUCTS: The usual apparel, housewares, and stickers with tons of toaster logos, including a diagram with toaster parts, separate logos with a man and a girl holding toasters, and women's T-shirts with the word "toast" sandwiched between two pieces of toast. If you see the shirt, you'll see how suggestive this image really is. Finally, there's the "I Love Toast" store, because "if you like toasters, you probably love toast!" Ya think?

VERDICT: It seems there's a museum for everything on the Internet. There are museums on toilets (number 349), famous hoaxes (number 345), and even sideshow freaks (number 128)! Why not toasters?

351 Bush or Chimp?
www.bushorchimp.com

By the name, this site does not mean that George W. Bush is dumber than a chimp. Nor is it implying that a chimp could make a better president (although James Carville believes that is so). As this site maker proclaims: "I'm not a member of any political party, and I have nothing in particular against the man. I just think he kind of looks like a chimpanzee." And, in a way, he does! This site shows several comparison photos in which GWB bears a striking resemblance to a chimpanzee.

PRODUCTS: BOC T-shirts, with about a dozen different comparison photos showing GWB making facial gestures, along with a chimp showing a similar gesture. There is also the Crouching Bush, Hidden Chimp shirt, showing a spoofed movie poster of *Crouching Tiger, Hidden Dragon*, along with a disturbing phrase by a woman named "Kathy," saying, "I love your website. I want BushorChimp.com to father my children." I want you to get help!

VERDICT: Nobody can deny GWB's resemblance to chimps, based on evidence here. The real question is, is Bush smarter than a chimp? Let's see, he graduated from Yale, he was governor for eight years in Texas, and he became president shortly after. On an interesting note, the bottom of the BOC page, there is a quip about how "Several of you out there have been emailing and signing in the guest book about how it is cruel to the chimps to compare them to George W. Bush."

352

Wisconsin Cheese and Cheeseheads
www.wisconsincheese.com

You may think Wisconsin is a really cheesy state. And you'd be right! We Wisconsinites like our weather freezing cold, our diets hearty and full of bratwurst and beer (none of those "salad-and-water" diets they have out in California), and, of course, our cheese cheesy! If you're one of those misguided Minnesota, Illinois, or Michigan folks (football fans know what I'm talking about), you'd best turn back now; this site may be a little too cheesy for the likes of you. If you're proud of your cheesiness, however, you'll find a great variety of Wisconsin gear (including genuine Cheeseheads), and of course, a prime selection of cheeses.

PRODUCTS: Wisconsin apparel, bobbleheads and collectibles, "over forty varieties of Wisconsin cheese," and of course, Packer and Badger gear. This site offers vacuum-sealed cheese and cheese baskets, as well as books on our great state. And what other book for Wisconsin than the *Tailgate Cookbook*, with tips on "Tail Gate Cooking Green Bay Packer Style." Speaking of the "Green and Gold," this site has a prime selection of Packer products, including ice scrapers, bobbleheads, mousepads, bumper stickers, and anything else to help you mount a "Pack Attack" wherever you go.

VERDICT: Of course I liked this store, as I'm a born and bred Wisconsinite, and always will be. The question is: can you readers in other states understand our fierce state pride, while being consumed in worship of your own pathetic state? Probably not. For Wisconsinites at heart, though, WisconsinCheese.com is a must visit.

353

The Bumper Dumper
www.bumperdumper.com

The Bumper Dumper: a place for things that go on the rear end. Of your vehicle! The Bumper Dumper is a toilet seat you can mount on an empty trailer hitch on the back your vehicle. Once you find a spot where you're certain nobody will see you (good luck), simply do your business and all the yucky stuff will go into a bag or bucket below the toilet seat. "Whether you are a hunter, fisherman, camper, or off-roader, the Bumper Dumper is a great item for all outdoor enthusiasts."

PRODUCTS: The Bumper Dumper can also be bought as a "stand alone" unit, letting you lean the frame against a tree. Finally, don't forget the "Bumper Dumper" T-shirts, featuring a front image with a toilet mounted on the back bumper. The back image shows a very, um, "sophisticated" family, waiting in line to use the Bumper Dumper.

VERDICT: So, I'm supposed to park my car in a remote forest, then do my business on the back end of my car? I could also stomp barefooted on broken glass, or get my legs waxed, but you don't see me doing that, now do you? I'll take the smelliest roadside rest stop over this disgusting device.

354

Mullet Junkie
www.mulletjunky.com

The makers of Mullet Junkie are more tonsorial scientists than fans of an extremely ugly haircut. Their mission is to hunt down, classify, and capture (in photo form) the various species of these horrendous haircut wearers.

PRODUCTS: Shirts, sweatshirts, and hats, like the "I Love Mullets" shirt, and the Mullet Junkies shirt. For those who don't have mullets but are still avid hunters, there's the Mullet Hunter sweatshirt. "With this new subtle design, the mullet probably won't see that you are a hunter, therefore making the hunt much easier (and safer)." I think it's the mullet wearers who are in danger: if some stranger were taking pictures of me, I wouldn't feel so safe.

VERDICT: We've all seen a mullet out in public. But for those on a mission to hunt these hairstyles in the name of science, this site is essential. As pointed out, the hunt can be dangerous in the natural habitats of these beasts. But once you view the extensive number of species cataloged here, you'll appreciate their efforts. If you want to become a hunter, or if you're one of the herd and want to show your pride, Mullet Junkie is an invaluable resource.

355

Patty Wack
www.pattywack.com

"Welcome all to my brand new twisted little playground." And twisted it is! You are greeted by a cartoon "host," wearing a suede blazer and a fez on his head. The rest of this site is a strange collection of photos under the headings "Oddities" and "Themepark Fashions." Photos show strange images, followed by a fittingly strange comment by the host. There's a picture of a jacket, along with the phrase, "Some wear diamonds, some wear pearls, but very few can pull off bird crap!" Wow, isn't that just hilarious!

PRODUCTS: The store's selection is very slim and very boring: mugs and mousepads with the Patty Wack logo, a '50s-style cartoon with the aforementioned host and a martini-style Tiki toothpick with an olive through it. Not very exciting.

VERDICT: I cannot imagine what kind of person would find this stupid stuff remotely amusing. It's like somebody snapped photos of random people at a zoo and thought they could pass as humor. Well, they're dry, disgusting, and more painful than a Whitney Houston song at a karaoke bar on amateur night. Don't expect a barrel of laughs at this website.

356

Killer Fonts
www.killerfonts.com

"What better way to let your boss know your true feelings than by resigning with the help of Lizzie Borden? How else would you confess ardent feelings about corporate takeover than through the script of Jesse James? And everyone will know you mean business when Jack the Ripper writes your cover letters." Yes! Now, you too can "enlist the most notorious psychopaths" of this century to help write letters, books, and birthday cards! This site has won a plethora of awards as well, including the "Cool Site of the Hour" from Cool Central.com, a web pick by thegist.com, and a pick by "The Blonde Ambition Hitlist." I could be on her hit list anytime!

PRODUCTS: Handwriting fonts from killers, dead presidents, dictators, brainiacs, cowboys and many more historical greats! Each font contains a small biography of the famous person, along with a sample of the font as it will appear on your computer. Take the case of famous serial killer "Jack the Ripper." He terrorized London in 1888 by killing and mutilating nearly a dozen women. Well, now Jack's legacy lives: on your computer!

VERDICT: Killer Fonts offers fascinating fonts at psychotically low prices! Now you can make masterpieces with Edgar Allen Poe's handwriting, or write stick up notes in the style of John Dillinger! If you're looking for an interesting font or two to spruce up your Word documents, you'll be pleased by Killer Fonts.

357 Ghost Village
www.ghostvillage.com

Here we have yet another "serious paranormal research" site. "Whether you are a ghost hunter, spirit photographer, you want to see ghost pictures, or you're interested in a true ghost story, Ghostvillage.com has something to offer you." "Spirit Photographers" sound like they belong on "Reality Shifters" (number 343), photographing auras or "bioenergy fields."

PRODUCTS: Shirts, hats, and mousepads, some with a Halloween-style picture of a ghost. They're "serious ghost hunters," but their logo looks like a guy with a sheet over his head. Go figure. There's also the I Saw a Ghost T-shirt, with a pair of evil ghost eyes on the back of the shirt. I've seen a ghost, too: on *Scooby Doo*. Finally, there are links to buy *The World's Most Haunted Places: From the Secret Files of Ghostvillage.com*. Yeah, the secretly fake files.

VERDICT: You already know what I think about ghosts and the paranormal and UFOs and whatnot, so I'm leaving you to judge the contents on Ghost Village for yourself. If you're the "the truth is out there," "we are not alone," "aliens killed JFK" kind of person, then you'll have a ball at Ghost Village. If not, well then you know what to do: click, close, and don't look back.

"Dinosaur kangaroos spotted in Chile!" "One-hundred-five-pound woman eats thirty-eight lobsters in record time!" What other place than the *Fortean Times*, a magazine printing news and research on "strange phenomena and experiences, curiosities, prodigies, and portents." The magazine was founded in honor of Charles Fort, an early twentieth century author whose accomplishments include "coin[ing] the term 'teleportation' and…perhaps [being] the first to speculate that mysterious lights seen in the sky might be craft from outer space." So, we have Fort to thank for cheesy, poorly done science fiction movies?

PRODUCTS: T-shirts, with the classic *Fortean Times* logo, the logo with a portrait of Charles Fort, and the Hierophant shirt. A Hierophant is defined as one who interprets arcane and sacred knowledge, but the picture has a man sitting under what looks like something you'd find in a futuristic hair salon.

VERDICT: The condensed biography of Charles Fort portrays him as a science fiction author who obviously had trouble distinguishing his own weird works from reality. However, without him, we would have never had *Star Trek*, *Star Wars*, or *Plan 9 from Outer Space*! Talk about being influential! In all seriousness, though, the Fortean Times is nothing more than another wacky, Internet tabloid on the paranormal.

359

The Banana Club
www.bananaclub.com

The International Banana Club and Museum is described as a "worldwide membership bunch," founded by Ken Bannister, T. B. (Top Banana)." The "Top Banana" is a native Californian who handed out banana stickers at photo conventions. The Banana Club has its own Banana Museum in Altadena with "seventeen thousand items known to all!" I wish they weren't known to me.

PRODUCTS: You can buy membership in the Banana Club for a measly ten bucks (plus $2 S&H). For this, you get "the EXCLUSIVE RIGHT TO EARN B.M.s (Banana Merits, you sickos) and get two degrees in Bananistry." Just be careful when you tell your friends that you've earned B.M.s. The "Master of Bananistry" and the "Doctorate in Bananistry," both "get you a medal and neck ribbon everyone will ask about! They look like Olympic medals!"

VERDICT: Joining the Banana Club is as useless as becoming a stamp collector, or joining a Britney Spears fan club. If you want to earn B.M.s (I can't possibly imagine why), or if you just want a little medal that can almost pass as a real sports award, then feel free to waste your money to join this corny club.

360

Empty Bowl
www.emptybowl.com

Who knew there was an extensive community dedicated to critiquing cereal? At Empty Bowl "you'll find reviews, feature articles, and general discussions about the greatest breakfast product on the face of the earth: cereal!" The greatest breakfast product? What about omelets, pancakes, and Belgian waffles? This site has an extensive archive of cereal reviews, including rare limited-time specials like the *Star Wars: Episode 2* cereal (please, no Jar-Jar marshmallows), and the *Powerpuff Girls* cereal. According to the review, *Powerpuff Girls* cereal is akin to eating "Rice Krispies and lollipop shavings."

PRODUCTS: Apparel, house wares, and stickers with phrases like "We take our cereal ceriously" (ah, the classic intentional misspelling), "We eat more cereal by 8 a.m. than most people eat all day" (that's not something to be proud of), "We are living in a cereal world and I am a cereal girl" (a quote from a classic *Sesame Street* parody of Madonna's "Material Girl").

VERDICT: If you're also a "cereal girl" (or "cereal guy"), and you're looking for some merchandise to show your passion for puffs or your fervor for flakes, this site can definitely satisfy your tastes. You won't find a better web resource on cereals than what's available at Empty Bowl.

361

Aunt Linda is the owner of a toy store and founder of the "National McDonald's Collector's Club." "Linda was the club's first president, then became the secretary, vice president and became president again. Now she is the president of the Great Lakes Chapter." Quite a tumultuous transition, huh?

PRODUCTS: Happy Meal toys are available in either MIP ("Mint in Package"), or L for loose, out-of-package toys (all, in other words, worthless). Available toys include the Duck Quacker Coder from the 1988 Disney *Duck Tails 1*, the Baby Piggy: the Living Doll from the 1988 Storybook *Muppet Babies* ("Living" and "Doll" do NOT belong together), and the Double Agent Watch from the 2001 *Spy Kids 2* series. You can also buy the 2004 Hamburglar Card Game, which contains instructions in English, Spanish, and French! El Bandito Hamburgesa!

VERDICT: I don't understand collectors. Their lives are centered around hunting down every single action figure; doll, cereal box, game, whatever, and they keep it in its original packaging. It's never used; it just becomes another decoration in a room full of outdated merchandise. If you've already taken the path of the collector, however, or are just looking for an old McDonald's toy, Aunt Linda can help you satisfy your collector's itch.

362

The Ultra Lounge
www.ultralounge.com

Ultra Lounge is home to "twenty-six volumes of the greatest music on Earth!" If you consider lounge music "the greatest music on Earth," that is. This site contains a large section with instructions for making cocktails as well, including a Black Velvet, Cuban Apricot, a Zombie, and of course, the James Bond Martini. Shaken, not stirred, Mr. Bond? How else may I assist you in stopping sinister super-villains bent on world domination?

PRODUCTS: The Ultra Lounge albums, with such snazzy titles as *Cocktails with Cole Porter*, *Vegas, Baby*, *Mambo Fever*, *Organs in Orbit*, and *Saxophobia*. *Saxophobia* contains many memorable tunes, like "Watermelon Man" by King Curtis, "I Dig" by Les Baxter, and "Goldfinger" by Count Basie and his Orchestra. You can also buy the standard apparel, house wares, and stickers with several '50s-style logos.

VERDICT: While I do find lounge music kind of interesting, I wouldn't want to listen to a whole album of it. It's like classical music, or Jackie Chan movies: okay in small doses, but less is so much more (*Rush Hour*, yes; *The Tuxedo*, no). If you dig this era of cultural music, though, Ultra Lounge is a swingin' place to be.

363 Ripley's Believe It or Not
www.ripleys.com

Believe it or not, this site is full of strange items and even stranger people. Videos at the "Odditorium" include the classic Fire Eater, along with the Eye Smoker, a man who can smoke a pipe through his eye, and the Human Plank, a man who can drive six inch spikes into his nose. You can also download computer wallpaper with a two-headed sheep, and take a look at the history of Ripley and his weird, wacky works.

PRODUCTS: Books, games, and other strange products. The "Miscellaneous" section features products such as Humpback Hits, Ripley's MagiCube, and Ripley's Giant Ring. "You can own a 'GIANT' ring designed for Johann Petursson, the Icelandic Giant who at 8' 4" was once billed as 'the World's Tallest Man.'" There's also a Ripley's board game, where players are given a fact and asked whether they "believe it or not." How about this one: $27,000 was spent on a government study to investigate why inmates want to escape from prison. Believe it. That's our tax dollars hard at work.

VERDICT: Ripley's is a combination of sideshow freaks, mutated animals, and people or animals with unusual skills. This is Ripley's biggest strength, as well as its biggest weakness. Some people will be amused, others will just see it as another glorified freak show. Ripley's is not about believing it or not, but liking this collection of freaks, or not.

364

Pets or Food
www.petsorfood.com

Have a hankering for some hamster? Do you salivate over seal? Do you find feral cats finger-lickin' good? Than Pets or Food is the place for you! Pets or Food is "dedicated to bringing together people and animals." Advertising themselves as humanists, Pets or Food is on a mission to "take in homeless animals and rehabilitate them to fulfill their destinies as either loving family companions or nutritious, protein rich meat supplements to those going without." We find them a home, or we eat them! What a philosophy!

PRODUCTS: There's the very expensive, but very tasty (hopefully) Komodo Dragon meat, available now for ONE HUNDRED THOUSAND dollars! Talk about premium cut! And this site offers rare Dodo Bird meat! After a biologist discovered a dodo crèche in a chain of islands off Brazil, he successfully bred the bird an entered into an "exclusive distribution arrangement" with Pets or Food. Now you can take "this incredible opportunity to discover the taste that led to the Dodo's extinction!" Right. Sure.

VERDICT: Despite a full purchasing interface with a shopping cart, it's obvious this site is a joke. They even have the nerve to ask you for your credit card number if you go far enough! Don't let this demented scam fool you; any site that offers extinct and endangered animals as food can't be good news.

365

Moon Shine Shades
www.moonshineshades.com

It's the 50s all over again! Looking for that retro lamp accessory that is just to die for? You'll find it at Moon Shine Shades, a Texas company that it clearly going back to the future. If you need a shade, a lamp, furniture, or even a screen door insert with a bucking bronco or cactus pattern, look no further.

PRODUCTS: Boomerang shaped tables, funky parts for making hanging lights, lighting sconces, and of course, lampshade parts and lampshades.

Round, square, oval, and rectangular shades. Shades with funky colors like "nicotine" and "chartreuse." Shades with patterns like "Orbit" and "Atomic," and my personal favorites: printed shades with images of Dancing Hula girls and mobile trailer homes.

VERDICT: This site is like squaresville, man. It is definitely stuck in a time warp, but a pretty neat time warp at that. I can't wait to order my "bowling pin" rectangular lampshade in aqua! Like most of the sites in this book, Moon Shine Shades fills a niche. Maybe it's a niche that should have remained unfilled, but a niche it is.

366

Circlemakers
www.circlemakers.org

This site is proof positive that there is a conspiracy afoot, that sinister forces are at work behind the mysterious phenomena known as crop circles. That is, if you consider pranksters with wooden boards attached to their feet a "sinister conspiracy." Circlemakers.org is a site where you can learn more about this fascinating community and learn how to make your own "genuine, dowsable, scientifically proven un-hoaxable circles patterns." So, I can learn how to destroy hundreds of dollars worth of crops, and let aliens and UFOs take responsibility for it? Cool.

PRODUCTS: At the "Consume" Circle Makers store, you can buy the official Circle Makers T-shirt, now available in "skinny" T-shirts, "for all the female circle makers out there." Hey, I dig a girl who's an expert in crop circle creation. Don't you, guys? If you're looking to get into the circle-making scene yourself, check out the limited edition *Beginner's Guide to Crop Circle Making*, a book "you won't find on amazon.com!" Really?

VERDICT: Maybe they should make a movie about circle makers, in a *Mission: Impossible* style format! Working by night, using sophisticated equipment (night vision and 2X4s), avoiding detection, all essential elements of the classic spy movie! Of course, you'd need the blonde bombshell, a pseudo-nerdy circle-making babe, and an evil G-man from the agricultural department bent on stopping our hoaxing heroes. But, ah, what could have been.

367

Michigan Lawsuit Abuse Watch
www.mlaw.org

We've all seen the classic abuse of the essential American right to sue whoever we want: the woman who spilled hot coffee from McDonald's on her lap, the guy who put his RV on cruise control and left the wheel, the toaster pastry that burnt down a house, all useless wastes of our tax dollars on a judicial system gone wild. The MLAW is dedicated to stopping these ridiculous suits. This site has a bevy of information on "Loony Lawsuits," "Wacky Warning Labels," and the "Whiplash Awards."

PRODUCTS: The bookstore has a number of essential books on the sheer idiocy and lunacy of America's stupidest court cases. Books include *The Case Against Lawyers*, by Court TV host and former judge Catherine Crier (everybody has a case against lawyers; even lawyers hate lawyers), *Buy this Book...or We'll Sue You!* by Laura B. Benko and Attila Benko, and *Whiplash! America's Most Frivolous Lawsuits*, by James Percelay.

VERDICT: You will like this site, or I'll sue you. You will like this book, or I'll sue you. If you tell me that Carrot Top's 1-800-CALLATT commercials are entertaining, I'll sue you. If you don't tell everybody that the lawsuits on this site are truly stupid examples of how ridiculous our court system is, I'll sue you. I have lawyers, and I'm prepared to use them!

368

LA Avenue
www.laavenue.com

Web Cams are the ultimate in entertainment. They've allowed us to watch corn grow, see moose grazing (number 203), and try our hand at spotting ghosts in "haunted" buildings. Now, you can see beautiful California from the LA Avenue web cam! An energy technician named Nick runs the web cam. Nick mounted a camera on his van and leaves it running by day so we can see where his job takes him in the colorful streets of Los Angeles. The camera is indeed live, and we get to see palm trees, shopping malls, gas stations, traffic jams, and other extremely exciting vistas.

PRODUCTS: Adult T-shirts, tank tops, and toddler shirts with a stylish design that would make Abercrombie and Fitch envious. Unlike that over-priced designer store, however (you pay for the name, not the clothing), the shirts here only cost ten bucks! But wait, why are the adult T-shirts and the toddler T-shirts the same price? Wouldn't the toddler tees be much cheaper to produce? Perhaps a baby boycott is in order; let's show them the power that the toddlers of America have in the marketplace!

VERDICT: Isn't this tech-savvy filmographer worried that someone will steal his web cam? Perhaps if the thief had the wits to keep the camera running, we'd see life in LA from a criminal's point of view! If it got big enough, it could become a new reality TV show, like *Criminal Eye for the Civil Guy*! If you prefer traffic lights and stop signs over car-jackings and vandalism, however, here's your chance to support this incredibly boring web cam.

369   Torture Museum
www.torturamuseum.com

This site is sick, barbaric, excruciatingly painful, and incredibly cool! This site covers "European Instruments of Torture and Capital Punishment," from the Middle Ages to today. European Instruments of Torture? You mean the Spice Girls? The site has an extensive political statement about how torture devices are inhumane, sickening, comparable to techno music, etc. The "Gallery" contains such infamous torture devices as the Inquisitional Chair (a chair covered with sharp spikes), the Iron Maiden, and the Heretic's Fork.

PRODUCTS: The book *Tortura Inquisizione Pena Di Morte*, by Aldo Migliorini. The title translates into *Torture Inquisition Capital Punishment*, for those not adept in Italian. Available not only in Italian, but English and Spanish! Now we can get a lesson in abominable instruments of pain in Español, or Italiano! Aye, no me gusto!

VERDICT: These devices are nothing compared to Rob Schneider movies. I mean, *The Animal? Deuce Bigalow: Male Gigalow? The Hot Chick?* Could anybody stand five minutes of those without permanent psychological damage? If you're looking to learn more about older, less effective instruments of torture, however, the Torture Museum is an interesting, yet painful learning experience.

370   I Want One of Those

www.iwantoneofthose.com

This site may be the ultimate in consumer driven honesty. Their motto? "Stuff you don't need…but you really, really want." And, by golly, they're right. This site has loads of incredibly cool, yet ultimately frivolous, expensive, and impractical stuff. Your disposable income will be quite quickly disposed of if you linger too long at this cornucopia of crazy products.

PRODUCTS: An inflatable Sumo suit to make you look like a two-ton Japanese wrestler. "Undoubtedly the most stupid—and therefore the best—costume in the world." A personal hovercraft, the Hov Pod is available for just under fifteen thousand pounds sterling. If you're in the market for a more "classy" gift, get the Humping Dog, a mechanical statute of a human leg with a cute little dog, well, ummm, humping the leg. That perfect gift for that perfect someone.

VERDICT: Wow. I just spent an hour at I Want One Of Those, and gee, is my wallet empty. I bought a Whirlpool Coffee Cup, some Exploding Golf Balls, and a Remote Controlled Fart Machine. Now I can't pay the rent or afford to buy food, but I really, really wanted that stuff!!!

371   Ses Carny

www.sescarny.com

You may say, "All those sideshow freaks are obviously fake; nobody can swallow a sword." Well, the Ses Carny sideshow is "New England's only 100 percent <u>real</u> Circus Sideshow & Human Freakshow…Years of performing and professional training have created one of the most hardcore, death defying circus sideshows you'll ever see." Despite this "hardcore" attitude, Ses Carny insists that they can offer "Fun For the Whole Family!" How can you show a human dartboard in a family friendly way?

PRODUCTS: The Ses Carny Sideshow T-shirt, with the back listing the various acts of the Ses Carny sideshow: Fish Eyes, Glass Eating, and the painful, yet alluring Bed of Nails. There's also the Ses Carny Feel the Pain bumper sticker (pain is something people generally avoid, isn't it?), and the Ses Carny Autographed Eight by Ten Human Blockhead Picture, with a rather repulsive face, made all the worse by the nail jammed into his nose. So much for "fun for the whole family," huh?

VERDICT: If you want to see this perverse exhibition of freaks by yourself, go ahead. But please, don't subject any young children to the disgusting images you'll see on this site and in this show. Exposing a developing mind to this is almost as bad as letting them watch *Big Brother* unsupervised.

372   Rock and Roll Bad Boy
www.rockandrollbadboy.com

Who wants to rock and roll every night, and party for all the day? This guy. "We have seen the future of Rock and Roll, and its name is Brett Meisner!" Not surprisingly, this quote comes from Brett Meisner. Features on this "bad boy's" site include a "Meisner 101 Hollywood Survival Guide," and the "Hard Truth," listing the "10 UNDENIABLE TRUTHS OF ROCK MUSIC." These truths include "Music does not sound better on pot" (true, despite what some loser stoners think), "Rap Music is a Passing Fad" (let's hope so!), "MTV Ruined Rock Music" (MTV ruined a lot of things, rock and roll included), and "The CIA Killed Jimi Hendrix, Janis Joplin, and Jim Morrison" (when does a crazy conspiracy theory count as a rock and roll truism?).

PRODUCTS: "Money, So They Say, Is the Root of All Evil Today." Pink Floyd fans will know that one, but the truism of this phrase doesn't seem to bother Meisner, or anybody else in America. There's a side wallet (also known affectionately as a fanny pack), custom photo and a license plate frames reading, "Mess with the bull, get the horns!" What do aggressive bovines have to do with being a "Rock and Roll Bad Boy"?

VERDICT: Brett Meisner is obviously in denial of the fact that most will see him as a loser. However, this is one loser I sympathize with. He's a rare breed in these days of rap, pop, techno, and all those other sad excuses for music. Smart and tasteful music fans will agree with most of the "undeniable truths" here (excluding the wacky murder conspiracy theory).

373

Valley of the Geeks
www.valleyofthegeeks.com

Valley of the Geeks, of course, refers to California's Silicon Valley, the cradle of the technology behind today's computer age. "Valley of the Geeks is an award-winning, non-commercial, satirical website I work on when I'm not busy with my full-time job in a Silicon Valley startup company or training for a marathon." He's an athletic geek! "Where else but in Silicon Valley could you have guys like Phillipe Kahn having a Toga Party at Comdex, Larry Ellison buying a Russian MiG jet fighter?" Sounds like the valley is one weird, overindulgent, geeky corporate community!

PRODUCTS: Apparel, hats, stickers, and postcards that "make great gifts and also subsidize the cost of running the website." If you're really in a charitable mood, though, this site encourages sending "small unmarked bills." Riiiiiight. The shirts have tech geek acronyms, which at times can be a foreign language to those who aren't as smart and geeky as we are (notice the "we" there).

VERDICT: It should be obvious to the reader that I am as comfortable at this site as I am among my own kind. You must understand, we geeks are a complex breed: our social conversations are governed by foreign technical terms. FYI, I'd be ROFLMBO if I were watching a Will Ferrell film. Yes, I'm JK, so DMY. True geeks will definitely find a home here at VOTG.

374

Iced Out Gear
www.icedoutgear.com

Are you down with Iced Out Gear? This store is here to sell you genuine "bling-bling," much like Pimp Hats (number 69). Why buy IOG? Check out the "We Are Legit" section, to see that IOG ain't foolin' ya. Four young hip-hop fans were trying to find a legit place to get some hip-hop clothing and jewelry." Since no other place offered reasonable prices on "bling-bling," much less "bomb" customer service, IOG was born, and now they the hizzie-shizzie! Whatever that means.

PRODUCTS: Scope out the wide selection of "bling" in the "Check it" section. The selection here includes name belts, custom "pimp cups," accessories, and the "ladies section." Some selections for all the fine, foxy ladies out there include the Pink band/White bubble face ELITE watch, a watch with a pink band and a shiny sliver surface. Finally, there's the Shoe Spinners, which are shiny plastic circles that can be attached to shoes.

VERDICT: This site is just sad. As many of the products here are below $50, I'd imagine that a genuine "playa" would see right through this. Then again, I'm somebody who wouldn't care whether I was wearing Calvin Klein jeans or Wal-Mart jeans. Whatever's cheaper. However, even I can see that this site is for wannabes.

375

Child Calm
www.childcalm.com

It's the safe sedating inhalant! Child Calm "helps quiet restlessness, promotes restful sleep, tames tantrums, and eases tension." Sounds like a cure-all for hyperactive children! How does it work? "Lavender and chamomile plant oils contain naturally occurring soothing properties. These...bring a calming effect as they are breathed in." There's a personal story by the founder of Child Calm, explaining how his hyper-activeness as a child made him feel miserable, embarrassed, rejected, blah blah blah. So, when he got older, he invented Child Calm to help "save every kid from the kind of experiences I went through." So, a sedating inhalant is his contribution to society. Sounds like he really made a mark!

PRODUCTS: Child Calm comes in a mist and in an oil form. The mist can be used in a child's room, as well as on pajamas, pillowcases, sheets, and in cars. The oil can be placed in a ceramic cup or tissue so it can diffuse into the air. Still not convinced of the calming power of Child Calm? Check out the obligatory "testimonials" section. G. M. of Illinois says, "When my four-year-old begins to whine or melt down, I spray 'fairy dust' on her to calm her. She loves it!"

VERDICT: I always saw aromatherapy as a softie entrée into the world of inhalants. Sure, now your child is settling down with Child Calm, but don't be surprised when your adhesives and paints start disappearing a few years from now.

376

Manties
www.manties.net

"Panties are for the gals; MANties are for the guys!" Manties are "for those nights and days when you want to be and feel a little special, naughty, and very sexy." This is already creeping me out. "Once you try a pair, you will wonder why you never tried them before." I'm NEVER trying these unholy underpants!

PRODUCTS: This site gets even more disgusting as you browse their selection. Lace and Bows, Fancy, and Embroidered Manties are available in brief and hi-cut varieties. Feeling sick, yet? It gets worse. MUCH worse. The Seven-Day hi-cut and brief Manties are "designed to replicate the quality and look of vintage yesteryear, while also incorporating modern designs, so you get the best of both worlds all rolled up into one." This description also implies that these revolting undergarments were around in the '60s and '70s. Our society hasn't evolved much in terms of dignity.

VERDICT: These are sick. These are disgusting. These are disturbing. These are just wrong. My lifelong mission will now be to purge this sick site from my memory, forever. If you have any interest in these, these...THINGS, then you should seek some help, NOW.

377

Monkey Phone Call
www.monkeyphonecall.com

This service charges ten dollars to call people and imitate a monkey. Really. This is what they do. "Monkeyphonecall.com offers realistic Monkey Phone Calls for people in the United States!" How realistic? "With MonkeyPhoneCall.com you get a professional call, not a cheap imitation!" "Professionals" paid to act like monkeys on the phone? I'd hate to see the "cheap imitation"!

PRODUCTS: First, read what people are saying about this unique phone service. Jon H. of Austin, TX says it was "The best $10 I ever spent!"

The "Sucksters," an online e-zine, proclaim that "After three decades, its very own market bubble, and untold billions of hours of deferred personal hygiene, the Internet has finally fulfilled its original promise: putting you in verbal contact with someone making monkey noises." I thought the original promise involved credit to its great creator, Al Gore?

VERDICT: Ten dollars for some practical jokester to call you and act like a monkey? There's so many other ways to spend ten dollars: a movie ticket, a funny T-shirt (like the hundreds in this book), ten double cheeseburgers from McDonald's! If you wish for a "professional" monkey imitation, however, Monkey Phone Call.com can indulge you in your wacky wish. But for ten dollars, you can do better. Or, do it yourself.

378 Stop Staring Clothing
www.stopstaringclothing.com

"Hello kittens, and welcome to Stop Staring. Here you will find the coolest and sexiest clothing inspired by the '40s and '50s." Kittens? Hardcore feminists would probably shut this site down just for calling women "kittens." Comparing a cute woman to a lazy animal that licks itself and coughs up hairballs if very offensive!

PRODUCTS: The Red Polka Dot Swing (a hideous polka-dot dress), the Black Swing dress (not to be confused with the more figure-hugging Black-Fitted dress), and the Chocolate A-Line dress (which truly makes the model wearing it look like a Hershey's bar, how delicious) are all stylish selections from the "Betty Collection." The "Separate" section includes sure-fire fashions like the 1950s Red Bathing Suit (a truly modest swimsuit compared to the skimpy, albeit supremely superior skin showing suits of today), and the Leopard Outfit ("abominable" is the only word to properly describe this outfit).

VERDICT: Women: do you want to look like the stereotypical oppressed housewife of the '40s and '50s? Do you enjoy wearing plaid, polka dot, and country rose dresses? Do you want to look totally unattractive to the opposite sex? If you answered yes, then Stop Staring can truly deliver on its promise: nobody will want to stare at you, except to chuckle at your truly tasteless clothing.

379

Cops
www.tvcops.com

The "Bad Boys" are coming for you…on DVD, that is! Drunks, druggies, robbers, violent husbands, they're all here, with an FAQ and reports of incidents from recent episodes. One arrest includes a man who was caught with methamphetamines in his pocket. He then asks to speak to his mother before going to jail, who then "lovingly reprimands him and demands that he gets his life together." I'm sure my mother would "lovingly" reprimand me if I was caught with illegal stimulant drugs!

PRODUCTS: Three DVDs of intense *Cops* action are available. If you buy the *Cops: Caught in the Act* DVD, you'll get "dangerous take-downs, high speed pursuits, [and] adrenaline-charged confrontations" that will "leave you breathless." Think that's exciting? Then you haven't seen the *Bad Girls* DVD, with "a very unladylike assortment of feisty, foolish female suspects who prove they can be every bit as bad as the boys." Who else but FOX could be such an equal opportunity insulter?

VERDICT: Remember, "all suspects are innocent until proven guilty in the court of law." Even if they're caught on film resisting arrest or in possession of drugs, they're still innocent? The corrupt justice system aside, *Cops* is still a great show filled with the dark humor on life on America's crime-ridden streets.

380

Zapato Productions Intradimensional
www.zapatopi.net

"Amazing discoveries," "important theories," "life-enriching tools," and other "frivolous diversions" are what you can find on Zapato Products Intradimensional, along with a load of senseless, bizarre, and clearly fictional stories. The brainchild of Lyle Zapato, this stuff is farther out than Ann Heche's psychotic-induced outer-space adventure. Remember: "you should browse through [the site] many times, as some content is only accessible in the fourth dimension." But I can only access the fifth dimension! They're being "dimension-discriminatory."

PRODUCTS: The definitive guide to the Aluminum Deflector Beanie, which can also be found in the original 505 (number 12). This device is "all the budding paranoid needs to know how to fight the nefarious forces of mind control." You got the "budding paranoid" part right. Along with these deviously deranged devices are T-shirts and mugs allowing to support the "endangered tree octopus" and the "Republic of Cascadia," a state designed to be free from government propaganda.

VERDICT: This site is an obvious joke. The conspiracy-theory parts employ incredibly dumb "safety" devices: tinfoil hats and fly swatters are not sufficient to resist the government's evil agenda to brainwash us. This site may be right about some things (i.e., all PBS programs employ some form of brainwashing), most everything is a twisted figment of Lyle Zapato's imagination.

381

Hot Lix
www.hotlix.com

Have a craving for cricket candy? Do you desire the sweet taste of worms? Hot Lix specializes in exotic snacks, some with dead insects inside. In fact, Hot Lix is so popular, it has "surpassed our expectations for acceptance, perhaps due to the increased demand for insects as food." How good are these insect confections? *Playboy* says, "the worms taste really good." *Forbes* says it's an "ideal conversation starter." And, Philip Caruso of *Newsweek* says that the worm pops are "the rage in California." Only in California.

PRODUCTS: Insect candy and liquor, as well as Chili Lix, for "a little bit hotter lix." You can "fulfill a burning desire" with Chili Lix, cinnamon-flavored lollipops with chili peppers in the center. For the "sissies," there's also Cinnamon Lickers, which are Chili Lix without the chili. In the "Not Lix" section, you can find T-shirts and mugs available to order with the Hot Lix lip logo.

VERDICT: Exotic foods are far from favorites of mine. I prefer strawberry lollipops, perhaps from bank deposit canisters (who said they were just for kids?). And eating insects is just plain gross. Then again, you might enjoy indulging in these exotic treats, and if so, you can't get more exotic than Hot Lix.

382

The Museum of Jurassic Technology
www.mjt.org

This is one weird museum. The mission of the Museum of Jurassic technology is somewhat ambiguous. The MJT "traces its origins to this period when many of the important collections of today were beginning to take form. Many exhibits…were, in fact, formally part of other less well-known collections and were subsequently consolidated into the single collection which we have come to know as the Museum of Jurassic Technology."

PRODUCTS: The MJT store was established by the Society for the Diffusion of Useful Information. The philosophy of the bookstore is as follows: "The rarest and most precious knowledge is not that which is imposed, but rather, that which is absorbed, inhaled almost, from the ephemeral substance of the world in which we are contained." Huh? Duh….museum no make sense me to. The museum store sells books, "commemorative china," apparel, and of course, membership.

VERDICT: This museum is weirder than the Troll Forest (number 165), or Zoltron (number 189). Their purposes are about as clear as a Monty Python film. If you can decipher the mission of this mad museum, then you're either a history nut or just a regular nut.

383

Horse Balls
www.horseballs.com

Horse Balls is dedicated to keeping horses and other animals happy. How do they want to do this? By selling a ball-shaped horse toy, of course! "Give your horse a Horseball and he will nose it, kick it, pick it up by the handle and toss it, run and play with it." Not only is this creative device entertaining, but also "a healthy way to channel a horse's energy." The benefit of "therapeutic recreation" is that horses will not develop bad habits, like destroying screens, doors, stalls, and fences. So, if I don't buy a horse ball, my horse is going to break down my fence? An effective scare tactic is afoot here.

PRODUCTS: The Eggbutt horse ball comes in seven colors, four of them with their own unique scents! Now your horses can have balls that smell like sugar cookies, molasses, peppermint, or maple! There's also the Horse Balls T-shirt, with the rather naughty phrase, "Let me show you my horse balls." An animal toy retailer taking advantage of the suggestive nature of their name? What has happened to this once innocent market?

VERDICT: Horse balls can be great fun even if you don't have a horse. And, since horse balls come in four different scents, we humans can spend hours sniffing the alluring aromas of horse balls! Hey, it worked for Scratch and Sniff stickers and scented markers. Why not an equine recreational tool?

384   Banana Guard
www.bananaguard.com

They say, "necessity is the mother of invention." That certainly wasn't the case when they invented Banana Guard. But, if you're "fed up with bringing bananas to work or school only to find them bruised and squashed," then Banana Guard may be your savior. Designed to "fit the vast majority of bananas" (you're discriminating against the banana minority!), the Banana Guard has features like ventilation perforations to prevent "premature ripening," and a "sturdy locking mechanism" so your banana stays safe.

PRODUCTS: Banana Guard is available in Ravishing Red, Outrageous Orange, Mellow Yellow (also a refreshing lemon-lime soda and a popular psychedelic song by Donovan), Sublime Green, Skyhigh and Brilliant Blue, Passionate Purple, Pretty in Pink (this Banana Guard variety certainly isn't pretty), and the ever-so-necessary Glow in the Dark banana guard. Does every blatantly unnecessary product have to be available in Glow in the Dark?

VERDICT: Banana Guard is overpriced, mainly because it is so utterly useless for anything besides transporting bananas. What else are you going to need a Banana Guard for? Perhaps they'd be good for shipping bananas to monkeys in the zoo (monkeys are bananas about bananas), but otherwise five dollars is extremely exorbitant for a single purpose banana carrier.

385 Milo's Tongue
www.milostongue.com

Milo's Tongue is a site dedicated to the tongue of a Chihuahua named Milo. This site encourages you to come in and "not be intimidated by [Milo's] beauty." Beauty is the last thing I'd associate with this hideous canine tongue. The photos on this site come in three ratings: "Cute" photos are presented with the obvious assumption that some people won't find anything about Milo cute, but nevertheless "present Milo's tongue in a completely tasteful manner." Doesn't help, since this site is tasteless to begin with. The "Twisted" category is "slightly more 'in your face' than the previous category." Finally, "Anti-Cute" photos are "Suitable for those of you who hate cute." I don't hate cute, I hate this dumb dog's disgusting tongue!

PRODUCTS: Magnets, mugs, and T-shirts with Milo and his tongue. All products have a picture of Milo with his tongue hanging out, saying, "Believe it." I believe it, if "it" is the fact that this site is revolting, offensive, and just plain gross.

VERDICT: Milo's Tongue is the most revolting body part on a living creature since Jay Leno's chin, John Goodman's gut, or anything about Hillary Clinton. Although tongues are meant to taste things, it's obvious this site is completely tasteless. Milo's tongue is like staring into the sun: very, very, harmful for your eyes.

386 Hamster for President
www.hamsterforpresident.com

Potus, a hamster bearing the name of the acronym for "president of the United States," is "gentle and harmless," and if elected promises to "run on his wheel all night, sleep all day, and let you, the voters, govern yourselves." What a novel concept! This site contains the campaign plan, Potus's platform on various issues, and a "qualifications" section, which is essentially a slam on every Republican of this century, combined with the usual blab on being cute, a la Demetri (number 318).

PRODUCTS: Hamster for President puzzles, coffee mugs, sweatshirts, and mousepads (why not hamsterpads?). No Potus gear is available yet, but you can buy the 2000 Vote Ms. Ganjette gear, with the cute hamster who ran that year (like a million other Internet candidates), and the phrase, "Better than the alternatives."

VERDICT: The "for presidents" site type seems to be quite popular, along with the "church of" type and the "museum" type. We've had Demetri (number 318), Mike the Headless Chicken (number 105), and now a hamster. So many presidential candidates, so few serious politicians to endorse them. So sad for Potus and his Internet rivals.

387   Dog Horoscopes
www.doghoroscopes.com

Presented by the Mystic Dog Newf, president of the Canine Astrological Society, Dog Horoscopes offers weekly horoscopes for dogs, as well as special birthday and compatibility sections. You can also see the "Sir Loin Tips" page, with dog care tips by Sir Loin, a graduate of "Bowser University" with a degree in "Puppyism" and a Master's Degree from Cambridge University in "Dogma." Cambridge always did have such low standards. Most of the tips are no-brainers, especially "Dogs shouldn't be given as presents, or to children under the age of five," and "Never name your dog after a living relative." DUH!!!

PRODUCTS: A plethora of books on pet psychology, including *The Rosetta Bone: The Key to Communication Between Humans and Canines* by Cheryl Smith, and *Doga: Yoga for Dogs*, by Jennifer Brilliant and William Berloni. *Doga* is described on Amazon.com as telling the story of how "Dogis Benny, Buster, and Cricket practiced in obscurity for years, perfecting their dogic principles." Practice how? Scratching themselves and fetching sticks? Revealing you inner butt sniffer?

VERDICT: Despite the appreciated spiritual attention for Man's Best Friend, Dog Horoscopes' bookstore is largely useless. If you want to know what the stars have in store for your pooch, though, you've found a sign at Dog Horoscopes.

388

Pursuit Watch
www.pursuitwatch.com

Tired of relying on reruns of *World's Wildest Police Chases* for your need for high-speed pursuits? Pursuit Watch is the premier Internet service for people who have felt as though they've "missed out on something" in missing a high-octane, high-adrenaline genuine police chase. According to the "Info" section, "Our members get the biggest kick out of this one-of-kind service that alerts you by phone, cell-phone, numeric and alphanumeric pagers, or by email when a chase is broadcast live on TV in your region."

PRODUCTS: You can try a sixty-day trial of Pursuit Watch for free! After that, it's $4.95 per month. There are a few catches, however. You can't view Pursuit Watch unless you have a satellite with Los Angeles feed, which leaves non-Californian cable users out in the cold. Also, "Some chases only last for a few minutes, while others last hours. We put out our pages as soon as TV coverage begins, and so we don't know how long it may last. Usually by the time a news helicopter gets over the scene, the pursuit has already gone on for quite some time." What a ripoff!

VERDICT: If only Pursuit Watch was around when the blood-pumping White Bronco chase captured the nation! True, it was 35 MPH for most of the way, and OJ's run from the law didn't result in any jail time.

389

Infiltration
www.infiltration.org

Cue the *Mission: Impossible* theme, this time for you! Infiltration "offers a mix of the practice and theory of urban exploration in areas not designed for public usage." Whether you're a budding burglar or just want to be James Bond, Infiltration can help you infiltrate boats, abandoned sites, drains and catacombs (I know I have a local catacomb network I infiltrate regularly), hotels and hospitals, and much more.

PRODUCTS: Subscribe to the *Infiltration* magazine! Infiltration can teach you "the art of urban exploration, a sort of interior tourism that allows the curious-minded to discover behind-the-scenes sights and have a lot of free fun." Sneaking into museums and construction sites is interior tourism? Infiltration is full of "editorials, exploring advice and information, articles on recent expeditions, and interviews, all illustrated with maps, pictures, and diagrams."

VERDICT: I'm sure the authorities wouldn't mind you sneaking into restricted areas and private properties after reading this magazine. So what if it's "restricted" or "private" or has an ominous "Don't Trespass" sign? This magazine can help you in defying the law and feeling like a movie super spy at the same time.

390   Big Boys Balloons
www.bigboysballoons.com

Big Boys Balloons is a collector's site for balloons! As "a service to fellow balloon fetishists and balloon lovers" and "a source for big, unusual, and hard to find balloons," BBB specializes in selling really, really, big balloons. So big, in fact, that multiple grown men can sit on them while inflated! Some of these mammoth balloons are "exclusive to Big Boys Balloons." I've been looking all over for that giant balloon, and now I've found it!

PRODUCTS: Round balloons, Airship balloons, and Unique balloons. The round section contains balloons like the German Round balloons, the Smiley Face balloons, and Fantasia Round balloons. The Airship balloons are the big ones: the Italian Airship balloon can fit four grown men while inflated. In a disappointing surprise, the Austrian and American balloons are significantly smaller. Discrimination is everywhere, even among balloon retailers! I blame the vast right-wing conspiracy first exposed by Hillary Clinton. You know it exists.

VERDICT: Doesn't everybody want a gigantic balloon in their house? Their uses are limitless: furniture, decorations (remember, it's art), party pieces; their practicality is unmatched. Not only that, they're cheap, too: less than a dollar for some of them and only ten bucks for bigger ones! If you're looking for unbelievably useless giant balloons, this is truly your "one-stop shop."

391

Find a Grave
www.findagrave.com

Haven't you always dreamed of knowing where Madge Blake, (the overly anxious Aunt Harriet from the *Batman* TV series) is buried? Maybe you're just dying (pun intended) to see a picture of Liberace's crypt, and get directions on how you can see it in person. And who knew that Falco, the '80s singer of "Der Komissar" and "Rock Me Amadeus" was dead (car accident, 1998), much less that he is buried in Vienna, Austria?

PRODUCTS: Books like *Your Guide to Cemetery Research* and *Hollywood Remains To Be Seen* are available. Find a Grave Greeting Cards are "high quality, unique, cemetery-themed cards" and provide five different styles of cards with photos of headstones and more. "Let your family members and friends know about your enthusiasm for cemeteries!" Uhhh…yeah. Of course, there are T-shirts and hats, and my personal favorite, the Map to the Stars' Bones, which helps you find the final resting place of that special entertainer.

VERDICT: In this era of instant celebrity, isn't it refreshing to know that after your fifteen minutes of fame, you can have an eternity of being worshipped in your final resting place? Even after the installation of security cameras and the use of guards with dogs, fans flocked to the grave of Jim Morrison of the Doors to party, use drugs, and write graffiti. Boy, isn't it nice to be remembered?

392

Ant Farms
www.stevesantfarm.com

The ants march one by one, into your home! Before you get out the RAID ant killer, consider Butterfly Gifts' Ant Farms as a way to welcome the industrious insects into your home. An ant farm "makes a fun and educational project! You can observe some ant behavior like tunnel and chamber making, and see different ant 'jobs' like feeder ants that gather food and worker ants that dig." And remember, "Ants are very clean and will move all their refuse as well as dead ants away from their tunnels." What a pleasant thought.

PRODUCTS: "Watch as these hard-working critters burrow underground to create an amazing network of subterranean tunnels, walkways, and secret chambers." How can I watch them build "secret chambers" if they're secret? There's also the Ant Farm village, where ants can "travel from farm to town and back again through clear, flexible Antway Connector Tubes." I'm sure the ants can distinguish farms and towns from a hole in the ground.

VERDICT: Ants are like communists. All ants are equal, except for the queen (dictator), no ant gets rewarded for extra work, and there's no opportunity whatsoever for personal advancement. Fortunately, this is nature at work, not a corrupt regime of oppression and fear.

393

Mat Tracks
www.mattracks.com

Thanks to Mat Tracks, your car can be a tank now, too! "Tires to rubber tracks conversion can take as little as thirty minutes. As easy as changing tires, giving you tank-like tracks on all four corners of your four-by-four vehicle!" Whether you use Mat Tracks for recreational, industrial, agricultural, or exploration purposes, Mat Tracks can transform unstable SUVs into true all-terrain vehicles.

PRODUCTS: Mat Tracks sells a number of tread varieties for trucks and SUVs, the Litefoot series for ATVs, and the Track-tor-Assist series for front wheel assist tractors. If you're satisfied with the performance of these tank-like treads, you can become a walking advertisement with Mat Track apparel. The Litefoot apparel section sells shirts and hats with "Team Litefoot ATV track conversion" embroidered on them. Another Mat Tracks sweatshirt asks the rather vague question, "Where do you need to go today?" Anywhere but here!

VERDICT: Mat Tracks is another site with an extremely selective customer base. Suburbanites and city dwellers have no use for tank treads on their cars. Even an eight-track is more useful than any of these tracks. If you fantasize about having a tank, Mat Tracks can help the delusion you seek. Otherwise, this site is utterly useless.

394

Vanishing Tattoo
www.vanishingtattoo.com

The Vanishing Tattoo is "a global odyssey in search of the last authentic tattoos." Vanishing Tattoo is the story of how Thomas Lockhart became an "apprentice" by "hanging out with Japanese, American, and tribal tattoo masters, absorbing the expertise he would need to make his own mark within the tattoo tradition. For Thomas Lockhart, skin ink would become his art...his obsession...his entire life." If anything besides your family and friends becomes your entire life, then you don't HAVE a life.

PRODUCTS: One interesting book is *Tattoos of the Floating World* by Takahiro Kitamura. Kitamura "discusses the art of the Japanese tattoo in the context of Ukiyo-e, concentrating on the parallel histories of the woodblock print and the tattoo." There's also an apparel section on "Tribal Tattoo.com," with Kanji Tattoo Designs, Classic Tattoo Designs, the School of Tattoo design, and the Warm and Fuzzy Tattoo design.

VERDICT: The good news is that this site focuses on tattoos having to do with cultural backgrounds and ethnic traditions. The bad news is that covering your whole body with ink is still not attractive to some people, myself included. Everybody has a different opinion on body art, and mine stands at the belief that this stuff is just plain creepy.

395

Haunted Places
www.haunted-places.com

The Haunted Places directory is your guide to finding a place near you with ghastly ghosts, frightening phantoms, and the nuts who say they've seen them. This site contains a travel guide to paranormal sites, as well as tours and lectures by paranormal "experts," and opportunities to buy tons of books, T-shirts, and equipment with paranormal properties.

PRODUCTS: Through Flamel College, Haunted Places gives you the opportunity to become a "certified paranormal investigator!" It's like being a ghostbuster! Only, without the portable nuclear laser beams and your own Ghostmobile. The Haunted Places directory is available in book form, as is the exciting *William Shatner's Journey into the Paranormal* book. The book reveals the stranger side of the *Star Trek* star, telling about his paranormal encounter on an abandoned desert highway, and how the experience inspired his album, *The Transformed Man*. Haunted Places T-shirts are also available.

VERDICT: I wonder why so many people have said they've seen UFOs, ghosts, monsters, and the like? I'm all for being open-minded, but it seems odd that every person who reports these phenomena has attempted to center attention on themselves through TV, books, or the Internet. I wonder why I've never met any ordinary, sane people who don't want attention, money, or both for their crazy ghost stories? Hmm…

396

Archie McPhee
www.mcphee.com

Archie McPhee have been "outfitters of popular culture since 1980." The real Archie McPhee was a member of a jazz band that played in hotels and bars in Asia. You could say that the Orient knows more about jazz because of Archie McPhee. Later, his great nephew-in-law Mark (talk about a distant relative) formed a joke shop in Seattle that has transformed into the site you see here.

PRODUCTS: On my visit to the site, the featured product was the Male Nurse Action Figure. "Armed with a stethoscope and a clipboard holding an X-ray, this 5 1/4" tall, hard plastic Male Nurse Action Figure is ready to treat your symptoms and fix what ails you." You might be perturbed by the fact that this nurse is a man. Well, you should know that "Male nurses make up six percent of the nurses in the United States and only slightly more in Australia and the UK, but this number is growing. These men are blazing the trail as role models and mentors for generations to come." Trailblazing. Yes. This site sells hundreds of other products, from action figures to costumes to décor, and more!

VERDICT: Being a nurse is a noble profession, don't get me wrong. But I'd rather be aided by a female nurse than some creepy guy in scrubs. Other than this slightly unsettling action figure, Archie McPhee sells great stuff galore.

397

Cat Boxing
www.catboxing.com

Cat Boxing: "Blow By Blow, Swap By Swap, And Growl After Growl! Video & Pictures of Round After Round of Feline Fighting!" Finally, something useful cats can do! The main event is and always will be Bootsy vs. Nova, as they are "the sole inspiration for this site." That's no excuse to make them the only main event! We want some variety in our Cat Boxing! Rest assured, though, the "What's New" section gives us that variety, with Fez vs. Jadis and other fights, some with other animals besides cats. Bink vs. Melody is actually a cat vs. a dachshund (aka wiener dog). The event is shameful for the poor puppy, with the cat ruthlessly scaring the harmless dog away. She just wanted to be his friend!

PRODUCTS: "Pick a shirt or two and a 'cat' pad for your computer!" The shirts, mugs, clocks, hats, stickers, and lunchboxes with a picture of a black cat and the phrase, "Get Buried at Cat Boxing.com." I'd bury the cat, alive preferably, but I'd rather not be buried myself.

VERDICT: While this does show catfights, it's not the type of catfight I like. We all know that we'd prefer two angry blondes duking it out over who should get the hunky guy, who looks better, or whether Miller Lite is great tasting or less filling.

398

Jolly Walkers
www.jollywalkers.com

"Clowns are special people…let Jolly Walkers put a smile on your feet!" Clown shoes freak me out! While I still follow the philosophy of Ihateclowns.com (number 10 from the original 505), Jolly Walkers is a reliable outfitter for clowns everywhere. The big question is, of course, are they comfy? "Jolly Walker clown shoes are made with the highest level of comfort in mind! Find out for yourself with our MONEY BACK GUARANTEE!"

PRODUCTS: Clown shoes, supplies, and accessories. The shoes come in lollipop, Mary Jane, tramp, sneaker, checker, jester, and custom varieties. From the custom section are the Classic America clown shoes, with the red, white, and blue on them, as well as custom boots in fireman, police, and Santa style. All of the shoes are comically oversized, of course. There's nothing funny about the price, however: most of the shoes are over $250! The other supplies are slightly more reasonable, but even the Curly Clown wig is still $39! Who knew being a Bozo could be so expensive?

VERDICT: Clowns were never funny to me to begin with. There's something about the colored hair, oversized shoes, and big noses that didn't appeal to me, and even freaked me out. Like I said before, Ihateclowns.com is by far the best clown site ever, because it's about hating these gruesome goofs, not idolizing them.

399

Alien Dog Tags
www.earthbounddog.com

"Picture yourself lost in the galaxy…UFO sightings and Alien Abductions are on the rise…Will you return to tell the story?" With Alien Dog Tags from Earthbounddog.com, you can rest assured you'll return to Earth safely to tell your senile story to whoever will listen! "In case of alien abduction these dog tags may save your life. The crucial data an alien will need to get you back to Earth is die stamped into these dog tags." What if they don't WANT to take me back?

PRODUCTS: "Engraved with several methods of locating Earth in the Galaxy, an alien pilot does not need to understand any human language to use this information." Does this get any stupider? It does, with the money back guarantee that says "should you be abducted by aliens while wearing location dog tags and not returned safely to Earth, you will be entitled to a full refund of the purchase price." How can I collect the refund if I'm not on Earth?

VERDICT: Alien Dog Tags are one of the stupidest ideas man has ever conceived. Even if there were aliens that can abduct me, I'm sure they'd be smart enough to know how to return me to Earth. If they were REALLY smart, they wouldn't return me at all! Nevertheless, if you want a weird gift for the alien/UFO/conspiracy theory fanatic in the family, Earthbounddog.com has the weirdest one you can find.

400

Jonny Glow
www.jonnyglow.com

Touted as "One of the first MUST HAVE products of the Twenty-first Century," Jonny Glow is a set of lights that you can install along the rim of your toilet. "With Jonny Glow, trips to the bathroom can now be taken without turning on the bathroom light! Jonny Glow lights the rim of the toilet for use in the dark, eliminating unwanted mess." It's called a light switch. Use it.

PRODUCTS: Jonny Glow is easy to clean, and no batteries or electricity are needed to use it. Simply let it "charge up" in fifteen minutes of regular bathroom light, and it provides a bright ten hour glow! Jonny Glow is perfect for helping guys perfecting their aim, for saving electricity, and for a wedding or baby shower gift. You can also use it when camping: simply wrap Jonny around a tree and you're set!

VERDICT: Whoever the genius was that invented glow-in-the-dark technology, we thank you. Sites like Glow, Inc. (number 83), Putty World, (number 97), and even Banana Guard (number 384) can sell products that can be seen in the dark without any electricity. Jonny Glow is yet another example of this amazing technology. And like all the other glow-in-the-dark products, it's completely useless.

401

20th Century Properties
www.missilebases.com

Missile Bases.com is run by 20th Century Castles, who sell "unique underground properties." True to its name, "unique underground properties" translates into abandoned missile silos! "Built at a cost of millions, these heavily reinforced historic structures were designed to withstand nuclear attack. They bring new meaning to the word 'shelter.' Centuries from now they will remain." I don't care how long they'll be around, what good are they to me?

PRODUCTS: 20th Century Properties sells a video containing recent news clips covering their business, as well as historic government footage of their missile bases. If you're actually considering buying one of these obsolete military installations, the "properties" section has all the information you'll need to buy one. The Titan II site is available to purchase for $85,000, with a catch: the "Silo imploded and [the] entire facility [was] buried—must be excavated." Still there is "Much valuable salvage thought to remain." If you're looking for a more hospitable missile silo, try the Atlas E site, a missile silo with three full living rooms, a kitchen, three finished bathrooms, and a hot tub and sauna room! Luxurious AND safe from nuclear fallout! Now only $545,000! "Seller is eager!"

VERDICT: While the name may be outdated, 20th Century Properties is only for serious real estate moguls looking to invest in something that can stand the test of time. And what better way than a nuclear ICBM missile silo?

402   Maggot Art
www.maggotart.com

First they say you can eat bugs with Hot Lix (number 381), and now they say you can make art with them? Maggot Art is "a fantastic new teaching tool for use in the elementary school setting. Children get hands-on experience with insects that most people find truly disgusting—maggots—while creating a beautiful piece of artwork to share with others." Thank goodness I'm not in elementary school anymore!

PRODUCTS: You can email to get information on the maggot art kits and supplies, or you can buy Maggot Art T-shirts right here online! The black T-shirt features the Maggot Art logo, as well as the Spanish Dancer painting seen on this site's welcome page. The white T-shirt features the Maggot Art web address on the front, and an "actual Maggot Art painting" on the back.

VERDICT: Does this stupid "anything goes" philosophy for art never end? Since when do maggots covered in paint qualify as art tools? Maggot Art is a sad, pitiful, disgusting excuse for an art medium. If you have even the slightest bit of good taste, you'll agree that Maggot Art is a travesty to true art.

403

Bar Stool Racing
www.barstoolracing.net

Bar Stool Racing is "dedicated to one of the most unique sports evolving across America today." The sport is touted as one that involves everybody, especially "the guys who may have lost their 32" waist line." This site also has membership information for NOBRA, the National Organization of Bar Stool Racing in America. Where's the "stool" in that abbreviation?

PRODUCTS: NOBRA T-shirts are available, "this time in a variety of sizes including XX large for the more areo-dynamic of you out there." You mean fatter people? The pictures show the front belly view, NOBRA, and the Bar Stool Racing web address. "We pay the big bucks for models," the caption says of this picture. The back says "Bar Stool Racing: the sport your momma warned you about!" They also comment that "this guy looks thirty pounds lighter with his NOBRA Tee."

VERDICT: Bar Stool Racing is as pitiful as washing machine racing, snail racing, and baby racing combined. It has the same silliness of Sumo Wrestling (see number 84 for the official American Sumo site) and the monotony of NASCAR (let's watch cars go in circles for hours!). At least it delivers what it promises: a sport with vehicles that allow you to race and drink beer at the same time.

404

Cow Pie Clocks
www.cowpieclocks.com

This site guarantees that you'll find a gift here for that "hard to shop for person in your life." The answer for the guy or gal who has everything: a Cow Pie Clock! Made from "Farm Fresh" Utah cow pies, the, uh, "specimens" that make up these clocks "were carefully hand-picked from millions of organically grown specimens, sun-dried in the fields of Southern Utah. It's time for some pie." It's certainly not time for me!

PRODUCTS: Small, medium, and large Cow Pie Clocks for the outrageous prices of $39.95, $44.95, and $49.95 respectively! The clock is deceiving in its appearance, looking more like a discolored rock than cow crap. As if these weren't bad enough, you can also buy Cow Ball golf balls. Fortunately, the actual balls aren't made of this horrendous material, they are glued to the cow pie with a few tees and a custom inscription. Some sample inscriptions are "Golf…who gives a crap," and "Your only handicap is that you still try to play." You have a handicap if you're crazy enough to buy these crappy clocks (pun intended).

VERDICT: Would you eat off a plate made of cow dung? Would you wear a T-shirt with cow dung on it? Then why would you want a clock made of cow crap? It may be a unique gift, but it certainly isn't appropriate. Only buy these truly disgusting clocks for a truly disgusting person.

405   Women in Waders
www.womeninwaders.com

They're women, they're hot, they're fly fishing! "We realize you may never actually run across women dressed like this in your favorite stream, but with the Women in Waders calendar on your wall, you can dream about it everyday." Oh, dream I will. Yeah, right.

PRODUCTS: Women in Waders calendars for this year and earlier years, back to 2001! Each calendar has twelve photos, one for each month, all with women scantily clad in bikinis and knee-high brown waders. It's very sexy, if you consider women wearing brown rubber waders sexy. There are also Women in Waders prints, postcards, shirts, hats, e-cards, and even videos of hot women-in-wader action! Women in Waders claims that all the photos are "tastefully photographed," despite that this site is classless as well as tasteless.

VERDICT: The women on WIW are attractive. If they were photographed from the knees up, this would be a very hot calendar! And, it would sell pretty well too. Once you see the women in knee-high waders, however, something just doesn't seem right. Perhaps it's meant to be a sick fantasy for fly fishers. Perhaps it's the fact that it IS a sick fly fisher's fantasy.

406

Land of the Lost
www.landofthelost.com

Land of the Lost was about the Marshall family, a goody-two-shoes dad, son, and daughter who, while going on a camping trip, fell into a time warp caused by an earthquake. They ended up in a strange prehistoric world with dinosaurs, monkey people, and guys in highly, um, realistic lizard costumes who were known on the show as Sleestaks.

PRODUCTS: *LOTL* DVDs and videos, including the full first season and special volume 3 and volume 4 videos containing two episodes each as voted on LOTL.com. In the second episode of volume three, "The Zarn," Rick (the dad) and Will (the son) discover an alien spaceship in a "mysterious" marsh. From the spaceship comes a beautiful woman named Sharon. "Will and Holly become suspicious, but it's not until later that Rick realizes Sharon's a little too perfect." Gee, ya think?

VERDICT: *LOTL* is another one of those shows which never gained much popularity, but still has a small, loyal, cult-like following of fans. If you're a member of the LOTL cult, landofthelost.com will be a Godsend. If you're anybody else, though, you'll agree that it's time to move on and forget about this silly show.

....

407

Live Nude Cats
www.livenudecats.com

Warning: this site contains highly realistic depictions of cats in the nude. Select a picture and you'll find the photo at the bottom of the page. For example, the Palm Tree Paparazzi photo shows how in Costa Rica "the beaches are crawling with topless tabby action." The photo shows a tabby cat laying on her side who is, oddly, censored in her lower and upper regions. Hey, I came for nude cats, not censored nude cats!

PRODUCTS: A number of the pictures can be clicked on to show a different set of T-shirts, hats, clocks, mouse pads, stickers, and mugs. The Sweet and Innocent and Oriental Spice products show a nude cat in an open cardboard box. Unfortunately, the box isn't closed to prevent the passage of air to the scandalous felines.

VERDICT: This site was troubling for me, even traumatic. Seeing cats in the nude was something I just wasn't prepared for. Sure, you could say they're always naked, but this site really makes their indecency apparent. If you used to seeing a naked cat stroll through your house, Live Nude Cats won't bother you. But if you don't want to confront the naked truth of pseudo-explicit animal nudity, stay away from LNC.

408

Toshi Station
www.toshistation.com

"But I want to go to the Toshi Station to pick up some power converters!" That famous *Star Wars* line by then-superstar Mark Hamill has inspired the domain name for this, but the actual site is not about *Star Wars* at all. Rather, this site is about geeky movie reviews. There is also the Chain System Rating, where you input the basic elements of your favorite (or least favorite) movie. First, you choose the category (Sci Fi, Horror, Action, etc.) then answer the question, "Was this movie a sequel?" Depending on what you choose, there's a plethora of possibilities. A few questions have you checking the basic bad elements of movies ("Child actor in a speaking role," "Released directly to video or made for TV," "Talking baby/bird/dog/cat," etc. and the basic good elements (Robots, "Proper abundance of thundering explosions," "Combat sequence featuring five or more participants," "Afros or other funkified head fashion," etc.) with the result being a rating of zero to five chains, the more the better.

PRODUCTS: Books graded by Toshi Station. One of the better ones with an A- is *Jennifer Government* by Max Barry, a book about a future where corporations rule the world and everybody has their employer as a last name ("Hack Nike," "Billy NRA," etc.). On the lower end of the scale is the D+ *Powder* by Kevin Sampson, about "the trials and tribulations of a fictitious Liverpool band on the path to fortune and glory."

VERDICT: Toshi Station is worth checking out just for the Chain System questionnaire. They also have some interesting books that range from highly entertaining to highly painful. Toshi Station is must for movie and book geeks everywhere.

409 Roller Organs
www.rollerorgans.com

Roller Organs, also called American Music Boxes, were late-nineteenth-century audio players that played small twenty-note rollers featuring popular music titles like "Over the Rainbow," the "Pennsylvania Polka," and "Stars and Stripes Forever," available to buy for as little as eighteen cents, a steal for the time. This Roller Organ site contains tons of information on this historic machine, including pictures of early models, a history of the device, and a "Buy/Sell/Trade" forum to exchange different roller titles.

PRODUCTS: Books on Roller Organs, as well as repair parts and rollers. Rollers, available in reproduction, original, new, and grand varieties, can be bought with classic titles like "She'll Be Comin' 'Round the Mountain," "Pomp and Circumstance," and, in a pleasant surprise for *Wizard of Oz* fans, "Ding Dong the Witch is Dead!" Prices range from $15 to $142 for the rarer ones.

VERDICT: While maybe an artifact of a distant past, Roller Organs.com is definitely offering a piece of history for those interested. If you have the good fortune of being an owner of a working model of one of these antiquated apparatuses, Roller Organs can offer a chance to expand your collection of rollers.

410 British Lawn Mower Museum
www.lawnmowerworld.co.uk

"Enter the fascinating world of this internationally famous museum and have a unique experience." The fascinating world they speak of is the world of British Lawn Mowers! This site has all the information you could possibly desire on lawn mowers. There's a photo gallery with pictures of lawnmower manuals, and a gallery of old lawn mower models.

PRODUCTS: In addition to BLM postcards, pens, birthday and greeting cards, and collectible toy lawn mowers, you can also buy rare antique and reproduction lawn mower models! The Model Shanks Lawn Mower, a very old, manually powered lawn mower (no electricity here), is a replica of a one-hundred-year-old lawn mower, available in red, pewter, or bronze! The price is 39.99—in British pounds. Why can't everybody just use our currency system?

VERDICT: The British Lawn Mower Museum has information on the history of lawn mowers. WHO CARES? I'm all for learning, but lawn mowers are not something we need to know anything about. We have enough misery in mowing our own lawns to care about the history of what cuts them.

411 Just for Openers
www.just-for-openers.org

"If you collect beer advertising openers or corkscrews, this is the website you have been looking for." I, personally, would look somewhere else for something else, but you may have been looking for this site. Just for Openers was founded in 1979 by Donald A. Bull, a native of Wirtz, Virginia.

PRODUCTS: Corkscrew and opener books, including *The Ultimate Corkscrew Book* by Donald A. Bull, *Boxes Full of Corkscrews*, also by Donald A. Bull, and *Corkscrew Patents of Japan* by—you guessed it—Donald A. Bull. *Corkscrew Patents of Japan* contains tons of Japanese corkscrew patent illustrations that will "amaze and delight" you, and might just let you finally "identify some of the unusual corkscrews in your collection." At long last, I can identify my favorite rare corkscrew! Hallelujah!

VERDICT: I wonder why all the books on this site are by Donald A. Bull (who also made the site)? Hmm, you think this might be a shameless promotion of his books, rather than an educational experience on the history of corkscrews? Then again, advertising means sales, and sales mean money, and money makes the world go round. You can't fault him for trying to make a buck with Just for Openers.com, and maybe teaching you a thing or two about corkscrews and openers along the way.

412

I Am an Idiot
www.iamanidiot.com

The obvious truth is in the name. But, as the creator of I Am an Idiot points out, "Everyone is an idiot at something. A brain surgeon can be an idiot in front of a computer and a rocket scientist can be an idiot at boiling water. We can all laugh at each other and enjoy life a little more." And laughing is always a good thing, even if it is at the expense of your fellow idiots.

PRODUCTS: I Am an Idiot bumper stickers, with the domain name and an idiot cartoon face, presumably of the dim-witted creator of this site. "Here's your chance to show the world who is an Idiot...put them on your locker, car, backpack, or anywhere else you can think of. You could even put them on your 'friends' locker, but you didn't hear that from me." Sounds like a good idea; no better compliment for your friend than an "I Am an Idiot" sticker.

VERDICT: I Am an Idiot is as much of a downer as "You Are an Idiot" (number 372 from my first book). Only, this time, you're discovering your idiocy yourself instead of having it thrown in your face. But, like this site says, everybody's an idiot at something. Me, I'm an idiot at being an idiot. I'm just brain dead when it comes to admitting my own idiocy, and I'm proud of it.

413

Hidden Doors
www.hiddendoors.com

Anybody who's seen their share of old TV and movies know that every creepy castle, mansion, or secret evil lair has a ton of secret passages and hidden doors. Now, this company can help you have your very own secret passage! The Hidden Door company specializes in making regular, visible doors into bookcases, making for a very discreet and very cool hidden room. Need a place to hide when your evil in-laws visit? Vanish into a secret room. Want to escape the heat when your significant other is teed off at you? It's yours with a hidden door.

PRODUCTS: Hidden Door secret entrances are available on any standard door size. When closed, the door looks just like a bookshelf. The doors are available in the standard in/out swing, as well as wine racks, arched tops, and latching and locking varieties. A standard door will take about eight weeks to manufacture. How much will this luxury cost you? Why, only $1,845! What a bargain, eh?

VERDICT: The only person I could imagine buying a hidden door is some delusional, paranoid millionaire. Somebody who buys the door to protect themselves from the imaginary assassins out to kill them. Somebody who thinks the government is using radio waves and black helicopters to try and brainwash them. People like that would buy a hidden door. Anybody else with half a brain will have little use for this strange site.

414

Red and Proud
www.redandproud.com

Red and Proud is "the home of the redhead." If you have red hair, you can be proud of it at Red and Proud. The aim of RAP is to "celebrate and promote the lot of the redhead, whether it be culturally, artistically, or sporting." This site contains Red News, the Red Academy, which educates redheads about how they got their red hair, and the Famous Redheads list, naming celebrities with red hair.

PRODUCTS: T-shirts and tops, hats, stickers, magnets, pins, mugs, and mousepads. One creative shirt is the Redhead Acronym T-shirt. "Tell the world that you are Ravishing Exotic Desirable Hip Energetic Astonishing Dropdead gorgeous." That's great, but how about an acronym for the guys? I don't think guys want to be exotic, ravishing, and dropdead gorgeous.

VERDICT: I can think of the best redhead of all time and the worst one. Best: Anne Robinson, the original, superior host of *The Weakest Link*. Not only did she make the phrase "You are the Weakest Link, Goodbye" a permanent part of pop culture, she had the ability to completely destroy any contestant's sense of self-worth! The worst redhead? Carrot Top. From the best to the worst, Red and Proud is a top-notch resource for redheads everywhere.

415 Surfing the Apocalypse
www.surfingtheapocalypse.com

Surfing the Apocalypse is another crackpot conspiracy theory site, full of farfetched, ridiculous, paranoia-induced "news" stories. The maker of this site proposes that "On these pages you will find much thought provoking and 'unusual' ideas and theories, but as you weave the pieces together, somehow they all seem to connect and make some sort of strange sense!" How can the deaths of sixty hippos, practice on goats by army doctors, and the "face" on Mars (which was later proved to be an illusion after a picture from a lower height was taken) be connected?

PRODUCTS: The *Universal Seduction* book series. "A focus falls on alien abductees" in volume three of this series. "New categories are presented: 'Other Wordly Creatures' (Bigfoot et al)…a surreal NJ vortex with interdimensional pictures is presented...Mormonism is exposed and reincarnation is addressed." I knew those Mormons were up to something!

VERDICT: The article I found most interesting was the "Crop Circle Beer" article, describing how a Long Island man made a special beer with barley from crop circle fields. I'm predicting that this beer will cause its drinkers to become radioactive mutants, enabling them to fly, walk through walls, and shoot lasers out of their eyes. Check up on STA to stay updated with your favorite paranoid conspiracy theories.

416 Big John Toilet Seat
www.bigjohntoiletseat.com

The Big John Toilet Seat is "designed and manufactured for our growing population." In other words, as America gets fatter and fatter, we need a toilet seat that can hold the fatter end of our population. The press release for BJTS calls it "a simple but brilliant innovation," and also says appropriately that it's "one of those inventions that makes us all wonder, 'Why didn't I think of that?'" Half of America's fads follow that motto. Look at the Pet Rock. Even George W. Bush could have thought of that.

PRODUCTS: The BJTS features a "Stylish ergonomic design [with] a larger, more comfortable opening and a luxuriously contoured sitting surface that is roomier than any other toilet seat on the market." Roomier toilet seats for roomier people. That is, they take up the whole room! It's also built with "continuous stainless steel mount and hinge," which is guaranteed to provide "unbreakable strength where others fail." And BJTS has been cleverly engineered to fit both round and elongated bowls! Talk about versatility!

VERDICT: I can't blame people for not being able to lose weight. With so many countless ways to lose weight, it gets confusing. Useless pills or crappy infomercial exercise machine? Pilates or 5-Minute-Abs? While these obstacles are no excuse for giving up, BJTS can accommodate America's overweight until they find a weight loss solution for today's crazy world.

417   NYC Garbage
www.nycgarbage.com

Besides being another indication that the artistic world is going off the deep end, NYC Garbage is a site that sells an unusual gift: garbage from New York City, inside plastic cubes. The maker of this site describes his typical workday: "I scour New York City for trash. After filling bags with subway passes, Broadway tickets (who would throw those away?), and other NYC junk, I carefully arrange plastic cubes full of the stuff." They'll call anything art these days.

PRODUCTS: The plastic garbage cubes contain a wide variety of disgusting junk. One sample cube a Kit-Kat wrapper, a Diet Coke can, a cigarette butt, a match box, a Heineken label, a piece of string, a Marlboro cigarette box, and a parking receipt. Each cube has a sticker with a date telling when the garbage inside was picked, and a personalized signature and number from the artist, Justin Gignac.

VERDICT: What is this world coming to? Who would actually buy this junk? Even more blasphemous is that some people would call this art. If you want real art, visit your local art museum (and even that isn't all art). Don't settle for this, well, garbage.

418

Handy Fashions
www.handy-fashions.com

You'd think Handy Fashions would sell clothing accessories that do something useful, like carrying pens or paper pads. Instead, Handy Fashions is here to help protect you from the dangerous effects of cell phone radiation! Handy Fashions prides itself in offering "up to date fashion[s]" as well as "highly effective microwave protection." Handy Fashions products contain highly sophisticated "shielding textile material" that has a shielding ability of 99.9999 percent from "dangerous" cell phone radiation.

PRODUCTS: Handy Fashions' Mobile Cap "is the most effective tool to protect you and your children from microwaves whilst using a cellular phone. Don't take any risks, but still enjoy the convenience of modern communication technology." Funny, I never considered using a cell phone a "risky" activity, unless it's in the hands of some chatty person behind the wheel.

VERDICT: I've used a cell phone hundreds of times. I've even put my head up to the microwave to watch my Hot Pocket get warm and crispy countless times. If putting my head in front of a microwave hasn't harmed me yet, why should I need "protection" from a little cell phone? Handy Fashions is obviously praying on paranoid safety nuts to sell their ultimately useless apparel.

419

Air Disaster
www.airdisaster.com

As if fear of flying weren't already an epidemic, Air Disaster focuses on the rare disasters of airline travel. As this description points out, "Although the name is not politically correct, it is a straightforward, accurate, and easy-to-remember description of a website that focuses on airline accidents and incidents." Sounds good to me; political correctness is just an obstacle to free speech created by the liberal media. Air Disaster contains an accident database, with abominable accidents going back all the way to 1950.

PRODUCTS: Books and videos on air accidents, including the three volume *Air Disaster* series. The first volume "makes compelling reading" and features "excellent descriptive artwork, diagrams, and maps." Artwork of what? People screaming in agony among the wreckage? Among the video selection is the *Worst Air Disasters* video, with an image of a flaming airliner plummeting to its doom on the front. Comforting, isn't it?

VERDICT: They say flying is one of the safest ways to travel. You sure won't believe that after seeing this disastrous website. If you have any fear of flying, don't visit this site. Because after seeing all the air disaster stories on this site, you may never want to fly again.

420

Sylvia Browne
www.sylvia.org

"Welcome, weary traveler, you have arrived at a place of Spiritual Renewal." If you consider the site of a popular psychic who has appeared on the Montel Williams show at least one hundred times a place of "spiritual renewal," that is. Sylvia Browne began her career as a "professional" psychic in 1973. Within a year, her practice was so large that she established the Nirvana Center for Psychic Research. Sylvia comes from a long family line of psychics; her maternal grandmother was an "established and respected counselor and healer" in Missouri.

PRODUCTS: Sylvia's book, *Prophecy: What The Future Holds for You*, has a "detailed account" of what the future holds for mankind. According to Sylvia, the future holds the end of the stock market, "interfaith healing centers" where world religions join forces "for the good of humanity," and even cities with domes around them to protect from pollution and meteors! Right, Sylvia.

VERDICT: I'm going to peer into your past. A person you know has died in the past, oh, ten, fifteen, twenty years. This person was a friend, or maybe a relative. You knew this person well. This person is missed very much in your family. This person died in a very sick state, but they loved you very much. There! Isn't that amazing.

421

W Ketchup
www.wketchup.com

"You don't support the Democrats. Why should your ketchup?" According to W Ketchup, the only flavor W Ketchup comes in is American. What does the W stand for? "Our official position is that the 'W' stands for 'Washington.'" Yeah, right. W Ketchup's other advertising tactic says that buying Heinz ketchup funds the liberal agendas of Teresa Heinz Kerry and her husband. What's more important, paying less for ketchup or not funding a liberal agenda? Decisions, decisions.

PRODUCTS: A minimum of four bottles must be purchased when buying W Ketchup. Why four? "The added handling costs of unpacking, repacking, and shipping a single bottle would make it the most expensive ketchup you've ever tasted." The price of W Ketchup is twelve dollars for four bottles, not including shipping. It's already the most expensive ketchup I've ever seen!

VERDICT: As much as I don't want to fund the Heinz family in their political agendas, I buy whatever ketchup is cheapest. I don't care if it's Heinz, Roundy's, Best Yet, Hunt's, or whatever. I appreciate a product if it's 100 percent American, but it should be 100 percent American AND a 100 percent good deal. W Ketchup is not a good deal.

422

Naked Dancing Llama
www.frolic.org

Step into the world of the Naked Dancing Llama, and "prepare to be filled with llama wisdom!" Since 1995, the NDL has given advice to visitors on everything "from their personal lives to complex math problems." The NDL even ran for president along with thousands of other Internet candidates like Mike (number 105) and Cthulhu (number 316).

PRODUCTS: As the NDL says, "Just because I am naked doesn't mean you have to be." If the T-shirt is the only way for NDL followers to keep their clothes on, then I highly recommend it. We don't need naked dancing people. The NDL T-shirt comes in two varieties: the "frolic quote" and the "lick quote." The frolic shirt spreads an insightful message: "Together we shall teach the world to frolic like a llama." Doesn't everybody need a little frolicking every once in a while? The "Lick" quote isn't quite as meaningful: "Don't lick something unless you really mean it!" Um, right. Wouldn't think of it.

VERDICT: I cannot understand the fascination with llamas. They're just furry South American animals. Is it the name? Do people find the word "llama" funny? The NDL is another lame llama site aimed at using primitive humor to take advantage of these cute, helpless Andean animals.

423

Life Gems
www.lifegems.com

Life Gems are dazzling pieces of beautiful jewelry, except that they're made from dead people! First, you get the body of your dead friend or relative cremated. Then you send their remains to Life Gems. By now you're thinking, "How can I trust some diamond company to handle the remains of my loved one?" Their "process guarantee" describes how they carefully handle the remains, including a unique sixteen-digit identifier, which belongs to your family, "and your family only."

PRODUCTS: The Life Gems are "created by placing carbon, the primary element of all diamonds, in conditions that recreate the forces of earth." In other words, Life Gems are made just like ordinary diamonds, except that the base material is human remains instead of rough diamond deposits. Up to one hundred Life Gems can be made from one individual, so almost all of your friends can have a piece of you once you die.

VERDICT: While I would be uncomfortable sending off my dead relative's remains to some stranger, Life Gems seems legit, and is a unique alternative for those considering cremation for when their loved one passes on. If you're looking for a unique, albeit odd, way to keep your loved ones with you forever, Life Gems can offer that.

424

Art Crimes
www.graffiti.org

This site, appropriately dubbed Art Crimes, is about the "art" form known as graffiti. Despite the fact that this is considered vandalism, the act of ruining property that hard-working people try to keep up, this site is offering a resource for graffiti "artists." While Graffiti.org does not endorse breaking the law, they do think that "art belongs in public spaces and that more legal walls should be made available for this fascinating art form."

PRODUCTS: Trucker caps, jewelry, shirts, and of course, "art" materials like spray paint cans and caps. There's also a children's book called *Lilman Makes a Name for Himself.* Supposedly "suitable" for elementary school and preschool readers, the book tells "the story of our hero, the young artist." The story is also described as a "positive, self-affirming story." Self-affirming vandalism? They'll let kids read anything these days.

VERDICT: As you can tell, I don't condone these "art crimes." I've seen the overpasses of bridges covered with hearts containing initials, obscenities, and other crap that shouldn't be considered "art." If these artists find someplace legal to do their work, good for them. But don't deface the property of hard-working people with your own junk, then try to get off the hook by calling it "art."

425

Rocket Guy
www.rocketguy.com

Mr. Walker, master inventor and engineer extraordinaire, "cordially and enthusiastically invites you to share his amazing world of invention, ingenuity, and the pioneer spirit." I can see why he chose the name: Rocket Guy sounds better than "The amazing world of Brian Walker." Rocket Guy is also home to "Project Rush," a plan to build a rocket that can shoot its occupant fifty miles into the air, only to stall and drop back down to Earth. No orbiting the Earth, no going to the moon. Just up, and straight back down.

PRODUCTS: Rocket Guy sells a cornucopia of space and rocket-related toys. One such toy is the Air Bazooka, which translates into "glorified Nerf gun." Like this description says, "It really has no specific scientific aspect but it's a load of fun." Shooting foam arrows is always fun! If you're five, that is.

VERDICT: Rocket Guy is essentially a glorified Chuck E. Cheese ticket shop. The toys here are the kind you can get for ten or twenty tickets. The really cheap, flimsy, poorly made toys. In fact, the toys here are as poorly made as a Ford Pinto, but not as flammable. Rocket Guy's selection of products is largely juvenile, with little to offer the serious scientific hobbyist.

426   Bubbles.org
bubbles.org

Tiny bubbles may make Don Ho happy, but do they make you happy? If so, then Bubbles.org may be able to satisfy your bubble-blowing hobby. This site has a brief bubble history section, which states that in the nineteenth century, the Pear Soap Company in England released the first soap bars, which not only kept the English squeaky clean, but also made bubble blowing a popular hobby! Bubble blowing was limited to "bubble pipes" until the middle of the twentieth century, when toy companies made simpler bubble blowing devices. Talk about a great history lesson!

PRODUCTS: There's a "limited supply" of Professor Bubble's *Official Bubble Handbook*, which is assumingly a guide to blowing the best bubbles. What kind of professor is Professor Bubbles? What kind of degree does he have? A Masters in Bubbleology or something? In addition to Professor Bubble's somewhat suspicious guide, the "best bubble blowing machines ever made" are here in the form of the Bubble Frenzy Machine.

VERDICT: I don't like the sound of this Professor Bubbles guy. I bet he's not even an expert in bubbles! He's trying to scam us into thinking that he's the world's foremost authority on bubbles, when the real credit goes to the hardworking folks who wrote the handbook and made the machine! Professor Bubbles? More like Professional con artist!

427 Madonna Inn

www.madonnainn.com

The Madonna Inn is not a hotel run by the Queen of Pop. Rather, it's a California central coast landmark that is, if the pictures are any indication, the embodiment of cheesiness. Looking more like a fairytale mansion than a hotel, the "world-renowned" Madonna Inn has one hundred eight rooms, "uniquely decorated with a special theme and color scheme, no two alike!"

PRODUCTS: The "Signature Items" section contains shirts, tote bags, aprons, and towels with the Madonna Inn logo, as well as the *Phyllis Madonna Book*, a book chronicling the construction of this hideous hotel. Sounds like an interesting book. But, for $47.95, not interesting enough. In the souvenirs section, you can buy snowglobes, salt and pepper shakers, and "pink sugar." No hidden meaning here, it's really pink sugar.

VERDICT: This hotel contains many themed rooms, and they're all super cheesy, super ugly, and super stupid. Their products are equally corny; any place that sells pink sugar shouldn't be in business. If, by some crazy chance, you want to stay in this tacky inn, this site has all the information you need.

428 International Federation of Competitive Eating

www.ifoce.com

The International Federation of Competitive Eating, touted as "America's fastest growing sport," is a site dedicated to a sport of pure gluttony: eating more hot dogs, pies, donuts, or whatever than your opponent. This site highlights news in the "sport," as well as the mandatory "safety" section, which "insists that all sanctioned competitive eating matches take place in a controlled environment with the proper safety measures in place." What safety measures? Pans for barfing in?

PRODUCTS: IFOCE T-shirts, navy caps, beanie caps, and coozies. Perhaps the coozies are implying that the IFOCE also sanctions competitive drinking competitions! With water, of course. The standard

Team IFOCE T-shirt has the IFOCE logo and the phrase, "Everything (Nothing) in Moderation," with everything crossed out and nothing in its place. Nothing? What about prescription drugs, or alcohol? You can also buy the official newsletter of the IFOCE, the *Gurgitator*. Such a nice name, huh? Finally, it's important to note that all T-shirts are available up to XXXXL, so participants large and small can buy T-shirts.

VERDICT: I wonder what kind of people participate in this crazy sport? I'm betting that they're all thin, athletic, and in great shape. Competitive eaters, overweight? Now who would think that? The International Federation of Competitive Eating might as well be called the International Federation of Overweight Over-Indulgers. Health nuts need not apply for this gluttonous sport.

429

Get out of Hell Free
www.goohf.com

They may not be quite enough to save your soul from eternal damnation, but they do make sinfully great gifts. A columnist was told by an angry reader that he was going to hell for writing a controversial story. The writer told this radical activist that a minister he knew approved of the story. Her response: "the minister [is] going to hell too!" The maker of these cards figured, "if a self-appointed fundamentalist could condemn people to hell with the snap of her mind, he certainly had the power to get them out again." Quite a story for a little joke card.

PRODUCTS: The GOOHF cards, in the style of a Monopoly "Get out of jail free" card, can be bought in bulk for "all your mass salvation needs." "Someone at the door interrupting dinner wants to convert you? No need, you can tell them you're already saved. They'll be trying to figure out the card as the door slams." Ah, yes, door-to-door religionists. They're a small step above door-to-door salesmen, who are a small step above telemarketers, who are a small step above the devil himself.

VERDICT: GOOHF cards are great joke gift for your friends and family burdened with annoying people in their lives. They almost look like real Monopoly cards! Too bad there's no "Get out of taxes free" cards. We still have to pay the IRS, but at least we can have instant salvation with Get out of Hell Free cards.

430

I Work with Fools
www.iworkwithfools.com

Don't we all? I Work with Fools is a place where "you can read or anonymously share work related stories about the foolish coworkers and bosses we all deal with daily." The mission of IWWF is to provide stressed workers with a laugh, because "Sometimes the only way to get through these damn work days besides surfing sites without getting caught is to have a good laugh." Stories range from a drama queen concocting family crises to get off of work, to a senile coworker yelling "Okay" at least thirty times a day, and even an IT Helpdesk worker telling a coworker that the system crashed because "they were not using an approved mouse pad." Duh, mousepads can cause crashes? Um, I should check if my mousepad is, uh, misunapproved, otherwise my system might be, um, crashable.

PRODUCTS: I Work with Fools T-shirts, mousepads (these are system approved), hats, and stickers. All products have the phrase "I Work with Fools," and a fittingly frustrated face. If you're really gutsy, try buying a mug or a lunchbox, then bring it to work. If that doesn't get you fired, I don't know what will.

VERDICT: I've heard many horror stories about coworkers. IWWF is a good site to visit to get a little pick-me-up, especially during a stressful workday where the incompetence of your co-workers is all too apparent.

431

Mr. Bling
www.mrbling.com

First we had "Iced Out Gear" (number 347) for all our big phat pimpin' bling-bling. Now, you can put the "bling" in your mouth! Mr. Bling "offers the world's best craftsmanship and at half the price compared to the leading maker in gold, white gold, and platinum teeth." Who exactly IS the leading maker in gold, white gold, and platinum teeth?

PRODUCTS: Custom jewelry, earrings, and of course, metal teeth. The Starter Kit is required with the purchase of any set of gold teeth, which helps you create a molding of your teeth. After you've sent Mr. Bling the impressions of your teeth, you can select the teeth and finally begin with the teeth to the tizzo in da rizzo izzo! I have no idea what I just said! If you want the bling from Mr. Bling, though, you better be willing to dish out the dough: the cheapest teeth are about $200.

VERDICT: I'd be kind of paranoid if I had gold teeth. You never know if some aggressive mugger might want to pull out your teeth. I also remember an unpleasant image from the movie *Leprechaun 2*, in which the greedy psychotic leprechaun forcefully yanks a bloody gold tooth out of a bum's mouth. Nevertheless, if you want some bling-bling in your teeth just like those indecipherable masta rappers, Mr. Bling can help you.

432   Inflatable Church
www.inflatablechurch.com

It's a holy sanctuary of God…in inflatable form! Presented proudly to you by InnovationsUK.com, this is the world's only Inflatable Church! "Tie the knot wherever you wish…YOU decide, we will provide a church for you!" The Inflatable Church allows you to have a wedding anywhere, from your backyard to the beach or, if you desire it, the middle of nowhere!

PRODUCTS: The Inflatable Church is forty-seven feet long by twenty-five feet wide and forty-seven feet high. The details of this inflatable house of God are "heavenly, complete with plastic 'stained glass' windows." Wouldn't that be stained plastic windows? The inside is adorned with an inflatable organ, altar, pulpit, pews, candles, and a gold (plastic) cross. Worried about guests bouncing around instead of watching your wedding? Worry not, the church has a hard floor. "But please NO SMOKING!" Gee, ya think?

VERDICT: While the Inflatable Church is good for a wedding anywhere, the inflatable fun doesn't end there. There's also the inflatable pub, the inflatable marquee, and the inflatable nightclub! Who needs to go to a rave when you can have one in your own backyard? Just make sure you invite some guests; it's not a party when you're the only patron.

433

Junkyard Sports
www.junkyardsports.com

Junkyard Sports is about sports that use everyday objects, like pans, balloons, and even trashbags to create an experience that focuses on "fun and participation rather than winning and competition." Oh yes, everybody wins! How nice. Junkyard Sports are touted as great not only for after-school programs and health and fitness education, but also retirement programs, anti-obesity services, and peace initiatives! Old people, fat people, AND hippies can benefit from Junkyard Sports!

PRODUCTS: Buy the *Junkyard Sports* book, by Bernie DeKoven, for "Cross-age, cross-ability, cross-gender, cross-cultural, environmentally friendly fun!" Well, Junkyard Sports certainly is politically correct. This book features more than seventy-five demonstrations of different varieties of six major team sports. The "endless" varieties of games can be played anywhere, with anything, by "almost" anyone. Why not just "anyone"?

VERDICT: While Junkyard Sports does present some interesting variations of games with common household objects, it's almost like the book's aim is to help bring peace and harmony to the world, rather than give us fun alternatives to traditional sports. Fun sports with everyday objects? Yes. Making the world a better place for everybody? No.

434

World Beard and Moustache Championships
www.worldbeardchampionships.com

The World Beard and Moustache Championships has its roots in Europe, dating back to 1990. But it was first introduced to America in 2003, in Carson City, Nevada. In this landmark event, "A panel of distinguished judges determined which beards and moustaches in seventeen separate categories merited their owners the championship trophies and the coveted world champion titles. Special prizes were also awarded to the youngest contestant, the contestant who traveled the farthest to attend, and the people's favorite." From the looks of these photos, I can't imagine how ANY of these people could be "favorites."

PRODUCTS: WBMC T-shirts, hats, beer mugs, and a WBMC video! The video is a "comprehensive video documentary" on the 2003 WBMC in Carson City. One T-shirt has a picture of Willi Chevalier, the 2001 "Freestyle Goatee" World Champion. He looks more like a resident of Dr, Seuss's Whoville than a regular human.

VERDICT: To make any comparison of the WBMC to the Olympics is obscene. Diving, gymnastics, even a 0-0 soccer game is better than this! The WBMC is a sad, sad excuse for a competition. The WBMC should have stayed in Europe where it belongs.

435 World's Smallest Versions of the World's Largest Things
www.worldslargestthings.com

Large things are popular among some folks, as evidenced by Great Big Stuff (number 156), but this museum highlights the smaller versions of larger things. The full and proper name being The World's Largest Collection of the World's Smallest Versions of the World's Largest Things Traveling Roadside Attraction and Museum (whew), this museum has miniature replicas of the world's largest things. Examples include the World's Smallest Version of the World's Largest Ball of Rubber Bands, which is made of miniature rubber bands commonly used in dental braces.

PRODUCTS: T-shirts, magnets, and other unusual roadside attraction-related gifts. The Babe Bits are "authentic chips of paint" from the giant version of Babe (Paul Bunyan's giant blue pet ox) in Bemidji, MN. Isn't scraping chips of paint from a landmark considered vandalism? Other gifts include the Cawker City Cuttings, a twine snippet from the World's Largest Ball of Twine, as well as nightlights and snow globes.

VERDICT: This museum is confusing. It's hard to tell which is largest, which is smallest, and which is the actual artifact. The WLCotWSVotWLT museum (try saying that five times) is an interesting tale of American roadside attractions and a treat for fans of world records and the world's largest and smallest things.

436 Quantum Sleeper
www.qsleeper.com

Bio-chemical terrorist attacks? Earthquakes and tornados? Kidnappers and murderers? Not a problem with the Quantum Sleeper! The Quantum Sleeper is a "high-level security system designed for maximum protection in various hostile environments." Your own house, a hostile environment? The Quantum Sleeper can even be fitted to protect against tornados, hurricanes, floods, and earthquakes! Talk about protection!

PRODUCTS: How safe is the Quantum Sleeper? The 1.25 inch polycarbonate plastic plating is bulletproof. In fact, the plating can stop a .357 Magnum bullet! In other words, a gun that would, under normal circumstances, literally blow your head clean off, can't even touch the Quantum Sleeper's armored plating! The control panel inside also gives you access to a full entertainment system, including a CD player, a DVD player and TV, and a personal computer! Also featured is a "toiletry system." Last I checked, going to the bathroom in your bed was not a good thing.

VERDICT: I can understand locking the doors, buying emergency survival kits, and other safety measures. But the Quantum Sleeper is safety overkill. In the other hand, having a TV and personal computer inside a bulletproof bed is kind of cool. Still, it's not worth buying what is, essentially, a luxury casket just to be able to surf the Internet in bed.

437 Scary Monsters Magazine
www.scarymonstersmag.com

The *Scary Monsters* magazine is a retro-style Transylvanian-esque magazine about werewolves, zombies, vampires, and the various incarnations of Frankenstein's monster. Never before has there been such variety in the depictions of zombies and werewolves: they look different every time! Then again, there was never an official "look" for the living dead. This magazine runs features like the "Journal of Frankenstein," a *Monster Memories* yearbook of their past issues, and other pieces of scary monster madness from the days of the black-and-white horror flicks.

PRODUCTS: In addition to offering subscriptions to the monster mag, you can also buy other monster-related gifts, like the Sam Scare Mask, a mask of a zombie man wearing a pair of creepy sunglasses. Since when are zombies sensitive to the sun? I thought that was vampires, or is that werewolves? I get so confused. You can also buy the videos of old clips from *Zacherley's* TV shows, a creepy monster show from the '50s.

VERDICT: The *Scary Monsters* magazine is a mix of old-school Transylvanian horror from the golden age movies, and a warped blend of modern humor. This store also offers some souvenirs from signature movies, like the Bates Mansion model from the movie *Psycho*. If you're a fan of not-so-scary, but somewhat humorous monster literature, the *Scary Monsters* magazine is a good pick.

. . . .

438

Prison Flicks
www.prisonflicks.com

Are you intrigued by the incarcerated? Do you desire detention centers in your movies? Prison Flicks is about movies set in or centered around prisons. As this site says of prison movies: "Basically anything you can do in a movie can be done in a prison movie." High-seas adventures, action, even love stories. Prison Flicks argues that "putting the characters in prison just makes it all so much more entertaining." Well, of course. Don't we all love seeing inmates as heroes?

PRODUCTS: Enough prison movies to fill a jailhouse are here, with links to buy them on Amazon. There are reviews of prison classics, like *The Great Escape* and *The Shawshank Redemption*, prison cult classics like *Escape from LA* and *Escape from New York*, and prison failures like *The Prisoner* with Jackie Chan (almost as good as *The Tuxedo!*), *The Rock* with Sean Connery and *Boa*. *Boa* deserves special mention here. In it, prehistoric snake terrorizes a prison twelve thousand feet under the Antarctic surface.

VERDICT: The best and worst of prison movies are here, and there <u>are</u> some good picks to be found. There is one thing I don't get: *Chicken Run*, a prison movie? Mel Gibson as a cocky rooster (no pun intended) saving chickens from a cruel farmer is NOT a prison movie. True, there's a breakout element, but a country farm is not a prison.

439

The Official Site of the eBay Wedding Dress Guy
www.weddingdressguy.com

They sell some crazy stuff on eBay. Haunted dolls, used underwear, you can even rent a guy to beat you up on eBay. But one eccentric eBay bidder has made a website out of his crazy auction. This site describes the story of the EBWDG's "satirical account of how he came to model his ex-wife's wedding dress and subsequent humorous updates literally left people all over the world crying from laughter." The EBWDG has a blog where he tells us about his new life as a stand-up comedian.

PRODUCTS: EBWDG T-shirts, clocks, mousepads, mugs, and more with a photo of the EBWDG in the eBay wedding dress! As you've probably figured out, the photos are extremely disturbing. There are also stickers with the phrases "I (heart) WDG" (I'm sure he loves you too), "I Don't" (I'm sure he wishes he said that to his ex-wife), and "Run Away! Run Away!" (you don't have to tell me twice!).

VERDICT: Thanks to the wonders of the Internet, the EBWDG's ex shall live in humiliation for the rest of her life, knowing that her ex-husband got famous off of her breakup with him. Isn't the Internet wonderful?

440

Casket Furniture
www.casketfurniture.com

It's furniture that you can always use—dead or alive! Casket Furniture is "your source for custom casket furniture, custom bedroom furniture and office furniture, casket novelty products, caskets and coffins, casket plans, and casket wear." Casket Furniture's products are meant to be "unique alternatives" that can help reduce funeral costs. They're unique, that's for sure!

PRODUCTS: Many varieties of casket furniture, as well as regular caskets, regular furniture (almost too regular for this morbid webpage), and Casket Novelties. One unique casket novelty is The Dali Portrait Casket Mirror. "Add a touch of the morbid to your languid lair. Simple coffin shape will send shivers down your lovers' spines. Glass not included." How am I going to find a casket-shaped piece of glass without paying a load of cash? Another Casket Novelty is the The Jefferson Casket Cigar Box. "Bill Clinton has nothing on this cigar box. For the politically corrupt aficionado." Bill has nothing on this one? Well, as he would say, it depends on what the meaning of "has" is.

VERDICT: Casket Furniture may be unusual, but it's also economic. Why have your surviving loved ones pay money for a casket when they can just carry you out of your living room while still on the furniture? If you're looking for some unique furniture pieces that can also save you a load of money once you kick the bucket, look no further than Casket Furniture.

441

I See Pet
www.iseepet.com

I See Pet allows you to "love your pet anytime, anywhere." You install a web-cam-like device and speaker in your house, and you can talk to your pet over the Internet. Baby talk to your fish from thousands of miles away! Never miss the next time Fido has an accident! You can even feed your pet using a remote control feeding system. It's high-tech, it's convenient, and it's an utterly unnecessary waste of your money!

PRODUCTS: Set up ISP with your network so you can access ISP anytime, anywhere! This site contains an extensive FAQ answering all computer questions you could possibly have. From installing ISP on a router network to retrieving a lost password (your pet as a password might be a good option), ISP makes connecting easy, sort of. To see what's in store for you once ISP is installed, check out the "Life with I See Pet" section.

VERDICT: Is it a coincidence that I See Pet has the same acronym as Internet Service Provider? I think not. It's a sign that the Internet, as useful as it is, exists so we can have stupid, excessively luxurious devices like I See Pet. While the Internet's biggest market is porn (no taxes + twisted perverts = big bucks), there's also a large market for very convenient, but ultimately useless devices like I See Pet.

442
The Leg Lamp
www.theleglamp.com

If you've ever seen the Yuletide classic *A Christmas Story*, you'll remember the Leg Lamp, the "major award" that Ralphie's father received as a bonus. Now, you can indulge yourself with this exotically erotic lamp, complete with its own "major award" certificate! The Leg Lamp site is the "original" leg lamp from the Christmas classic; accept no substitutions!

PRODUCTS: The Leg Lamp is a "clever" decoration that will "get more attention than anything you've ever had." Well, obviously. It's perfect as a gift for frat houses, bars, dens, and even…playrooms?! What kind of sick parent would put this in a child's room? And, "with your choice of stocking, shoe, and lampshade it can be customized to fit any decor." I don't think any heterosexual man would really give a darn if it matched the décor or not.

VERDICT: It's good to see that the women who purchased this lamp can tolerate something a little risqué. It shows that they're not easily offended, and that's a good thing. Too many people take life too seriously. Everybody needs a little bit of humor in their life. Offensive, maybe. Funny, heck yes! The Leg Lamp is a great example of a gift about learning to take life with a laugh and a smile.

. . . .

443
Classic Alien Paintings
www.classicalien.com

Aliens don't often come to mind when thinking of classical artwork. Well, that's about to change with Classic Alien Paintings. "On this site, we present a range of famous paintings with the added twist of replacing the main characters with an alien art theme. We also have some erotic art originals, again populated by alien beings." "Erotic" and "alien" do NOT mix. Period.

PRODUCTS: Any of the alien paintings in the gallery page can be purchased here. There's the *Dancers* painting, with several aliens dancing as well as the *Father's Blessing* painting in the style of Michelangelo's artwork in the Sistine Chapel. I'd obviously think Michelangelo's vision of God would include aliens. Wouldn't you? The *Planting Their Seed* painting, has an alien replacing the man in Grant Wood's *American Gothic*, and the rest of the paintings are the aforementioned "erotic art." Very, very, disturbing.

VERDICT: It seems aliens are all the rage these days. First they invaded movies, then they invaded TV, and now they're invading the Internet. Is Earth next? Or is their influence limited to our "creative" forms of expression? Only time will tell if this artwork belongs to the ages, or in the garbage.

444

Pimp Juice
www.letitloose.com

Did you ever think that skinny losers could be instantly transformed into pimps? Well, you still shouldn't, because it's not going to happen. But the makers of Pimp Juice, an energy drink created by rapper Nelly, are trying their hardest to peddle their product to wannabe pimps. However, "pimp" isn't what you think it is here. Rather, it's an acronym that stands for Positive Intellectual Motivated Person. Uhhh...sure. This site has news on PJ, and lets students apply for the $5000 P.I.M.P scholarship.

PRODUCTS: Buy a twenty-four-pack of PJ, with twenty-four cans of "liquid energy." It'll just cost you about forty-eight bucks. Two dollars per can? Ouch! Being a positive intellectual motivated person isn't as easy or cheap as I thought it would be. You can also buy a shirt that says, "I AM A PIMP," with "Positive Intellectual Motivated Person" below it. Yo, man, you a pimp! What? Positive whatchucalit? There are also hats and jerseys with the words "Pimp Juice" on them. Strangely, positive intellectual motivated person is nowhere to be found on these duds. I wonder why?

VERDICT: Pimp Juice is an admirable effort to give back to the community, but I doubt many actual P.I.M.Ps are going to buy this to be a P.I.M.P. I may be a P.I.M.P, but most folks are not. They want to be a pimp, not a P.I.M.P. No matter what, PJ can help you become a pimp, whichever kind you want to be.

445

Wonder Farms
www.wonderfarms.com

Wonder Farms sells furry balls with eyeballs sticking out of them, called Softys. Really, that's what they are. Wonder Farms is a "mysterious and magical place ideal for growing Softys. They are a unique form of life that grow like plants but have fur like animals." This farm sounds a little too "mysterious" and "magical" for me. And remember, Softys "are self-sustaining creatures, but they require love to keep them happy. The more they are fondled the happier they are." I hope that's an error in the translation!

PRODUCTS: Fuzzo, Cozy, Cooter, Pinky, and Winky are all Softys you can buy to love. One Softy, Fuzzo, is "furry and green with four pink eyes. Each eye can be popped out of its pocket for extra-sensory perception. A special blend of 'love spirolina' give Fuzzo his rich green fur and a positive outlook on life." Spiro-what? By contrast to the gentle Fuzzo, Cooter is an orange Softy with one eye who "likes exploring small dark places with his eye and has a tendency to get into trouble." Cooter may be mischievous, but like his siblings, he looks like a deformed Tribble (the rapidly reproducing furry animals from the original *Star Trek*).

VERDICT: What will those crazy Japanese toymakers think of next? I wonder if they think America is as weird as we think they are? When we look at our dumbed-down, celebrity-obsessed culture, it's obvious that strangeness goes both ways. Wonder Farms simply indicates that they're a bit weirder than we are.

· ·

446

Mullet Wigs
www.mulletwigs.com

As if we didn't have enough mullet goodness with Mullet Junkie (number 354), you can now have your own mullet, free to wear whenever you want! Mullet Wigs sells wigs that makes you appear to have a mullet, without the hassle and shame of growing one. If you're "intrigued and fascinated by the cultural phenomenon known as the Mullet," then "you have come to the right place…Get laughed at! Get your ass kicked! Without having to grow a mullet!" If that's what's gonna happen to me, I'll pass on these pathetic wigs.

PRODUCTS: Choose a mullet wig from one of four classic styles: The Landscaper (a.k.a. The Ape Drape), the Trash (a.k.a. Kentucky Waterfall), The Class of 1987 (a.k.a. The Nebraska Neck Warmer) and the Female Mullet (a.k.a. The Bingo).

VERDICT: The Mullet Hunters could use some of these wigs. What better way to go on the hunt than to blend in with the native species? It's safer to take pictures of mullets when they think they're among their own kind. Regardless of whether you're a hunter or not, Mullet Wigs can bring out the true redneck in you, whenever and wherever you please.

447 Head Balancer
www.headbalancer.com

John Evans is the "Undefeated head-balancing champion." In the Guinness Book of World Records, Mr. Evans has an impressive six records. He can balance 96 milk crates, 548 soccer balls, 62 Guinness books, 11 beer barrels, or 101 bricks on his head. There's also a picture of John balancing a car on his head! How does he do that without snapping his neck? Mr. Evans is also a charitable man—so far he has raised 64,900 British pounds for charity!

PRODUCTS: The T-shirts feature a large photograph of John performing "his most popular and well-known record—balancing a Mini Cooper car in his head!" Mr. Evans "can manage this for over ten seconds, and…has performed the stunt all over the world, including [on] many television appearances." Well, I'm sure if I could balance a car on my head, people would want me to be on television too. The keyrings feature photos of Mr. Evans performing his famous balancing feats, and now each order comes with a FREE year planner, with twelve photos of Mr. Evans "in action!"

VERDICT: I wouldn't like the life that John Evans has. I wouldn't want to balance cars, bricks, beer barrels, and all that other stuff on my head! If this headstrong freak intrigues you, though, you can check out his site and maybe buy some stuff to help him out.

448 Star Spangled Ice Cream
www.starspangledicecream.com

Like W Ketchup (number 421), this site argues that if you don't support the Democrats, why should your ice cream? Check out the love/hate mail to see how much conservatives love this ice cream, and how much liberals loathe it. One man says, "I am a proud member of the vast right wing conspiracy. I will see if I can locate a distributor in the Houston area to handle your product." You're a member of the VRWC too? Maybe if there are enough of angry conservatives, it can actually exist! A more liberal writer says, "This is absolutely the most ridiculous thing I have ever seen. Why don't all of you imbeciles get a real job? Oh, sorry, there aren't any jobs. But as long as you're 'patriotic' you think everything will be fine. You people are PATHETIC!"

PRODUCTS: Flavors like Iraqi Road and Rushmallow (after conservative radio talk show host Rush Limbaugh), populate this conservative confection menu. A few other standout flavors are Smaller GovernMint (that's a flavor I can sink my teeth into!), and I Hate the French Vanilla. There's also Star-Spangled merchandise, with T-shirts and other gifts featuring some of the popular ice cream logos.

VERDICT: There are a few flavors missing from this patriotic palette. How about CBS Subjective Swirl, with a swirl of biased caramel reporting by Dan Rather? And don't forget Weapons of Mass Deliciousness; why didn't that get in here?

449 Modern Drunkard Magazine
www.moderndrunkardmagazine.com

Modern Drunkard Magazine is a crazy magazine written by "group of functional alcoholics based primarily in Denver, CO." Yes, they just did call themselves alcoholics. Do they mind that word? "No. We are taking it back from the fascists. Soon it will be considered a compliment." Alcoholic, a compliment. Yeah, sure. Another valid question is, "Are you drunk right now?" "Most likely." At least they're honest. Another is, "Do I have to be a drunk to enjoy your magazine?" "No, but it certainly helps." More brutal honesty there.

PRODUCTS: MDM shirts, hats, flasks, lighters, flags, and posters. There's the "86 Rules of Boozing" Poster, as well as a poster that says, "Now It's Time For My Real Job—Getting Loaded!" Your real job is pretty pitiful. "Hoist the flag of debauchery" with the MDM flag, a flag bearing two scabbards with a martini glass above them. Finally, you can subscribe to this loaded magazine. Twenty-four bucks gets you "six booze-packed issues that'll whip you into drinking shape in no time."

VERDICT: If there's one history lesson that everybody should remember, it's Prohibition. It didn't stop people from drinking, it just made them drink more. If you try to take away something people are regularly accustomed to having, there's going to be trouble. *Modern Drunkard Magazine* is a tribute to alcohol, which was, is and will always be a part of our culture.

· ·

450

The Bell Witch
www.bellwitch.org

BellWitch.org is dedicated to "preserving and popularizing the legend of Tennessee's infamous Bell Witch." The "visitor" in question is a supernatural entity who would, among other things, pull off bed sheets, sing hymns, and even slap members of the Bell family. Since when can ghosts slap people? The spirit was nicknamed the "Bell Witch" by Andrew Jackson, who supposedly visited the farm and witnessed the ghost's antics himself. Uhhuh. Sure. It's said that the spirit foretold the Great Depression, along with both world wars and the Civil War. It once even sang a song about brandy! What kind of psychotic specter is this?

PRODUCTS: Books on the Bell Witch are available, including one straight from the horse's mouth. *Our Family Trouble: The Bell Witch* by Richard Williams Bell, is an account of the Bell family's "experience," told by a descendant of the Bell clan. Another is *The Bell Witch: The Full Account*, by Pat Fitzhugh.

VERDICT: I've heard a lot of ghost stories, some of which are almost believable. But this one is nuts! A ghost that sings, gives death threats, predicts the future, and SLAPS PEOPLE? Visit this site and decide for yourself.

451

Yellow Bamboo
www.bamboovideo.com

Yellow Bamboo is a "an official self-development, protection, healing, and white magic non-profit association founded in Bali." Yellow Bamboo's videos allow you to tap your own inner energies to achieve "Rapid spiritual self-realization and personal development." Yellow Bamboo allows you to "attain more development in one month than ten years of yoga and meditation." I smell a "get-enlightened-quick" scheme here. You can even learn to "knock down attackers without touching them!" Talk about inner power!

PRODUCTS: The "free" videos are an introductory gift for starting your journey on the path to "personal power." These videos include the *Yellow Bamboo Initiation Ceremony*, which allows you to join this kooky clan without traveling to Bali. After you've been initiated, try the Level 1 *Yellow Bamboo Mantra and Pranayama*, a meditation exercise course "designed to empower you to achieve whatever you desire in life." What if I desire a hot blonde in a bikini?

VERDICT: Since when can yellow pieces of plant help me achieve psychic powers? Perhaps the masters of Yellow Bamboo learned from the pandas. It's not that farfetched to imagine that pandas have telekinetic powers, is it? If Pamela Anderson can write a book, maybe we can have telekinesis and instant healing powers, just like the pandas.

452

Feral Children
www.feralchildren.com

Feral Children is a site is about children often known as "wild children" or "wolf children." Feral Children are children who have "grown up with minimal human contact, or even none at all. They may have been raised by animals (often wolves) or somehow survived on their own." If you think the classic "raised by wolves" story is ridiculous, you'll be surprised to learn that children have been raised by many different animal types—even ostriches! What do they do, stick their heads in the sand?

PRODUCTS: Videos, books, and music about feral children, available from Amazon. They even offer children's books on feral children! One book, *The Wolf Girls : An Unsolved Mystery from History* by Jane Yolen and Heidi Elisabet Yolen Stemple, presents the story of "Kamala and Amala" and asks readers to determine whether the children in the story were actually raised by wolves or not. The music section features music inspired by feral children, including *Über den Wolken—Lieder aus 4 Jahrzehnten*, which translates into *Over the Clouds: Songs out of Four Decades*.

VERDICT: The truth is that wolves are very sophisticated animals. In fact, there has never been a report of a healthy wolf attacking a human. The notion of a child being raised by an ostrich is crazier than the wolf scenario. Regardless, Feral Children offers interesting insight into the world of children raised without human contact.

453

Head Blade
www.headblade.com

Head Blade: "The Ultimate Head-Shaving Razor." This razor is specifically designed to shave your head. No more clogging up less powerful razors with hair trying to shave yourself bald. Now, the Head Blade can help your head stay nice, shiny, and hairless. There's an FAQ here for the Head Blade, with one incredibly stupid question: "I can't read. Do you have an illustration that shows how to use this smart little invention?" Clicking the link proceeds to a picture explaining the Head Blade. If you can't read, I suggest you learn how. Now.

PRODUCTS: This store opens with—what else—a gorgeous woman hugging a mannequin's head. She appears not to have a top on, but we can't tell for sure (unfortunately). You can buy the Head Blade itself, along with accessories, apparel, and skincare products. Perhaps the oddest product is the Head Blade Pen, a pen with the Head Blade logo. Why do we need a pen with an advertisement for a razor on it?

VERDICT: Certain people look better with their heads shaved, no doubts about it. If you think you look good bald, you can either buy the Head Blade, or, you can wait until you get older and your hair starts falling out! You don't need a razor to shave off hair when you have no hair to begin with! Isn't getting old fun?

454

Choc Roach
www.chocroach.com

This site introduces you to the wonderful Choc Roaches, chocolate replicas of cockroaches. Both "genders" of Choc Roaches are made with "the same rich and delicious, melt-in-your-mouth Semi-Sweet Chocolate." Toasted almonds are the distinguishing feature between the two genders: the male Choc Roaches have almonds, while the females do not. Some people apparently appreciate the "feeling of authenticity" that they get from biting into an almond Choc Roach, because "it more closely replicates the experience of biting down on the real thing." That's not a very pleasant thought.

PRODUCTS: Mini-Packs are for the "timid" who are not ready to "make a commitment" yet. Midi-Packs are for "the almost ready to join the cause, but still a little shy." Finally, the Parti-Packs are for "the bold" who are ready to "make a statement." What kind of statement? "I like eating chocolate insects"? In addition to the roach packs are the RoachKebabs. They include tags with "instructions for use:" "OPEN MOUTH, INSERT ROACH & SUCK." If hearing that phrase doesn't induce nausea, I don't know what will.

VERDICT: We can at least be thankful that Choc Roaches are not real roaches encased in chocolate. Choc Roaches are slightly more refined than "Hot Lix" (number 381). "Slightly" is the key word here. If you can get over the fact that these confections are shaped like cockroaches, Choc Roaches might just be a tasty treat. Most people, however, will want this candy exterminated.

455

Toe Food
www.toefood.com

Toe Food has spent twenty years providing "edible foot products." Their target audience are people, companies, and organizations who are "always 'a step ahead' of the pack," and are "looking for that unique gift to 'stand out' from the crowd!" Two horrible foot puns in one paragraph! Talk about a "stand-up pair"!

PRODUCTS: Chocolate and candy feet products, like the Petite Feet, small, bite-size feet available in milk chocolate and white chocolate. Petite Feet are also available in bulk, and in sugar free! It's a delicious AND healthy way to stay a "step ahead" of weight gain! You can also buy Stinky Feet candy products, in regular variety (sour-apple flavored), Hot Stinky Feet (hot cinnamon flavored), and the Freaky Stinky Feet variety pack for Halloween season.

VERDICT: Ready for a slew of tacky foot puns? Here we go: Toe Food is a "step up" from traditional candy stores. In fact, the other confectionary sites are going "six feet under." They try their best to compete with Toe Food, but it's always "one step forward and two steps back" for them. So, if you're looking to "step up" to another level in confectionary quality, you can rest assured that Toe Food will "stand by you" in your quest for reasonably-priced feet-shaped candy.

456   Wooden Computer Peripherals
www.woodcontour.com

Not content having just your desk made out of wood? Now, why settle for boring plastic when you can have a wooden computer? Wooden Contour Computer peripherals allows you to buy computer accessories made out of wood! This site features an "exquisite line of solid wood PC peripherals specifically designed for those who appreciate the finer things in life." Each peripheral set contains a mouse, keyboard, and seventeen-inch flat panel monitor, all made out of a wood type of your choosing.

PRODUCTS: Each peripheral set is specially made with high-quality wood. The keyboards, mice, and monitors undergo a rigorous crafting and finishing process. Available in mahogany, red elm, beech, maple, cherry, teak, and other exotic wood varieties, the peripheral sets will cost you anywhere from $5,000 to $12,000! More proof that anything claiming to be a "finer thing" in life is extremely expensive.

VERDICT: Why would you even want a wooden mouse, or keyboard, or monitor? Wood is out of style! Sleek silver and black computer peripherals are in now, not some old-fashioned wooden crap! This outrageous set of computer accessories is way too stiff for the average budget shopper.

457

AOL Memorabilia
www.aolmemorabilia.com

AOL CDs, and beyond! "You say you want more AOL Memorabilia? I got your AOL Memorabilia right here!" I? You mean, you run this whole store? All by yourself? Get a life, dude. This AOL Memorabilia site is also a museum of sorts, with history harkening back to the days of 1.0, when they charged online time by the hour (I believe it was $2.95 an hour when we first got it).

PRODUCTS: Old AOL T-shirts, including the AppleLink Personal Edition T-shirt. AppleLink was a service that Quantum/AOL made for the Apple Computer company. Obviously, it didn't work out (or we'd all be surfing with AppleLink today), so the project was scrapped. But, the T-shirt remains! The T-shirt proudly bears the AppleLink motto: "Once you're linked, you're hooked." Yeah, we're all pretty hooked to AppleLink today. You can also buy the AOL Beach Bash T-shirt, which AOL gave out at their 1992 company picnic! It's tacky, it's old, and it's, um, historical. Yeah, that's it.

VERDICT: I still am baffled by how AOL can possibly manufacture countless amounts of those darned free AOL trial disks. You'd think they'd need to a small country to produce the plastic needed to manufacture those things! Manufacturing excess aside, AOL Memorabilia offers, well, memorable products for the AOL junkie.

458

Feather Wear
www.featherwear.com

First, we had "Designer Doggie Wear" (number 184) as an option for clothing our pets. Now, for the bird enthusiast, we have Feather Wear! Feather Wear offers designer bird clothing, but that's not their flagship product. Rather, Feather Wear is the maker of the Revolutionary Bird Diaper! "Safely travel with your feathered friends without fear of messy surprises!" I thought everybody liked surprises? "Convenient! Comfy! Colorful!" I can agree on convenience and color, but how do you know if birds find this dopey diaper comfortable?

PRODUCTS: Flight Suits is the more attractive name of the Bird Diaper. "Worry-free from embarrassing accidents (poop) or dangerous fly-aways." How does the bird diaper prevent your bird from flying away? Why, with bird leashes, of course! These Bird Leashes are Velcro, and are used "exclusively" with Flight Suits. In other words, you have to buy a Flight Suit for $19.95 before you can buy the bird leashes. You pay for what you get though.

VERDICT: When I hear the words "Flight Suit," I think of something jet pilots wear to protect themselves from the dangerous effects of G-forces. Or perhaps an old aviator jacket, like the ones worn by Charles Lindbergh and Amelia Earhart. Diapers for birds should not come to mind. Feather Wear products are convenient—perhaps a little too convenient—for bird owners, but useless for anybody else.

459 Surfers Against Sewage
www.sas.org.uk

Let's catch some radical waves, and save the world from pollution at the same time, dude! The Surfers Against Sewage campaign is crusading for "clean, safe recreational waters, free from sewage effluents, toxic chemicals, and nuclear waste." Oh, yes, you can find nuclear waste on any shoreline you visit, can't you? SAS uses a "solution-based argument of viable and sustainable alternatives" to challenge industry leaders and politicians to help clean up our shorelines. Solution-based arguments? I'd say that's a little vague, wouldn't you?

PRODUCTS: T-shirts, hooded sweatshirts, kid's stuff, accessories, and other clothing to support the SAS cause. Like any environmentally conscious site, they sell organic varieties of their products, including hats and T-shirts. The logo for this line of products appears to be some sort of fish. It actually looks like a mutated fish. Mutated from polluted sewage, perhaps? Smart message, dudes.

VERDICT: Surfers don't come to mind when thinking of improving the environment. Words like "gnarly," "radical," "bodacious," and "mondo" come to mind, but saving the environment? I guess it goes to show that those cool surfer dudes can also have a heart for the piscatorial playgrounds of their extreme sport.

460

I Used to Believe
www.iusedtobelieve.com

Do you remember some of the silly beliefs you had as a child? Did you think that babies came from the stork, or even that everybody likes the president? This site contains a full archive of silly beliefs from readers, sorted by topics like sex, religion, the media, and grown-ups. While there are several very cliché beliefs (i.e., the TV would suck you in, like the movie *Poltergeist*, if you watched too long), some of the beliefs are downright hilarious! One person thought that if "I ate something electronic, I'd have electric powers." Hopefully, you never actually tried that!

PRODUCTS: IUTB features the book, *Butter Comes from Butterflies*, by Mat Connolley and Scott Menchin. This book is a huge collection of the "silly, strange, and sometimes astonishing" explanations children have for have had for things. Like the kid who thought that grilled cheese sandwiches were really made with "gorilla" cheese! Mmmmm...toasted gorilla.

VERDICT: One belief I had, like many other people, is that watermelon and apple seeds would sprout up in my stomach and kill me! I still am paranoid of fruits with seeds. If you have the fortune (or misfortune) of remembering some of your ridiculous notions of how the world works, IUTB will be a welcome reminder of the innocence and naiveté we used to have as children.

461

TV Be Gone
www.tvbegone.com

Are you tired of those loud TVs in sports bars, showing games nobody wants to see? Can't find the remote when the Arby's Oven Mitt commercials come on? Or do you just like annoying people by turning off their favorite shows? TV Be Gone is your answer. It's a keychain remote that turns off TVs. Wow, that's so amazing! I can turn off a TV! The thing that makes TVBG different is that it can turn off "virtually any television!" That means you can turn off TVs at your friends' houses, at parties, and even in sports bars.

PRODUCTS: Why use TVBG? "Because a TV that is powered on is like second-hand smoke. Why should you be exposed to TV just because someone else is addicted to it…Some people may like breathing in someone else's smoke, but that's not for everyone. Similarly, not everyone wants to be disturbed with someone else's media." Who likes breathing in second-hand smoke? That's like somebody wanting to chop their fingers off, or wanting to listen to Michael Bolton!

VERDICT: I know if I'm watching *The Simpsons* or *The Price Is Right*, I wouldn't want some stranger turning off my TV. If I don't hear Bob Barker reminding me to spay or neuter my pet every morning, I can get pretty angry. On the other hand, if I were being subjected to *Judge Judy* or *Divorce Court*, then I'd want TVBG in a hurry.

462 Dome of a Home
www.domeofahome.com

The house of the future is here! Dome of a Home offers all the information you need on the world's greatest dome-shaped house. The Dome Home is a building constructed with style and practicality in mind. Actually, the primary purpose is to protect against natural disasters. The Dome Home, having survived Hurricane Ivan, is proof of how this simple, yet revolutionary new concept is the future of architectural design.

PRODUCTS: Buy the Dome of a Home T-shirt! On the front is a design with the number "2000," representing the current time period, showing the Dome Home on the beach above dolphins swimming in the ocean. On the back is the number "3000," showing the Dome Home underwater! So, let me get this straight: in one thousand years, the Dome Home will still be here, only it will be submerged under the ocean? Such a cryptic T-shirt. It looks cool, though. If you can't settle for a lousy T-shirt, you can rent out the Dome Home…for about $5,000 a week!

VERDICT: Dome of a Home is proof that the best designs come from the simplest ideas. A house modeled after a simple geometric shape? Perhaps one thousand years from now, we'll all have a dome of a home. Regardless of what the future holds for humanity, the Dome of a Home is a simple, stylish, and just plain smart idea.

463

Fog Screen
www.fogscreen.com

Now, not only can you watch your favorite movies and TV shows, you can now walk through them! The Fog Screen is a special projector that puts an image on a screen of thin mist. So, if you've ever wanted to turn on *Roseanne* and punch Tom Arnold in the face without breaking your television set, Fog Screen can make your dream a reality! Isn't technology great?

PRODUCTS: Rent out the Fog Screen for your next party or presentation. It works like a slideshow projector; just replace the standard screen with the fog screen. Perfect for showing home movies at family reunions and wedding receptions! Or, watch the big game on the Fog Screen! Watch as your drunk, idiotic friends try to jump through the screen and catch the ball! The possibilities are endless!

VERDICT: Like Holokits (number 72), Fog Screen is a promising new technology that just may be the wave of the future. Pretty soon, we'll forget all about HDTV and we'll be watching bad sitcoms and reality TV shows on a thin screen of fog.

- -

464 I'm Changing the Climate
www.changingtheclimate.com

Affluenza-infected suburbanites, beware; the hunt is on! While a small percentage of SUV owners use these behemoths for off-road expeditions and camping trips, most owners of SUVs are soccer moms and white-collar businessmen. I'm Changing the Climate has a mission to transform SUVs "from a status trinket to the badge of shame that it is! Join us as we direct our social activist energies toward the exciting new sport of Big Game SUV Hunting."

PRODUCTS: The sole product of this site is the I'm Changing the Climate bumper sticker. But you're not supposed to put this bumper sticker on your car; you're supposed to put it on OTHER cars—SUVs. By sticking an ICTC bumper sticker on the back of an SUV, you're engaging in the sport of Big Game SUV Hunting. There are rules of engagement for this sport: First, much like how hunters seek antlered bucks over small fawns, SUV Hunters should only look for big ones: Range Rovers, Ford Expeditions, Cadillac Escalades (yo, yo, I'm changin' da climate, dawg!), and, the ultimate SUV Hunter prize, the Hummer. Secondly, don't tag the gas guzzlers that are needed for business purposes. Go after affluent suburban owners who have SUVs just to "keep up with the Joneses." If it's obviously only used for "expeditions" to the downtown office, it's fair game.

VERDICT: This is a site I agree with! Why should people be proud of owning these giants when their idea of the enjoying the great outdoors is strolling some manicured golf course? If you're looking for a fun way to get back at affluent owners of these gargantuan gas guzzlers, order a box of stickers and take a suburban hunting trip.

465 Amanda Storm's Wrestling and Cookie Paradise
www.amandastorm.com

Wrestling and cookies: what better combination? Amanda Storm is a graduate of Killer Kowalski's Wrestling School, and she appears on *Atlas Championship Wrestling Television*. Amanda was also the star of an MTV documentary called *True Life: I'm a Pro Wrestler* (MTV makes such high-quality documentaries). Finally, Amanda also bakes cookies and sells them on this site. Talk about a jack of all trades!

PRODUCTS: Buy *Blakwidow: The Book*, which details Amanda's life as a pro wrestler. This book sounds like a captivating read! Be sure to check out the *California Challenge Submission Wrestling Video*, featuring Amanda and her friend Kristie in forty-five minutes of "highly competitive wrestling." Is watching two sweaty women wrestling for forty-five minutes a good thing or a bad thing? Finally, try a batch of Amanda's chewy chocolate chip cookies, made from scratch in Amanda's kitchen and sent directly to you!

VERDICT: Doesn't every guy want a woman who can do a choke hold AND bake delicious gourmet cookies? Amanda Storm is the perfect woman! Now you too can get a taste of what it's like to be Amanda Storm, along with a taste of those scrumptious homemade cookies.

466 Ill Mitch, Russian Rapper, Skateboarder, and Boxer
www.illmitch.com

"I am ILL Mitch. I come from Russia to America now I am free to do three favorite things. These are rap and ride on my skateboard and hit my boxing bag. But most favorite thing is rap." Isn't America great? This site gives you a glimpse at the enigma that is Ill Mitch. See him make meaningless, rap-style hand gestures! Watch him posing with his skateboard and his over-sized, dorky red helmet! And marvel while he spars with his old punching bag! Finally, be sure to check out the news section for the latest on Ill Mitch and his upcoming new CD!

PRODUCTS: Buy Ill Mitch CD now! "Hello to rap fans. This is my CD...Named PUNCH WHILE RAP. 'Turn it up!' they say." Please. Turn it down. NOW. You can listen to his song, "Fast and Danger," which is akin to listening to nails grind down a chalkboard. If you're looking for a gift that's guaranteed to disappoint, pick up the This Board is Fast and Danger shirt, with a cartoon of Mitch posing with his oversized red helmet and skateboard.

VERDICT: Ill Mitch's rapping is a disappointment to the genre. Not that any other rap song should even be called music, but this is really, really, REALLY bad rap. Bad as in Gerardo bad (if you don't remember "Rico Suave," consider yourself lucky). This Russian rapper is an example of how, sometimes, the American cultural melting pot can get a little ugly.

467 American Anti-Gravity
www.americanantigravity.com

Humans have always been searching for ways to defy the laws of nature. American Anti-Gravity is a chronicling of attempts to counteract the force that keeps us from floating off into space, along with a host of other efforts to make science fiction into science fact. Learn about Lightning Beam Guns, Jetfan's Coanda-Effect UFO, and the HFGW Gravity Beams—which teaches you how to make a "pure beam of gravitational energy" with super-conductors. Doesn't everybody have a superconductor?

PRODUCTS: Buy the American Anti-Gravity CDROM, with over four hundred megabytes of anti-gravitational goodness. This stunning CD includes information on "lifter" technology, which presumably uses devices that allow you to, well, lift things. It also contains information on Ion Propulsion systems, the Marcus Device, Superconductor Grav-Shielding, and De Aquino's ELF Anti-Gravity! I don't know what they are, either, but they sure sound cool!

VERDICT: This stuff is harder to understand than an IRS tax return form! Then again, if Britney Spears can understand anti-gravity (as shown from Britney's Guide to Semiconductor Physics from the original 505), maybe it isn't so complicated after all. Unless you're a physics professor, however, you won't understand American Anti-Gravity's extremely complicated and headache-inducing terminology.

468 Own Your Own Gargoyle
www.stonecarver.com

Who said gargoyles were only for Gothic cathedrals? This site allows you to own your very own Gothic-style gargoyle! Whether you want to creep out your neighbors with a gargoyle on the front porch, or creep out your co-workers with a desktop gargoyle, OYOG offers plenty of eerie, unsettling, and downright scary options for owning your own hideous stone beast.

PRODUCTS: Gargles of gargoyle designs are available, like the Dolce Mio, which translates into "My Sweet." This nine-inch-high bust depicts a hideous beast holding a bouquet of flowers. A stone demon offering stone roses; how romantic! The grossly misnamed Cutie gargoyles are described as "a different kind of pet rock." All the uselessness with bad looks to boot!

VERDICT: I've always been scared of gargoyles, and Own Your Own Gargoyle's offerings are more unsettling than attractive. It's obvious why Gothic architects thought these would scare off pigeons seeking a bathroom break. If you're a fan of Gothic architecture, or, if you're seeking a scary stone sentinel for your front lawn, feel free to indulge yourself at Own Your Own Gargoyle.

469 **Bio Hazard Alert Detector**
www.mcwhortle.com

McWhortle Enterprises is a company in the business of "biological defense mechanisms." Their products are geared towards protecting corporate executives and field workers from environmental hazards and terrorist attacks. Now, McWhortle is advertising a simple product that any average Joe can use, along with some intriguing investment opportunities.

PRODUCTS: For the first time, McWhortle is selling a commercial product to the general public: the Bio Hazard Alert Detector. With a simple power source of two AA batteries, can detect "microscopic levels of hazardous bio-organisms." It can detect weapons grade biohazards from fifty feet away. Great, now I know when there's a highly poisonous gas near me? Then what do I do?

VERDICT: Unless you're in a potentially dangerous work environment, the Bio Hazard Alert Detector won't be of much use to you. We're safe enough that we don't need to walk around with a device designed to detect poisonous chemicals. But, for overly cautious people, the Bio Hazard Alert Detector is, in their minds, a necessity. You make up your own mind on this gadget's usefulness.

470   **Psychic Twins**
www.psychictwins.com

Usually, a pair of hot blonde twins is a good thing. This case is no different—if you can forget about their crazy careers, that is! Linda and Terry Jamison are identical twins who also both happen to be psychos—er, psychics! The Psychic Twins appear regularly on Oprah Winfrey's Oxygen Network and even—what else—National Enquirer TV! They MUST be for real! The twins are also "accomplished actresses, singers, comedians, producers, designers, models, authors, teachers, healers, mediums, lecturers, painters, and book illustrators...and have done all of these things professionally!" It seems like being credible is the only thing they can't do!

PRODUCTS: The Psychic Twins' *Transformation* CD is chock full of "life changing affirmations," along with soothing "celestial" music. Think relaxation CDs, but with hot, blonde, psychic twins. To get this super-psychic CD, order online, or simply send $20 to the twins' home address! Open your mailbox, find a few twenties, sounds like a great job to me!

VERDICT: Are these chicks for real? Put it this way: the twins will be appearing soon on *Weird TV*, they have also appeared on the British show *American HOT*, and they once made an appearance on *The Osbournes*. Put that together with National Enquirer TV, and you get a good picture of how credible these "talented" twins are.

471

Ice Hotel
www.icehotel.com

Don't bother taking off your mittens and scarves, because this hotel is about as cool as it gets—literally. The Ice Hotel is the world's only hotel made completely out of frozen ice! Located in the village of Jukkasjärvi, a small village two hundred kilometers north of the Arctic Circle, the Ice Hotel prides itself on, among other things, the fact that their interior room temperature is never OVER 0 degrees Celsius! Talk about a "cold" reception! Ha, ha…what?

PRODUCTS: In addition to a full fledged souvenir shop, the Ice Hotel site also sells—what else—ice! The Ice Shop sells ice either as pure, raw material, or in the form of a magnificent ice sculpture. I've always wanted a big monkey made of ice. The souvenir shop sells Ice Hotel DVDs, books, shirts, and even thermal underwear, a necessity if you plan to visit.

VERDICT: If you don't mind freezing your butt off while sleeping, showering, and watching TV, the Ice Hotel is a chillingly awesome alternative to the dry, hot, desert city of Las Vegas, or the tropical, humid beaches of Jamaica. If you want something a little more exotic for your next vacation or romantic getaway, the Ice Hotel offers a "cool" alternative.

472

Lost in Toys
www.lostintoys.com

Danger, Will Robinson, danger! Danger of the tacky kind, that is. For those who aren't familiar with the retro sci-fi series, *Lost in Space* was a series about a family who was sent into space in the year 1997 (funny, I didn't hear anything about that). The Robinson family would meet Space Vikings, android armies, time merchants, and a host of other crazy characters on their journey to Alpha Centauri.

PRODUCTS: Model kits, trading cards, T-shirts, calendars, and a ton of other collectables from the TV series and the movie. But the ultimate awesomely horrible gift is the Robot Ramblings CD set, a trio of CDs comprised solely of phrases from the Robinson's eccentric B-9 robot that looks more like a gumball machine. Hear such classic phrases as, "I have come to warn you about the robotoid" (we all know how dangerous he is), "That does not compute" (sounds like Microsoft technical support), and of course, the classic "Danger, Will Robinson!"

VERDICT: It's hard to believe that, as little as forty years ago, all of the corny futuristic space dramas were set in the year 1999, or 2005. Today, we're just as close to getting to Alpha Centauri as we were then. However, some things have come along which the writers of the fifties could have never imagined: cell phones, computers, reality TV, and rap music. Perhaps truth is stranger than fiction.

473

Clayton Bailey
www.claytonbailey.com

Clayton G. Bailey is a ceramic sculptor who creates extremely unusual sculptures. Some of his sculptures include a Hypothermic Jar from 1997 that, by the sculptor's own admission, "looks like a chocolate brownie." Another type of Bailey's sculptures is the Burping Bowl, which contains a "submerged ceramic creature" that will "periodically [lurch] up in the water and [emit] a loud belching sound." How pleasant. Whenever you visit a new section of the site, you can hear a loud, comical noise through your computer speakers (boings, whistles, etc.).

PRODUCTS: Buy "Mad Scientist Gift Items," like the UNOBTAINI-UM, which contains "The rarest of the known rare earths" and is "coveted by many but never obtained until now." Then, why is it called Unobtainium? You can also buy "Space and Robot Items" like the Robot Teapot, a porcelain robot that actually brews tea. You'd better have deep pockets, though: the Robot Teapot alone is five hundred dollars! Nobody ever said art was cheap!

VERDICT: Art seems to evolve into something weirder and stupider with each passing day. Clayton Bailey's work is, technically, art, but when you look at it you'll see stupid sculptures like something at a garage sale. For the prices on these porcelain art pieces, this site is really ridiculous.

474

Oozing Goo
www.oozinggoo.com

Lava Lamp fans, your time has come! The aptly named Oozing Goo is a self-described "Lava Lamp Syndicate" that sells lava lamps and provides instructions for making them yourself. Learn about the disputed history of Lava Lamps, and see several different versions about how this loony lamp was invented. Or, discuss Lava Lamps on the "Lava Line" forums.

PRODUCTS: Lava Lamps are available in the eight-ounce mini Lava Lamp, the twenty-ounce medium Lava Lamp, the best selling thirty-two ounce Midnight Lava Lamp, and the whopping fifty-two ounce Aristocrat Lava Lamp, which is described as "Cary Grant meets Jerry Garcia." That's like George W. Bush meets Scott Peterson: not proba-ble! A link to buy other novelty lighting, such as sparkle lamps or black lights, is also on this webpage.

VERDICT: Lava Lamps have always been a groovy decoration option, and Oozing Goo offers oodles of those options for you. If you want to be creative and save money by making your own, Oozing Goo provides the necessary information. If you just want to buy your own profes-sionally made Lava Lamp, you have several great models to choose from. For anything you could want about Lava Lamps, Oozing Goo is the place.

475 Reading Toes: The Book

www.readingtoes.com

The art of reading toes is a "method used to obtain self-knowledge, and to analyse personalities and behaviour patterns by interpreting the position and shape of toes." Imre Somogyi, the author of *Reading Toes*, "developed a theory that toes are mirrors and that the shape and position of your toes show who you are." Think palm reading, except uglier.

PRODUCTS: *Reading Toes*, the book, can be purchased on Amazon.com. In *Reading Toes*, Imre Somogyi explains the enlightening revelations that led to the discovery of the method. And, of course, he teaches you how to read your own toes, and the toes of others! Each toe represents something different. For example, the right pinky toe represents the earth, fear, and insecurity. How did you get this from looking at feet? A reader commenting about *Reading Toes* says, "It works!" and explains how the book "makes you understand that harmony can only be achieved when you accept that other people are different from yourself." I could have figured that out without looking at my feet.

VERDICT: How can you learn about your personality by staring at your toes? Everybody's feet look the same to me. Sure, some are bigger than others, and some are uglier or smellier than others, but we all have ten toes that look, for the most part, exactly alike. Reading Toes is a bunch of new age nonsense, and that's the "toe-tal" truth.

476 Experimental Interaction Unit

www.eiu.org

The Experimental Interaction Unit is a unique look into the future of technology. The creators of EIU are striving to "employ state-of-the-art techniques" to create technologies which will "simultaneously study, distract, and assault our future interactions with machines." English, please? The technologies being researched here include Dispersion, the very scary biological pathogen vending machine; the I-Bomb, the bomb of the future designed to destroy computers and machines on a massive scale;

and the Gallery Shooting Gallery, a gun you can fire at another human being via the Internet! Scared yet?

PRODUCTS: Buy the Official EIU T-shirt, with the EIU logo on it, or the Personal Tactical Technology poster, with pictures of microscopic biological pathogens on them. Or, buy the video of the Dispersion machine at the Arts Electronica 1999 show. Finally there's the I-Bomb informational video, a video detailing the development of the I-Bomb.

VERDICT: This stuff is scary! Whatever their intents, their so-called "scientific research" will frighten you, shock you, and make you wonder what the future holds for us.

477 Tsui Design and Research
www.tdrinc.com

Eugene Tsui has been called "the seminal architect of the twenty-first century." His twenty-first-century design ideas look more like something out of a bad science-fiction movie. In addition to designing theme parks and office buildings, Tsui also has made plans for a floating city and the Ultima Tower, a two-mile-high residential living complex! A weird idea with a name to match!

PRODUCTS: You can buy *Evolutionary Architecture: Nature as a Basis for Design* by Eugene Tsui. The book proposes architectural concepts based on nature's structures, such as buildings shaped like dragonflies and spider webs. Also available is the *Shenzen Ecological Theme Park Concept Book*, with concept artwork of unique, unusual, and downright wacky designs. There are also the Eugene Tsui posters. One depicts Tsui wearing a cape, and the other is a strange picture of Tsui's head crossed with what appears to be a seashell. From what I've seen, this guy does have a seashell for a brain. Finally, there are the hilarious futuristic clothes, like the one-piece athletic jumpsuit that's so ugly it makes Zoobaz pants look tame.

VERDICT: If Eugene Tsui is the architect of the future, I certainly don't want to be around when the "future" buildings start going up. I mean, a floating city? A spider-shaped theme park? Jumpsuits that look like something a cheesy superhero would wear? I'll take today anytime over the future, thank you very much.

478 Peter Pan's Home Page
pixyland.org/peterpan

I can fly! At least, that's what this nut thinks. This is the personal page of a fifty, yes, fifty-year-old man who likes to dress up in green tights and shirts and pretend that he's never going to grow up. Starting this site "so that Tinkerbell would have an easier time finding me," this man goes on to describe his hobbies and explain his reasoning for his bizarre behavior, saying that "society has deified the gender boundaries they've established, especially the rules of what boys should and should not enjoy doing."

PRODUCTS: If you "donate" money to keep this site up, you get a gift along with your "donation." Donate sixteen dollars to get a signed "flying" picture of the author of this site leaping into the air, pretending to fly. Donate twenty dollars for a Be a Pixie mousepad, a mousepad with the same picture. Finally, donate twenty-five dollars to get a T-shirt with—you guessed it—the same picture. Talk about high-quality production values.

VERDICT: I don't care if you want to stay forever young in spirit; dressing like Peter Pan and leaping into the air is just plain weird. What do this guy's friends think of him? Does he even have any friends? I'd rather hang around with Wacko Jacko at Neverland ranch than spend time in this guy's version of Neverland. And asking for "donations" in exchange for cheaply made products is pretty stupid as well. If you consider yourself the slightest bit normal, you'll stay far away from this perturbed pixie.

479 Weirdo Music
www.weirdomusic.com

Weirdo Music, "your portal for weird and wonderful music," takes a look at several alternative music choices. The reviews section evaluates several odd titles like Hmmm..., Kraftwerk, the Prime Time Sublime Community Orchestra, the Thurston Lava Tube, Uncle Neptune, and Two Headed Puppy. The latter review says you shouldn't expect "exceptional vocal or musical stunts or incredibly inventive song writing." Instead, just expect "pure entertainment." I'm supposed to enjoy the album when the singing and lyrics are crappy? Looks like the artists aren't the only weirdos on this site.

PRODUCTS: Links to several weird music shopping sites are available, like Subliminal Sounds, a site offering such groovy titles as Tari Bert's *R So So*; "Groovy '60s sounds from the land of smile!" And, where would this "land of smile" be? Subliminal Sounds also is candid about its goals, saying, "I need a lot of money to help everyone on this planet earth." Correction: you need money to help one person on this planet: you.

VERDICT: This site has some really wacky titles! Any site with an album called *Hair Goes Latin* on it is a winner in my book. If you're looking for some weird alternatives in your music library, Weirdo Music is about as weird as it gets.

480

Utilikilts
www.utilikilts.com

More Scottish kilt goodness, this time for the freedom-loving handyman! Utilikilts prides itself on their "comfortable alternative to trousers" with their Men's Unbifurcated Garments, or MUGs. Unbifurcated? Is that even a word? Be sure to check out the calendar section for the latest news on Celtic festivals and events, as well as the photo galleries for great professional photographs of kilt wearers.

PRODUCTS: Buy the Original Utilikilt, "the kilt that made Seattle famous!" A rainy, depressing United States northwest city isn't a place I'd associate with kilts. Nevertheless, the original kilt is "sturdy and comfortable" with large saddle pockets. It's "durable," "comfortable," and "versatile!" Also available are the Denim Utilikilt (like jeans, in kilt form), the Workman's Utilikilt (doesn't every workman wear a kilt?), the Survival Utilikilt (I will survive, baby), and the Leather Utilikilt (cowboy kilts)!

VERDICT: As The Kilt Store showed us, you can never get enough of that free feeling only offered by kilts. And now you can even be free and comfortable while fixing the lawnmower or that leaky faucet! It's freedom, versatility, and comfort, all in one stylish Scottish package.

481 Longmont Potion Castle
www.longmontpotioncastle.com

Fortunately, or rather, unfortunately, this is not another one of those kooky, new age magic sites. Rather, Longmont Potion Castle is "an infamous series of telephone calls that have been described…as 'the most absurd phone pranks on the market.'" Absurd would be perfect for describing these crank calls. Many of them are simply men laughing with the occasional "I don't know, bro" or "you crack me up." They don't crack me up, that's for sure.

PRODUCTS: You can buy LPC T-shirts, if they strike your fancy. One T-shirt has the name Mike Jourgensen, along with the phrase "late at night" against a blurred, blue picture. As if that weren't stupid enough, there's another with the word "abdomen" and a senseless drawing where an eye and two faces are the only clear images. Finally, if you desire something totally idiotic, boring, and downright dumb, you can buy tapes or CDs of these pathetic prank calls.

VERDICT: This is the worst thing since the eight-track tape. They're not even funny. They're not even intelligent. And they're definitely not worth your money. Listen to a few of them and you'll agree: if this were a real castle, it would be invaded, destroyed, and written off in history as a prime example of stupidity.

482 Ostriches Online
www.ostrichesonline.com

You've tried mink fur coats, you've got enough leather, so why not try the new rage in animal fashion: ostriches! With over twenty thousand ostrich products, forty-five thousand newsletter subscribers, and twenty-eight thousand satisfied clients in over 125 countries, Ostriches Online is your one-stop shop for everything ostrich!

PRODUCTS: Try boas, fringe trimmings, masks, fans, and other apparel made from ostrich feathers. The ostrich feather cape is a stylish alternative option for formal wear. Marked down from the

$1,750 retail price tag (yes, you read right), you can now get an ostrich cape for the low price of $262.50—if you buy one hundred of them. That's over twenty-five thousand dollars! Be sure to also try the boas, purses, and dusters. Dusting with ostrich feathers; the ultimate pointless indulgence.

VERDICT: Who knew ostriches were in such high demand? I certainly don't know anybody who would want a full wardrobe of ostrich feather clothing. Not only that, these clothes are uglier than an episode of the Maury Povich show (best known for meaningful topics such as, "Is it a woman or a man?"). Still, if you have a desire for a full-fledged ostrich wardrobe, open up your wallet at Ostriches Online.

483

Birdman
Weapons Systems
www.birdman.org

Touting "Unfriendly Products for an Unfriendly World," Birdman Weapons Systems Online is a site dedicated to providing you with the "most powerful weaponry concepts [known] to modern man." According to BWS, "Evil resides in ALL of us no matter what we do," and at the rate society is going today, we're all going to destroy each other sooner or later. So, when the time comes to defend yourself from your bloodthirsty neighbors, you'd better have the biggest guns, and that's where BWS comes in.

PRODUCTS: BWS is where you'll find the world's only hand-held nuclear pistol! The .50 BMG round of the Nuke 50 pistol packs as much power in a single shot as twelve hundred tons of TNT! Now that's a REAL weapon of mass destruction! Also available is the Mountain Dew shotgun, which lets its wielder fire unopened twelve ounce cans of Mountain Dew at extremely fast and extremely lethal speeds! Do THIS Dew!

VERDICT: Like BWS says, today's world, for the most part, is not a friendly place. So, when exercising your second amendment right to own a lethal weapon, why not get the most powerful weapons on Earth? The bottom line is that you will never be truly safe until you have your own hand-held nuclear pistol, as if that weren't obvious already.

484

Space Food Sticks
www.spacefoodsticks.com

This site is even more proof that food in stick form is never a good thing. Space Food Sticks are the original freeze-dried sticks that astronauts used to eat on their missions into space. What do these sickening sticks taste like? Some customers have compared their taste to Powerbars (not a good thing), but also say that "there's something chewy and unique about Space Food Sticks that is quite indescribable." I can describe it in one word: yuck!

PRODUCTS: In association with the "Funky Food Shop," SFS offers the original astronaut food in three pairs of two for ten dollars. Ten dollars for six disgusting freeze dried sticks of God-knows-what? You can also purchase the original Neopolitan astronaut ice cream. Let's see, should I buy freeze dried ice cream for $1.67, or should I buy a jumbo pack of delicious milk chocolate M&Ms for about the same price? Decisions, decisions.

VERDICT: If Space Food Sticks are as disgusting as the astronaut ice cream (a food which I had the unfortunate displeasure of tasting), I wouldn't taste them if I were on a desert island! Although, if I had fifteen rivals on that island, I'd gladly feed them the space sticks, because I'd do anything to get that prize of one million dollars. A purely hypothetical situation, of course. Somebody would be crazy to do that in real life…right?

485

The Pharaoh's Pump
www.thepump.org

There are many arguments over why the pyramids were built. Some say they were tombs for pharaohs; others say they were astronomically-oriented structures with religious significance. According to this book, the pyramids were actually Egyptian water pumps! The articles on this site chronicle the research behind how and why the pyramids were supposedly built for this theoretical function.

PRODUCTS: *The Pharaoh's Pump* book is, according to this site, "probably the most controversial of all books written about the Great Pyramid." Doesn't sound too far fetched to me, but then again, "controversial" sells. Mel Gibson isn't a billionaire because he made a traditional movie, now is he? The book tosses out the traditional notions of the pyramids and replaces them with the theory that the pyramids were essentially sewer systems.

VERDICT: This is an interesting theory of the dozens attempting to explain the purpose of the puzzling pyramids. We may never know what the purposes of the pyramids were, but we can still make wild guesses, and that's just what the Pharaoh's Pump is.

486

Car Living
www.carliving.com

Many things are considered art today, and now you can count living in cars as one of them! Car Living, which is defined as "staying in a vehicle for one night or…longer," is, according to this site, perfect for just about anybody! Whether you're a young woman or an old man, college student or wealthy suburbanite, car living is a perfect as a hobby, vacation, or even a permanent residence. Yeah, I'd choose a small car with no bathroom, kitchen, or bedroom over my house.

PRODUCTS: *Car Living Your Way: Stories and Practical Tips From Those Who Have Been Down the Road* by A. J. Heim is the essential guide for anybody interested in car living. The book starts with chapter one, "Car Living Defined," and moves to chapters like "Reasons for Car Living," "Mental Preparation," and even "Car Living and Feng Shui." Crazy? Perhaps. But living in a car is crazy to begin with.

VERDICT: I cannot imagine living in a car for even one day. How do you cook decent meals? How do you bathe? How do you communicate with friends and family? The Car Living book answers all these questions, but chances are you'll take a small apartment or motel room any day over this loony lifestyle.

487

Tiny Pinocchio, the World's Smallest Dog
www.tinypinocchio.com

This site is a look into the life of the world's smallest dog. Tiny Pinocchio, also known as Noki, is just a little bit bigger than a twelve-ounce can of Coke! When he was born, he weighed only two ounces, but now that he's a "big boy," he weighs a whopping one pound! Noki is so small, that he has to be put in a birdcage when company comes over, so people don't step on him! Good idea, unless you want Tiny Pinocchio to become Flat Pinocchio.

PRODUCTS: Own the Tiny Pinocchio designer pin, made by Noki's "human sister." You'd think that since Tiny Pinocchio is small, the price would be too. Wrong! This pretty pin will cost you about twenty-five dollars! Not every price is bigger than Noki, though: the Tiny Pinocchio CD will only cost you about five dollars. Still, for these prices, you wonder why you can't just buy the darn dog.

VERDICT: Everything about this site is too large! If you have the world's smallest dog, shouldn't you have the world's smallest website? If you have the world's smallest dog, shouldn't you have the world's smallest prices?

488

Left-Handers' Day
www.left-handersday.com

This is the official site of Left-Handers' Day which, on August 11, commemorates the annual celebration of "left-handers superiority!" And why are left-handed people superior? Does their left-handedness make them stronger? It certainly doesn't make them cooler! Left-handed day is meant to remedy our tendency to favor right-handed people by "designating your personal space as a LEFTY ZONE where everything must be done left-handed!" Have fun being lonely in your little "Lefty Zone."

PRODUCTS: Utensils, office supplies, and other tools modified to suit left-handers. Examples include the Left-handed Ruler, a ruler that lets lefties use rulers without obscuring the numbers. Perhaps the stupidest product is the Left-handed Keyring, with the phrase, "I Have a Right to be Left-Handed." The keychain is meant to remind you that "We may be left-handed, but we are usually right!" Um, "right," or should I say, left...

VERDICT: This is a great store for left-handed people to get the products they need. Products that are usually oriented to right-handed folks. But why do they have that "us vs. them" mentality? Then again, we all know that the right is right when it comes to the important issues…that matter to right-handed people, of course. What did you think I was talking about, silly?

489 Personal Computing Environments
www.mypce.com

I'm all for having the best technology, but this is going a bit too far. These personal computing environments, or PCEs, are meant to create "ultimate environments" for computer and video game junkies. Resembling something found in a NASA training center, the PCE caters to "an exploding global population that is increasingly tethered to computers to manage nearly all aspects of their daily lives." Come on, we don't entrust our lives to technology—unless you count the television. We are not worthy, oh glorious cable box!

PRODUCTS: The PCE: essentially a high-tech adjustable dentist's chair with a couple of high-tech television monitors suspended at eye level and an adjustable bar to hold a keyboard. You can customize your own PCE to suit your individual needs. Whether it's high-intensity computer gaming (for videogame geeks like me) or graphic design for your software company, there's a PCE for you. With the PCE's surround-sound system and high-definition LCD monitors, computing is "as exciting as driving a sports car." Maybe as exciting, but not quite as expensive. One PCE is about $2,200; still a lofty price tag, but nowhere near the sports cars it claims to match.

VERDICT: While the PCE may be cutting edge, it's not really practical for home use. It appears to take up the amount of space of a small personal office. For videophiles or audiophiles that want the best of the best in high-powered computing, however, the PCE is where it's at.

490   Human Descent
www.humandescent.com

Human Descent is where you'll find some the strangest, sickest, most disturbing Frankenstein's-monster-like creations on the Internet. There are hellish hybrids of animals everywhere on this site, including lizard birds, duck frogs, lion owls, dog people, cat weasels, penguin roosters, and other appalling abominations awaiting you at Human Descent.

PRODUCTS: Human Descent T-shirts, calendars, mugs, mousepads, and other accessories with pictures of the hybrid animals on them. There's the dolphin toucan, the Wolfird mug (wolf and bird), the Deerird mug (deer bird), and many more unusual products.

VERDICT: This is disturbing. More disturbing than Richard Simmons.com (number 91). More disturbing than Rogaine for women. More disturbing than a lot of things. But, it's strangely compelling to see these mutations, even if they're obviously digitally altered photos. For a most unusual visual experience, Human Descent is an interesting incarnation of abnormality.

491   Perfect Sideburns
www.perfectsideburns.com/PShome.html

Forget the Perfect Pancake, the Perfect Omelet, or the countless other "perfect" as-seen-on-TV products; make way for the Perfect Sideburns! It's so easy to use, and it (hopefully) works! Kenneth Steinfeldt says of the Perfect Sideburns, "Ya, it's true, you can teach an old dog new tricks! Prolook was the best bone anyone ever threw me." Good boy! You want a treat?

PRODUCTS: Buy this accessory, and you'll have Perfect Sideburns within minutes! Simply cut the Perfect Sideburns gauges to the shape you desire, put the gauges on, lather and shave, and presto! You've got absolutely perfect, absolutely flawless, absolutely hideous sideburns! Now available at the low "introductory" price of $12.95! What a bargain! Hey, does this piece of crap we're selling actually work?

VERDICT: Of the many as-seen-on-TV products, nothing is more essential than the Perfect Sideburns! We don't need any omelet maker, or vegetable chopper, or Hepa-filter, or handless cell-phone speakers—all we need is the Perfect Sideburns! Who cares if there's a large chance it does nothing it says it does? There's nothing more vital to success and prosperity than great sideburns! And isn't that worth taking a chance on?

492   Monopoly in the Park
www.monopolyinthepark.com

This monstrous Monopoly board is a giant replica of the original Parker Brothers game—with valuable real estate pieces from Silicon Valley! For families, parties, company picnics, and washed-up, unemployed dot-com millionaires, the giant Monopoly in the Park board is perfect!

PRODUCTS: You can rent Monopoly in the Park for your next outdoor get together. The rules are the same, except now you're the game piece! And don't be shy to dress the part, either. Participants in MITP can "don gigantic token-shaped hats," or even "wear jailhouse garb." Go directly to jail. Do not pass Go. Do not collect two hundred dollars. And do not play this game when it's raining.

VERDICT: There's a reason the property pieces are from Silicon Valley: so former owners of sites like Pets.com can rent MITP and remember the days where everybody said, "You're going to be the next Bill Gates." And it seemed that way—that is, until the dot-com bubble (which was the primary cause of the "booming" Clinton-era economy) burst, and all those sites went the way of New Coke. Those were the days for those owners, and Monopoly in the Park is a cathartic experience for them—and a fun game for parties and reunions, too.

493

Enlighted
www.enlighted.com

What better way to accentuate your snazzy new threads than with some flashing lights? Founded by engineer/fashion extraordinaire Janet Cooke Hansen, Enlighted sells jackets, vests, suits, and even bras with flashing lights attached to them. Now we have a new reason to stare—at clothes, of course.

PRODUCTS: While most Enlighted orders are custom-made to your liking, the gallery showcases some of the more popular designs. Examples include the EL (electroluminescent) wire jacket, which is covered with about three hundred feet of flashing wires. You can have the wires in any shape you want, including words. Why act like you're single and desperate when you can just say it on your jacket? Like anything custom made, however, this stuff costs a lot: one foot of EL wire is ten dollars. That means if you want the suggested three hundred feet of wire, you'll have to dish out three thousand dollars, plus the cost of the garment! Who knew cheesy novelty lighting was so expensive?

VERDICT: These clothes are tackier than a Disney romance movie! Who would want to pay thousands of dollars for cheesy flashing lights on clothing? This flashy fashion (no pun intended) is as tacky is it is overpriced. If you want attention, there's cheaper ways to get it than attaching expensive flashing lights to your clothes.

494

Airplane Homes
www.airplanehomes.com

It's the trailer home for millionaires! Airplane Homes takes a Boeing 727-200 fuselage and completely refurnishes it to be a fully functional residential property. Enter via the air stair doors or the wing stairs to find a kitchen, carpet or wood flooring, a fully functional bathroom, and of course, the standard overhead compartments on real airplanes.

PRODUCTS: Put a two-thousand-dollar deposit down on your airplane home today! Once finished, the total cost of the airplane home is

$314,000; expensive, but not too expensive considering real estate prices in New York and California. Alternately, go shopping for your airplane home on eBay! Yet another example of how eBay can help you get any item your twisted little mind desires (my favorites are the used underwear and haunted computers).

VERDICT: I think living in an airplane would be cool. The luxuries of first class, the undeniably unique quality—it's an irresistible combination! If you're seeking a creative, unique idea for your next home, consider the advantages of living in an actual airplane with Airplane Homes. Now if only they could actually fly…

495   Miss Black Widow
www.missblackwidow.com

This site is a "dedication of years of interest and personal research" regarding the Black Widow spider also known as *Latrodectus mactan* or the rather affectionate Murderous Biting Robber. Miss Black Widow is full of information on the anatomy, environments, and even mating rituals of the Black Widow spider. One interesting fact on this alluring arachnid is that an average Black Widow will consume over two thousand insects in one lifetime! And we thought we ate a lot!

PRODUCTS: Black Widow spider products here come in sterling silver jewelry, purses, handbags, and even shoes! The jewelry section contains two Black Widow designs, as well as designs modeled after astrological signs, such as Aries, Cancer, Capricorn, and Gemini. Perhaps the strangest product is the Black Widow Fragrance, a perfume "so feminine and alluring, it will entice and arouse the desires of any of our male species!" Perhaps if I didn't know the name, it would.

VERDICT: While it is certainly interesting to learn about Black Widow spiders, I'm not exactly going head over heels for the other products, especially the jewelry. I'd rather see a woman wearing a puppy necklace, or a horsie bracelet; they're so cute and cuddly. Call me girly, but I don't care for those icky spiders, and I don't care for this store.

496

Guitar Table
www.guitartable.com

Here's an idea for your next funky living room addition: a table made out of
guitars! Handmade in Evanston, Illinois, from the same materials used to
build acoustic guitars, each guitar table is made of the top and bottom of a
single guitar. After construction, each guitar table is finished with high-
gloss acrylic resin for extra durability. All the looks of a guitar without the
music! I always knew they were meant for something better.

PRODUCTS: You can order any of the guitar tables featured on this
site's homepage. Guitar Table No. 19 is a "special" guitar table with
"red on red." Actually, the better description is "red hot flamboyant
pink on super snappy pinkish red." For something a little more traditional, try Guitar Table No. 10, a guitar table made of tan and brown
wood. Guitar Tables run in price from about six-hundred dollars to
eight-hundred dollars.

VERDICT: What a neat idea for home décor! Not only can guitars play
great music, they make great tables once they've outlived their usefulness! Perfect for retro or music-themed rooms. Even for the prices,
Guitar Tables are an awesome idea for home decorators in the market
for a cool, hip, and alternative idea.

497

Facial Workout
www.facialworkout.com

Instead of waiting for wrinkles to appear on your face or using makeup to
cover up the ones you already have, consider a new preventive measure. No,
it's not a cream, and it's not a drug. Rather, it's a new form of exercise!
Facial Workout offers an alternative idea for preventing or getting rid of
wrinkles, without the expensive cosmetic surgery.

PRODUCTS: The Facial Workout, by G.B Colin, is the "safe, natural,
and non-surgical" choice for a facial Fountain of Youth. FW explains
how unlike our heart or lungs, we have "conscious control" over our

facial muscles. Whether we're smiling at a great TV show or scowling at an angry acquaintance, we exercise complete control over our facial muscles. FW explains how to take advantage of this to "diminish lines and wrinkles" and "[be] kind to your face." I didn't know my face had feelings.

VERDICT: Sure, the Facial Workout is an alternative for a youthful face, but why do bothersome exercise when we've got our best friend in cosmetics? Botox! Just one injection from a sharp syringe, and your wrinkles are gone! Botox also makes you happy! We can't help but smile (if the muscles work) when we've got a bunch of chemicals injected into our faces! Or, just buy the Facial Workout book and do a few exercises. The choice is yours.

498

Water Joe
www.waterjoe.com

It seems like they're adding all sorts of stuff to water these days to make it a more desirable drink. First it was artificial flavoring, and now it's—surprise, surprise—caffeine. As this website says, "everything begins with an idea," and the idea here is that some people don't like coffee or Coke, the most acceptable solutions for some quick energy. So, why not put caffeine in water? And thus, Water Joe was born.

PRODUCTS: Water Joe is currently available at stores in Wisconsin, Illinois, Minnesota, Indiana, Michigan, and at Publix Stores in Florida. If you're living elsewhere, or are too lazy to go to the store, you can order WJ online. Some "creative uses" for Water Joe suggested in the animated intro are putting it in your fish bowl ("watch those little guys swim!"), and "Make your ice cubes with it." Cold AND caffeinated!

VERDICT: While the idea of spiking water with a quick-energy chemical may not be original, it's a good idea for people seeking an alternative to coffee or soda for their all-nighters and long driving trips. Let's just hope WJ doesn't go the way of Jolt, or Surge, two other failed attempts at energy drinks with decent taste (obviously, Red Bull doesn't count). Now if only we could get this stuff down to California—what a flavor of the week it would make.

499   **Dog the Bounty Hunter**
www.dogthebountyhunter.com

The endless loop of the Baha Mens's "Who Let the Dogs Out" isn't the only stupid, over-the-top, pointless thing about this site. Who's stupider is Duane "Dog" Chapman, the Bounty Hunter, a self-appointed enforcer and guardian of justice who sounds like he should be locked up in the pound rather than on the streets catching bad guys. The one trick he does know is how to fetch criminals. With over six thousand captures, Dog is, according to *Midweek Magazine*, "The best bounty hunter in the world." And we all know how reputable *Midweek* is!

PRODUCTS: "Six men can carry you, or twelve men can judge you. You decide!" How about neither? This phrase is quoted as being a "Dogism," and it's the worst slogan since McDonalds' "I'm Lovin' It" jingle. How about, "I'm hating your crappy commercials?" There are two T-shirts and a hat available, both with Dog's logo and the word "RUN" on the back. That's probably the ONLY good idea on this site.

VERDICT: It's great that Dog is a genuine do-gooder, and it's better that he's good at what he does. But, of all the dumb nicknames, why "Dog"? Roll over, dog! Fetch, dog! Catch a criminal, dog! Good boy! Only Ice-T and Ice Cube match that name for sheer idiocy. Dog may be skilled at putting bad guys away, but this mutt is about as dumb as they get.

· ·

500   **Giant Microbes**
www.giantmicrobes.com

What better stuffed-animal for your kid to cuddle up with than a soft, fuzzy, disease-carrying germ? Giant Microbes sells stuffed microbes modeled after the ones that can give you stomach aches and stuffy noses, and even some that can kill you. You want a fuzzy common cold virus? You've got it. Want a cute little Black Death microbe to sleep with? You can find it here.

PRODUCTS: Giant Microbes are divided into separate categories according to how dangerous they are and what their purposes are.

Think of the difference between a Stomach Ache and Ebola as the difference between a stuffed bear and a stuffed puppy. There's the more common "Health" category, with pathogens like Ear Ache and Sore Throat. Don't forget the dreaded but darling "Calamities," with diseases like Sleeping Sickness and Flesh Eating. Just what I want to cozy up to at night: a flesh-eating virus.

VERDICT: I knew there were weird stuffed animals out there, but this is going too far. Who would want a stuffed animal that's supposed to be a fungus or disease? And the Ulcer plush doll is disturbing to say the least. The worst part is that they have the nerve to charge you money for these things! I'd pay to get these disgusting dolls out of my house! When it comes to stuffed animals, Giant Microbes is about as disgusting as it gets.

501   House Gymnastics
www.housegymnastics.com

House Gymnastics, formally known as Harrison and Ford House Gymnastics (wonder where they got the name?), is described as a "cross breed of yoga, breakdancing, climbing, and gymnastics in a domestic setting." If you already think it sounds crazy, wait until you the pictures. High jumping down the stairs, bridges over the bathtub, and wedging above a doorway are all a day in the life of a house gymnast. And I thought not using the railing was dangerous.

PRODUCTS: The *House Gymnastics* book is an indoor acrobatics guide that will "take you from your armchair to the hallway, the fridge, a window ledge, and back again without spilling your housemate's tea." My housemate's tea? No wonder they're so crazy. If you'd rather not break your neck doing these "daring" moves, you can watch the H&F team do all twenty-five moves in twenty-five minutes on a DVD. Not a lot of DVD for your money, is it?

VERDICT: The lesson here is obvious. Whenever we see some kid on the news who's broken an arm or fractured an ankle trying to be a real-life Spiderman—we just blame House Gymnastics. Now wasn't that easy? Unless you're a trained professional, doing House Gymnastics will give you a trip to the hospital rather than a high adrenaline thrill.

502

Puppet Terrors
www.puppetterrors.com

These circus sideshows are more than just creepy freaks; they're psychotic serial killers! Puppet Terrors is an "independently owned freak show" of homicidal clowns and monsters straight out of the scariest horror movies. Characters include Bunky the Clown, a clown with green hair and a sharp knife, and Death Row Joe, a Frankenstein-like monster with a penchant for pain. Scary stuff.

PRODUCTS: Puppets, stickers, and comic books featuring the Puppet Terrors crew. The comic book, *Puppet Terrors: Murder, Mayhem, No Strings Attached*, is about Bunky the Clown and Death Row Joe, two toy puppets who walk, talk (with much profanity to boot), and "on occasion, get into trouble." While Bunky and Joe discover that they're not the only toys in the world, much to their bloodthirsty, maniacal delight, an army of killer toys is amassing at the South Pole, ready to unleash untold horrors on the world of humans! I can forget about a good sleep tonight.

VERDICT: I always knew clowns were no good. Just look at I Hate Clowns from my first book. Now is the time where I truly "can't sleep, clowns will eat me." Whoever dreamed up this psychotic circus has some serious psychological issues. Puppet Terrors is, for lack of a better term, terrifying.

....

503

Pet Obsessed
www.petobsessed.com

The name says it all. Pet Obsessed allows you to immortalize your pet through digitally altered classic paintings! The works of van Gogh, Rembrandt, and Da Vinci can be altered to replace famous figures in art with your pooch, kitty, lizard, bird, or any other pet that you're way too attached to!

PRODUCTS: Putting your pet in a painting is easy as one, two, three. First, select any famous painting from the picture gallery.

Then, provide one to three pictures of your pet. Fill out an order form and presto! You've got your own digitally altered masterpiece, starring your pet! Want your lizard in da Vinci's *Mona Lisa?* You've got it. Want Rover in Michelangelo's breathtaking Sistine Chapel painting? It's yours. The possibilities are endless! However, all the paintings are composed digitally, so you're paying for a cut-and-paste job, not a custom-made masterpiece.

VERDICT: This site's name couldn't be more appropriate. If you love your pet so much that you want him or her in a famous painting, you are truly obsessed. Is obsession a good thing? For great music or a creative TV show like *The Simpsons*, maybe (I myself am a Simpsons fanatic). But with a pet, it's dumb, deranged, and downright disturbing.

504 No Pants Day
www.nopantsday.com

It's exactly what you think it is! That's right! The first Friday of May is No Pants Day, the day where you go about business-as-usual—except with no pants! This site gives you some creative ideas for making your own special No Pants Day. Bars and restaurants are encouraged to give discounts to those brave enough to leave their trousers at home. Businesses are encouraged to make Friday "Extremely Casual Friday." And of course, individuals are encouraged to, obviously, not wear pants!

PRODUCTS: Buy No Pants Day T-shirts! Whether you wear them exclusively on No Pants Day, or any other day of the year, they're a bold fashion statement. The T-shirts come in two varieties. One shows a triumphant figure in boxers waving a flag made of pants. The other has a "No Pants" sign (like no smoking). And of course, you'll want your No Pants Day boxers for when No Pants Day rolls along—everybody needs a good explanation.

VERDICT: What an original idea! First we have Talk Like a Pirate day, and now we have another fun day that reminds us not to take life too seriously. Of course, for some people No Pants Day might not be possible. It would be a bad PR-move for the president to participate, not to mention a tabloid field day. But, for those who can, liberate yourself on the first Friday of May by going without pants!

505

Drive Ins
www.drive-ins.com

The drive-in movie theater is an endangered species these days. People sneaking in without paying, outdoor "noise pollution," real estate prices, and angry neighbors have all contributed to the downfall of one of America's last classic institutions from the bygone eras of the '50s and '60s. This site is a guide to help you find the last of these endangered attractions at a location near you, along with nostalgic articles and stories about drive-in days of yore.

PRODUCTS: For die-hard enthusiasts and others seeking a nostalgic drive-in experience, there's the Pocket Edition Drive-In Locator, a worldwide quick reference for locating drive-in movie theaters. Books like *The American Drive-In* and *Those Were the Days* offer a look back at the glory days of the drive-in. Finally, the *It's Intermission Time* DVDs and videos let you view authentic classics shown at drive-in intermissions back in the day.

VERDICT: I've put seeing a drive-in movie on my list of things I'd like to do in my lifetime, simply because it's such a rare experience in today's commercialized, money-monger world. Corporate America has become so obsessed with money that they've forgotten many of the old American values. I mean, Christmas ads before Thanksgiving? Is nothing sacred anymore? Corporate ethics aside, this site is a valuable resource for anybody looking for a good nostalgic experience.

Index

Unique Box Shop, 100
Utilikilts, 321

V

Valley of the Geeks, 250
Vanishing Tattoo, 264
Vegas Weddings, 130
Veggie Van, 28
Villisca Axe Murderers, 168
Vynsane, 50

W

W Ketchup, 282
War Store, The, 125
Warhol Store, The, 198
Watch Me Eat a Hot Dog, 96
Water Joe, 333
We Love the Iraqi Information
    Minister, 17
Weasel Balls, 114
Weather Shop, 138
Weird NJ, 18
Weirdo Music, 320
When Pigs Fly, 204
Whip Store, 124
Who Would Buy That?, 18
Wicked Cool Stuff, 69
William Hung Store, The, 10
William Shatner Store, 62
Wisconsin Cheese and Cheeseheads,
    236
Wishing Fish, 64
Women in Waders, 271
Wonder Farms, 298
Wonder Magnet, 43
Wooden Computer Peripherals, 305
World Beard and Moustache
    Championships, 290
World Kickball, 51
World of Celebrities Store, 196
World's Smallest Versions of the
    World's Largest Things, 291

Y

Yellow Bamboo, 302
Yoga Kitty, 35
Youth of Britain, 219

Z

Zapato Productions
    Intradimensional, 254
Zoltron, 127
Zombie Nation, 138

About the Author

Dan Crowley is an eighteen-year-old, honor-roll high school student who loves video games, reading, writing, and, of course, Internet surfing. Dan lives in Wisconsin with his mom and dad, two sisters, and a cute little puppy named Marnie. Dan is the author of the smash hit *505 Unbelievably Stupid Web Pages*. Since childhood, Dan has frequently written fictional stories for fun.